WALLACE H. GRAHAM

WALLACE H. GRAHAM

THE MAN WHO BECAME PRESIDENT TRUMAN'S PHYSICIAN

Wallace Harry Graham, M.D.

Foreword and Afterword by Heather Graham Foote
Introduction by Von V. Pittman, Ph.D.

Compass Flower Press
Columbia, Missouri

Dr. Wallace Harry Graham, 1910-1996

Published by Compass Flower Press
an imprint of AKA-Publishing
315 Bernadette Dr. Suite 3
Columbia, MO 65203

Compass
Flower
Press

Cover Image:
Major Wallace H. Graham; December, 1944; Brand, Germany

Library of Congress Control Number: 2019934694

ISBN 978-1-942168-73-7 Trade Paperback
ISBN 978-1-942168-93-5 Hardback

To my dear wife, Velma, who spent untold hours transcribing my dictation and typing my manuscript. I am forever grateful.

—*Wallace H. Graham*

CONTENTS

FOREWORD

After the bombing of Pearl Harbor, my father, Dr. Wallace Harry Graham was called into active duty. By this time, he and my mom, Velma had been married over five years. The family had already grown to include two young children. My mother kept us together as much as possible by following my father's unit on maneuvers. We moved into whatever rental housing was available in the nearest small town. This was extremely important for the integrity of the family, especially because of the upcoming time of extended separation due to my father's entry into the European Theater of World War II in 1944.

In his later years, my father often asked me if I had read his manuscript. I always regretted that I had to tell him I hadn't gotten to it yet. When he passed away, one of the cathartic processes I took on was to organize his papers, pictures, and finally read the manuscript to which he had referred.

Many of the incidents he recounted were familiar from his storytelling to me, Mom, my brothers and our children. But I found so much more of the man I knew. He was larger than life in his knowledge, derived from his unquenchable thirst for learning, and his kind and caring ways. My father always enjoyed pursuing a goal and having an objective. He was a man of vision. Even though he was a realist and forthright, he was an optimist. He usually saw the bright side of situations. This trait helped him immensely in preparing for the war as well as performing surgery in active combat zones throughout Europe.

He was able to find beauty and humor everywhere, whether in nature, his school-day boxing "career," or dire circumstances in the armed forces as a highly ordered and skilled physician and surgeon in the field.

I found his manuscript a fascinating look through his eyes, imparting his strong ideals and love for family, friends, travel, cultures, and life in general.

Needless to say, I laughed and I cried. Above all, I missed this man who was my father and everyone's friend. The people I met who encountered him all felt like they knew him, and all showed respect and a genuine affection for him.

The world was a better place when he was here, but more to the point, it is a better place because he was here. The effects of a man with his qualities last far beyond his physical life for many more than me and my family.

I am thankful for the values he gave me and proud that he touched so many lives.

—*HEATHER GRAHAM FOOTE*

INTRODUCTION

In January 1944, fifteen thousand American soldiers crammed together on the *Queen Mary*, headed for England to train and assemble for the D-Day attack on the Normandy coast. Near the end of their voyage, General George S. Patton came aboard to deliver an assertive discourse about the German army they would soon face. Captain Wallace H. Graham, a doctor assigned to the 24th Evacuation Hospital, found Patton's speech valuable, particularly his emphasis on relentless pursuit. Most of the American troops were skeptical, however, when Patton recounted stories about atrocities the *Wehrmacht* had visited upon opponents and civilians. But Graham says he knew them not only to be true, but an inevitability, part of the Hell he and his comrades would soon face.

Wallace Graham, like many of his peers would have to reconcile the nobility, duties, and hopefulness of medical practice with the horrific nature of war. To succeed in both while maintaining their humanity required considerable strength of character. This book reconciles the hellishness of battle with an enduring commitment to humanity. It should rank high among first-person accounts of modern mechanized warfare. Graham understood all too well the nature of the war in which he was about to participate. He would know it even better by the time it ended.

After graduating from medical school at Creighton University in Omaha, Nebraska, Graham served residencies and postdoctoral work in Vienna, and in several hospitals in Hungary, as well as at the University of Edinburgh, in Scotland. He saw firsthand the quickening buildup to war. Earlier than most Americans, he became convinced of its inevitability. In Vienna, he unsuccessfully tried to persuade his Jewish landlord to get his family out of Austria. Two days after he received his Master of Surgery diploma, German troops marched into the city to celebrate and solidify the *Anschluss* between Germany and Austria.

In Hungarian hospitals during his residencies, or 'hospitantships,' Graham treated gunshot wounds acquired by soldiers who had been sent by their governments as "volunteers" to fight on Generalissimo Francisco Franco's side in the Spanish Civil War. This, and his other residency experience before the United States officially entered the European theatre of war would serve him well just a few years later.

Shortly after his return to the United States, Dr. Graham was called to active duty in the Army, which he would find a hospitable—even rewarding—place to practice surgery. From the beginning of his active service, then throughout his career, he appreciated the military's resources, as well as its medical practice and organization.

Readers, particularly those who consume a great deal of military history, will find this book unusual in that Graham offers no grievances or complaints about the Army's bureaucracy or management system. And, he seems to have no need to settle scores at the individual level. Instead, he is extremely generous in crediting many of his colleagues by name. He also extols them as members of groups. He is generous in his praise of nurses, medics, and even the litter-bearers who moved the wounded, and the Graves Registration units that identified, then either buried the dead or prepared them for transit home.

Graham rose to the rank of Chief Surgeon of the 24th Evacuation Hospital as the allied armies moved through western Europe and into Germany. He and his colleagues often operated very close to artillery fire as they treated wounded Americans, allied soldiers, civilians, and even German troops, all with state-of-the-art care. And as was the case with most participants, war took a toll on Graham, physically and emotionally. He suffered a wound that crushed two vertebrae, but performed surgery the next day. When he encountered a young French brother and sister whose parents had been killed and their home destroyed by artillery fire, he unsuccessfully tried to adopt them and have them sent to the United States. He would worry for years about their well-being.

General Graham's observations are not limited to war and surgery. He was a shrewd and appreciative observer of the countries and people he encountered. His description of a rural Hungarian Christmas sparkles. And his extended treatment of the joy of celebration following the liberation of Paris is superb.

Before leaving Europe at the end of World War II, Wallace Graham would somehow catch the eye of President Harry Truman, who asked him to become his personal physician. When Graham declined, Truman "drafted" him anyhow. In addition to serving as White House Physician, he would maintain a surgery practice at Walter Reed Army Hospital. In time, he would reach the rank of Major General. He would become a sort of medical diplomat, attending to the ailments of several world leaders or members of their families. And he would serve as Harry and Bess Truman's personal physician until both of their deaths.

This volume is an extraordinary account of a doctor's first-hand observation of the build-up to history's largest war, then his participation in its resolution.

—*Von V. Pittman, Ph.D.*
United States Diplomatic History
University of Georgia

CHRONOLOGY

1910, 9 October	• Wallace Harry Graham is born in Highland, Kansas
1917, Summer	• Family trip to Colorado
1919	• Graham family moves to Kansas City, MO. Wallace is nine years old.
1922-24	• Grade School years:
	• Piano lessons, Paper route, Boxing debut
	• Scouting: to Eagle Scout at age fourteen
	• Neighborhood "gang": street baseball
1925-29	• High School years: Westport and Paseo High Schools, Kansas City, MO
	• Football Team
	• ROTC: Army Reserves age seventeen, partial summers at ROTC Camp
	• Boxing: Golden Gloves champion— Welter-weight division
1929-31	• University of Missouri, Columbia, MO Freshman & Sophomore years ROTC
1931-34	• Central Missouri State College, Warrensburg, MO—B.S. Degree 1934
	• ROTC
1934-36	• Medical School: Creighton University School of Medicine, Omaha, NE; M.D.
	• 1st Lieutenant, U.S. Army
1935, 15 September	• Marriage to Velma Ruth Hill, R.N.
1936	• Massachusetts General Hospital: Summer Internship; Kansas City General Hospital
	• Rotating Internship completed
1937, July	• Boarded SS *Washington* for Europe with Velma
1937-38	• Surgical Residency: Vienna, Austria University of Budapest, Hungary Segzed, Hungary
	• The Royal College of Surgeons, Edinburgh, Scotland

1938	• Return to United States with Velma
1938, November	• First child, Wallace Scott born
1939, December	• Second child, Heather Ellen born
1939-41	• Shared office with his father, James Walter Graham, M.D.; set up Family Practice
1941, April	• Active Duty, U.S. Army, Fort Leonard Wood, Missouri
1941, 7 December	• Pearl Harbor, Hawaii: Japanese attack on U.S. soil.
1941, 24 December	• Attained rank of Captain, U.S. Army
	• Army training and maneuvers, Fort Leonard Wood, Missouri; Camp Breckenridge, Kentucky
1943, January	• Army training and maneuvers, Memphis, Tennessee.
	• Attained rank of Major, U.S. Army (cover photo)
	• Entered WWII; Duty: Combat Surgeon, 24th Evacuation Hospital, attached to 101st Airborne Division
1944, January	• Promoted to Lieutenant Colonel
June	• Landed on Omaha Beach "Easy Red;" Took part in Allied Invasion
1945, August	• Attained rank of Colonel
1945	• WWII European Theater of War ends.
	• Wallace Graham called to Potsdam, Germany

*This span covers the material written by
Wallace Harry Graham.*

Wallace Harry Graham's life chronology resumes in the Appendices.

CHAPTER ONE
GROWING UP IN HIGHLAND

The day of my birth, 9 October 1910 in Highland, Kansas, began quietly, with brilliant red, yellow, and orange leaves from nearby oaks, gums, and maples fluttering down with the gusts of wind, amid shafts of sunlight. An occasional far-off rumbling was heard, and sprinkles of rain dampened the leaves and browning grass. My father, scrubbed and gowned, sat quietly by my mother's bed, watching as the hands of the Big Ben clock moved. As labor increased, so did the storm's intensity, with increasing crescendo of rumbling thunder and winds blowing in from the prairie flatlands far beyond the gentle, rolling hills surrounding the little town of Highland. Inside the house two neighbor women busily boiled water and gathered towels and cloths in preparation for the appearance of a new member of the Graham household. At last, amid a loud clap of thunder and a burst of lightning, came the lusty cry of a healthy boy. The attending women went about doing necessary chores, the tension eased, and my father and mother were greatly relieved. The storm abated, and rain followed steadily for the rest of the day. I was not the first child born to the family. Nine years before me in 1901, my brother John had been born in Saint Joseph, Missouri. It was there where my father was an intern and then resident surgeon in Ensworth Hospital. My parents later moved to Highland because the town, and indeed the entire county of Doniphan was in need of medical help.

My recollections of growing up in Highland are very pleasant. My brother and I had a variety of pets, and our parents were tolerant of them so long as we fed and housed them.

We had owls (screech, barn, and brown), found at different times where they were dropped from nests or injured in some other way. We made huge pens with tree branches and stumps to approximate their habitat, and fed them mice until they were well enough to be free. By the time they could eat a whole mouse we knew it was safe to let them go.

At one time we had a mother opossum with nineteen little ones. We had a raccoon, which we enjoyed watching as it washed its food in the water of a little pool we made, and a pair of gray flying squirrels, pigeons of many varieties, rabbits, white mice, ferrets, a crow, and such farm animals as bantam chickens and guinea hens.

I recall vividly that my favorite pastime was to roam the woods with my friend Raymond King, whose nickname was 'Tater' because of his favorite food, the potato. We walked silently along creek banks as we played Indians. We were either barefoot or in moccasins, as my mother had read us stories of Indians who walked quietly through the woods so as not to frighten the many busy animals of the forest. At times we were as boisterous as imagination demanded. Our favorite headgear was a band; with the feather of a red-tailed hawk in the back. We were especially interested in a family of muskrats in the bank of the stream. We watched intently as they dug holes in the side of the bank and in the process made slick mudslides where they apparently had great fun sliding down to the water. Farther down the creek we watched a family of beaver gnawing and felling trees to increase their dam. By this stream we learned of the hatching of frog eggs into pollywogs and their growth into adult frogs. A family of deer grazed with the cattle close by and the two small boys staring in wonderment seemed not to frighten them.

In Highland our summers were warm and carefree, and winters provided a different type of enjoyment. When snow came it was a sign for Tater and me to make an igloo where we played as if we were Eskimos. We had our weapons (plenty of snowballs) to throw at each other or anything in general. When we came in the house from playing in the snow, Mom would have warm sugar cookies for us.

Another winter delight was sledding. My dad and I made a bobsled and tied it to the buggy or springboard wagon, and Dad took us for rides. To make it more exciting he hurried the horse with a flick of the whip and a "Giddy-up" and off we went, laughing and shouting for Dad to make the horse go faster. My friend and I would also go sledding by ourselves. One time I found a steep hill and decided to have a good, swift slide, ignoring a crossroad near the bottom. Going down the hill like the wind on my Flying Arrow, I spied a horse trotting over the crossroad, pulling a surrey with fringe on the top. I knew I could not turn fast enough to avoid hitting the surrey so I took a desperate chance in that flashing second and guided my sled between the front and back wheels. There were other winter joys such as sitting around the fireplace at night, eating popcorn, and listening to stories, fancying myself a part of them.

I am glad I lived in Highland with the privilege of contact with nature—the prairie, rolling hills, woodlands, flowers, birds, and four-footed creatures. I loved to watch the ground squirrels, groundhogs, and the prairie dogs, and discovered that the prairie dogs lived in the same burrows with ground owls. Not so compatible was the black-footed ferret which would occasionally take over a burrow and eat its host. Sage hens and prairie chickens were abundant on the prairie then, but now are practically never seen there. Huge jack rabbits with black-tipped ears sometimes galloped alongside our horse and buggy. Many times in the woodlands I heard the four hoots and whir of the northern owl, and looked at it with wonder among the limbs of majestic elms, oaks, and hickories. There are other pleasant memories: I remember how the earth felt with its thick, elastic cushion of leafy mold on which I learned to walk noiselessly. Here I never heard the sound of a car nor even the creak of a wagon; to me, the woods and the prairie were lands of enchantment.

The marshlands and meadows around Highland were filled with flowers in spring—violets, dutchman's breeches, jack-in-the-pulpit, Sweet William and lady's slippers. I remember the beauty and harmony of their colors and subtle fragrances. My mother had taught me the names of many flowers. She also taught me the uses of medicine from the may apple, dandelion, poke, sassafras, and sweet gum, along with the particular qualities of other trees and plants. Together, we enjoyed gathering watercress, early poke leaves, dandelion, lamb's quarters, mustard, young thistle, wild lettuce, and chives, all of which became a tasty dish known as "greens." I was also taught measures of safety and survival and how to find one's way by the stars at night if necessary.

My father made the most elaborate kites I had ever seen, with pockets to capture the wind. Painstakingly he made them of bamboo or light wood, to which he applied glue and beautifully colored tissue paper, finishing them off with long tails made of rags. With this treasure I made my fastest run down a slope so that the wind could lift my kite and was delighted to see these creations lift into the sky. One of my pleasures was to lie in a green pasture while my kite was flying and I held the end of the string. Many an hour I spent with my face turned to the heavens, where I could imagine fascinating figures in the cumulus clouds. I also dreamed of faraway places and gazed at on the horizon, believing I could see the buffalo running and the Indians riding wildly on their beautiful horses and painted ponies.

On rainy days the barn loft was a retreat, and I dreamed of great expeditions I would take as I lay in the hay listening to drops run into rivulets down and off the roof. I dreamed of leprechauns, gnomes, and dancing fairies. Some of the fantasies probably came from stories my mother read to me, especially one she accompanied with music, "The Hall of the Mountain King," where the broom danced. I also remember her playing a Hungarian rhapsody, and I could imagine frenzied activities of playing, dancing creatures as the music built to its peak of excitement.

We had many games to make life interesting and fun. We played marbles, mumblety-peg, hide and seek, cowboys and Indians (Tater and I always elected ourselves Indians), horseshoes, scrub baseball, shinny, Indian wrestling, ice skating, Indian lore, and trail making.

One day I decided I would climb to the top of the town's water tower, which seemed like just another game. There was no ladder, only crisscrossed iron bars in x-shape extending to the top where there was a railing and ledge. Looking up, the height did not intimidate me and I began my adventurous climb. After reaching the first leg of my journey, however, I looked down, and a sense of fear gripped me. But my decision was to get to the top, so step by step I climbed, finally reaching that top ledge so I could view the world. It gave me a sense of exultation, and I walked around the ledge conjuring tales of Indians out on the prairie.

After some time, and it being late in the afternoon, I began to wonder how I would get my foot down to the first iron criss-cross under the ledge. A woman from town happened to see this kid on the water tower and shrieked with fear. The scream brought more people, followed by the town firemen, who shouted at me, and one fireman began to climb. I yelled that I could come down myself, but was still concerned about that first step under the ledge. I thought that if I got up I could get down, so I held onto the ledge while my feet dangled and felt for that first wedge of iron. Amid shouts of the crowd below I swung my right foot and lowered slowly until my toes felt the first crossbar. The shouts below, if I recall correctly, were not altogether encouraging. Some were imploring me to stay and hold fast, others shouted "go back", and the kids whooped it up and said, "sure you can make it—come on down."

I knew I could make it if I could bunker down enough to get under the ledge and get my hands on the first crossbar—the one above the one my feet were now on. I felt fairly secure with both feet and slowly I caught the top crossbar with my hands. The descent was no problem now although I did not feel so hundred percent brave when I looked down. It would have been much more simple when I had started down if the woman who saw me had not started to shriek and scream calling the other people and the town's volunteer firemen. Dusk was falling as I descended to the base. I was rather expecting accolades on my accomplishment, but instead my mother gave me stern disapproval even as she put her arms around me. My father strongly and sternly admonished me saying that if I tried such a "fool stunt" again I would receive a much warmer reception. I fully understood what he meant.

Highland boasted no paved streets, and on rainy days mud bespattered the horses and wagons. Few cars traveled in those days. The most prevalent mode of transportation was horses and buggies, or spring wagons. When an occasional car ventured the road on a muddy day, it was no rarity to see wheels sunk to the hubs. The usual remedy was placing logs, boards, or cinders in the mudholes to gain traction. Frequently it was necessary to hitch a team of mules or horses to the impotent auto and pull it to more secure ground.

Summer evenings in this small town were never dull, as they were often spent with storytelling or we could always look forward to an occasional prayer meeting, revival, or Chautauqua. I remember hearing Billy Sunday who was loud, commanding, and certainly dramatic. He would slam the chair to emphasize a point. Occasionally a group of wrestlers came to town for an exhibition, and put out the word that they would take on anyone who dared offer himself as an opponent. Not many ever accepted the challenge. Saturday evenings sometimes brought band concerts from the platform in the town square. People came for miles to listen to our fine band. One evening while I was listening to the music it stimulated me so forcibly that I could not keep my feet quiet, and I got up from my chair and began to dance in the aisle, whereupon the bandmaster invited me to come up to the platform. This I did with enthusiasm, and when the music started again I commenced my dance. I tapped, jigged, twirled, and spun. At the end of the initial concert the bandmaster gave me a dime, and people threw pennies up on the bandstand platform. He asked if I would like to perform on every concert night, to which I readily agreed, but don't remember how long the contract was in effect.

My most lasting memories were neither of the life of nature nor of the small town, but of my parents. My father, Dr. James W. Graham, was dedicated to medicine and surgery. He had grown up in Tarentum, Pennsylvania, where he roamed among the pines in the Alleghenies. He told me colorful stories of his life there. I could always go to him for answers to my many questions, and we later enjoyed exchange of ideas. Dad was no sports fan, as he would not take time from his duties, but did manage to see me box, and I believe he came to watch a few track meets. After I became a doctor also our discussions of diagnosis and therapeutics often became intense, but there was always a good feeling between us and we ended our talks in good humor. Dad was five feet, nine and a half inches, a stocky man with square shoulders and erect posture, fair of complexion, freckled skin, his balding head capped with sandy red hair and a large natural curl in the center. His face was chiseled, with sharp nose, square jaw, full and sensitive lips, a network of furrows around his eyes, and minor furrows on his cheeks and forehead placed there by the plow of time. He radiated dignity, intelligence, strength, and kindness, with the twinkle of humor in his eyes. He was modest and unobtrusive.

My mother, Elizabeth Marie Veneman Graham, was considered tall for a woman, five-feet, seven and a half inches, posture erect, shoulders square. She carried her auburn hair in a knot at the back of her head. She invariably caused a second look from passersby, which I always noticed when we walked together. Her manners were exquisite, and unconsciously aristocratic, giving the appearance of one who had been everywhere and had command of situations. She appeared austere, but possessed a warm compassion. I often thought her more kind to animals than to my father, and so remarked. Her answer was that my father was an intelligent man who could understand logical situations, even though he might not act accordingly, whereas animals could not reason and deserved special consideration.

My mother seemed a bit sharp and needlessly impatient with my father because of his method of arbitration on controversial matters, whereas she was always decisive. Love was sincere, although Mother and Father were temperamentally opposites. My father's voice never turned to condemnation. Mother was ultra-penurious, whereas my father had no serious thoughts regarding money. My mother, being very frugal, was prone to give my father considerable problems when he would buy anything new, although certain utilities were necessary.

One night while I was sleeping, I was awakened and heard my mother giving my father considerable argument. I heard my father saying, "All right sweetie, everything will be fine." However, she continued the tirade. This disturbed me considerably so I thought of a solution. Thereupon I stood on my head at the top of the stairs and rolled down like a ball, whooping and howling. Of course, I had been fully aware that the steps were carpeted and I would not injure myself. This trick accomplished what I set out to do. Immediately the argument stopped and all attention was devoted to me, while I moaned and groaned. I was then placed in bed, and everything was happy and calm.

My mother was an excellent cook and kept a neat house. Mom was continually busy, up and running from six in the morning till after nightfall. She was a strong-willed woman who had high principles and maintained them, expecting others to do exactly the same.

Mom was an excellent pianist, and it was her desire to be either a concert pianist or to use her knowledge of many subjects. Her wrists were thin, her hands delicately molded into tapering fingers. Instead of playing her beautiful piano she cared for the household. She was trying to obtain this objective prior to her marriage by teaching and advancing along this line, saving what she could. She did not resent the marriage, but she did, I am sure, object to the cessation of the necessary effort to obtain her goals. She knew it was a sacrifice, and more than once remarked that "Two collegiate degrees and here I am with red, raw knuckles tied to this washboard."

As a youngster I thought we lived in a huge house, and did not discover until later that it was small and barely large enough for the family. Water came from a well outside the kitchen door, with a long rope and bucket tied to the deep end, the other end over an iron-wheel pulley. My mother collected wash water from a drain off the roof, and stored it in the cement-lined cistern on one side of the kitchen door. The buildings about the property were the woodshed, chicken house, doghouse, and outhouse. Eventually, we had plumbing and running water. The privy and well were abolished in favor of a sink, bathtub, and flush toilet. We had a small handle-pump to bring water from the cistern to the kitchen. Saturday night was bath time in an up-to-date tin tub, which was elongated and with a slanting back.

Our house possessed a very special modern convenience—a telephone. Phones in our town were all party lines. We turned the crank for Central who gave a certain number of rings for each individual on the line. Ours was two longs and a short, but when other people on the line heard the ring they often picked up their receivers to listen in on the conversation, sometimes interrupting and adding their comments.

We had a large stove in the kitchen and a potbellied stove in the front room. Both were wood burners. Embers glowed in the cooking stove most of the time. Among my morning chores was keeping the wood-box filled, feeding the dog, Shep, who was a friendly mix of collie and shepherd, feeding and watering the chickens, gathering eggs, then scrubbing up.

We had two cellars; the one under our house was entered through slanting doors connected to the house's south side. About ten stair-steps led into the cellar where we stored fruit. One of my chores was to wrap apples separately in paper and to put them in containers in the cellar. This kept them cool and crisp. I also had to help sort the potatoes, remove sprouts, and cull the bad ones which were easily discerned by their odor. Late one night we heard noises in the cellar and my father went outside, closed the heavy double doors, and placed a large padlock on them. Several weeks later my mother related that we had an unwelcome visitor who entered the cellar with empty baskets intending to relieve us of a newly picked crop of fruit. Dad changed the borrower's mind by locking him in the cold cellar overnight.

My parents held the idea that a tired and busy boy was a good boy. They taught me how to make a garden including how to remove potato bugs, and to care for cabbages with sulfur and other methods of eliminating bugs. I helped feed chickens, several pigs, and the cow. I learned how to milk the cow and was proud of how much milk I could get in the bucket. Also I helped my mother make soap from lye and hog grease in a huge black iron pot. My mother had me help her prepare onions and corn for drying and hanging up to prevent rodents from eating them. I remember vividly that when the horseradish was ground to be bottled, my eyes burned form the pungent aroma, but it was delicious on meats in small amounts at the dinner table. I also recall helping prepare corn for hominy; after shucking field corn and removing kernels, we soaked the corn in lye water, after which we rinsed it many times and then picked off the little dark pieces that attach kernels to the cob. We left them to dry—producing hominy. The cabbage heads were shredded and made into sauerkraut. Apricots and apples were dried or the apples made into spicy apple-butter. I churned butter by hand in a wooden-bucket churn with a plunger paddle, and sat there pumping for hours it seemed before butter separated from the milk; the residual buttermilk I poured off and either drank or saved for cooking or drinking. I was quite proud of the yellow butter which resulted from my efforts.

Every year in late November or December, neighboring farmers helped Dad slaughter pigs to take to the smokehouse. I remember helping keep the smokehouse in action by feeding embers with wood chips and bark. At hog butchering time huge boiling vats were prepared with roaring fires fed by split logs. The hogs were slaughtered before dawn at the far end of the field. The hog was first shot, and then hung by the tendon attachment in the back feet. This was to aid the bleeding process. After this, the hog was placed in boiling water and scrubbed with heavy wire brushes, removing hair and bristles. The hog was then split in half and eviscerated, the liver and all organs were properly handled, sectioned, wrapped and labeled, and the intestines thoroughly cleansed and sectioned in appropriate lengths. The skin and fat were cut in blocks, pressed, rendered by being boiled in the huge black kettles. The grease from this was then poured in large cans and set to one side. Chitlins and cracklins were made. Experts then carved parts for hams, shoulders, ribs, tenderloins, chops, tripe, head cheese, and sausage. Nothing was wasted.

While the adults were busy, the children ran around laughing, playing, and chewing chitlins and cracklins. A tasty rind could be chewed for hours. Certain sections of meat were ground into sausage by adding sage, red and black pepper, and salt. The feet were parboiled after scrubbing, then placed in the pickling vat. Hams were then chosen, some to be hung in the smokehouse and some to be rubbed with brown sugar, pepper, salt, and salt peter, then placed in a muslin tight sack and hung as sugar-cured ham, with cloves and spices added later. This was my introduction to another part of farm life, noting that every part of the pig was used—except the squeals. I received a broad education in a few days of work where neighborly families gathered, contributed equally in produce, and divided the work, then had a grand dinner the following week.

Our family was not poor, but we did not live affluently. I was told at an early age that the best education would be afforded my brother and me if we would apply ourselves and obtain scholastic results. My brother John was away at whatever school my parents thought would afford him a good education, which did not always coincide with what my brother wanted. My parents explained to me that if I wished spending money or wanted to save, that would be my responsibility. They encouraged me by establishing a small bank account. I remember one of my first ventures was to sell produce from my parents' garden. Since I had done most of the planting, they approved of my making a contract with townspeople and with the local hotel owner for my produce. I cut asparagus and tied it in bunches, picked green beans and put them in quart containers, and pulled radishes and onions and washed them. I don't remember how much I received, but thought it a princely sum.

We had a glut of pigeons in the top of our barn where a sort of cupola housed them. Dad spoke of shooting some to reduce the population, but I begged him not to and thought of how I could make money and accomplish the desired result of lowering the pigeon population. I asked the hotel owner if he would buy them if I brought them in alive. He agreed, and we made a deal, until my dad was satisfied. The hotel owner served squab, and I gained extra funds.

To enhance my income, I decided to sell one of my special pigs to the tailor, Mr. Weaver. My mother had a large Chester white sow, which delivered thirteen pigs. Two were runts, which the sow would not suckle, so they were given to me. I was determined to raise them so wrapped them in towels and put them in a box behind the stove in the kitchen. I fed them milk by bottle with a nipple, and when they could eat more I went into the fields to get corn or whatever was available for pig food. I made a pen for them outside and before long they grew into normal size, and I thought the time was right to sell one. I talked with Mr. Weaver and told him I would sell him the pig for five dollars, which I thought an enormous sum, and Mr. Weaver prided himself on a bargain. I went home to tell my mother and father of my financial ability. I heard cries of anguish from my mother, but my father had a better solution. He marched over to Mr. Weaver, explained the situation, and returned the five dollars to get the pig back. I think they later sold the pig for fifty dollars which they put in my bank account.

There were absolutisms that Mother and Father both held, and one was cleanliness at all times. Mom would have hand and fingernail inspection before every meal. Orders were to put hands on the table, and if inspection was passed, Dad would return thanks and we would proceed to eat; if not, we were to go wash our hands, and not until we passed inspection were we allowed to eat.

Mom made quite an issue of table manners; it seems as if I can hear her—"now the napkin goes in the lap first and not as a bib" and "women sit to the man's right, hands in the lap except when eating. Do not play with crumbs or the utensils. Never scratch or fiddle with your face at the table. Do not slouch or tip the chair. Touch nothing until Dad returns thanks. Now, surely you know the utensils are to be used from the outside in— start with the instrument farthest from the plate unless the silverware is incorrectly placed. Never grasp the utensil as if you are handling a shovel or a broom. Eating with the fork European-style and using the knife as a pusher is perfectly acceptable unless you prefer the cross-over style." We had a dozen don'ts, among which was, "Do not rest the knife or other utensils on the edge of the plate like the oars on a boat. The knife, when not in use, is placed transversely across the top of the plate, and when the meal is finished the knife and fork are placed diagonally." All these directions were not as harassment or a lecture. There was a mountain more of dos and don'ts, all for our betterment. We later appreciated knowing these details to avoid embarrassing ourselves or others.

Life in Highland was very pleasant for me, but there were moments that were agonizing. I remember receiving the start of a paddling in front of my classmates in first grade because of talking when I should have been listening. Another time in class I raised one finger, meaning I had to urinate. This was during an academic test, and Miss Bly, my teacher, reminded me that I had been excused twice within the past few minutes to go, so she took me across her lap to paddle me in front of the class. She had on a beautiful new red dress, and with the first stroke of her hand across my seat, my plumbing burst and she screamed out, "What are you doing?" She let me down in a hurry and ran out of the room dripping and with a huge darkened and wet area over the front of her dress. My classmates were bursting in laughter, but I was chagrined and ran home fast. I was never paddled again. Later my physiological problem, the enuresis, and the stuttering which I had developed, came under control with the love and security my parents gave me, and their patient explanations.

On special occasions my brother John came home from military school at Wentworth. I loved my brother and was very proud of him in his spic-and-span uniform. He was the pride of the town. He always treated me kindly. But like me, he had his moments of embarrassment, as when he took a girl out for a ride in the buggy. The old horse, Molly, had a problem with gas after having eaten a load of green oats, and retaliated in a blast with every trot. As John and his girl, the town beauty, rode along behind Molly, they faced a bombardment from the rear of the horse. He was humiliated but when he was older he recounted the story on occasion with at least a bit of humor.

Saturday nights in Highland the streets filled with wagons, buggies, and occasionally a car. Townfolk gathered to buy, visit, and gossip, while munching roasted peanuts, chestnuts, or popcorn from the whistling machine where the man scooped aromatic, buttered, fluffy corn into bags.

It was a thrill to go down to our small railway station. I found it exciting to watch the massive iron train (the iron horse) enter the station, huffing, puffing, and steaming. The engineers and conductors were awesome figures to me; the engineer sat high in his seat behind the engine like a king on his throne, and waved to us gawking, admiring smallfolk. Even now, the far-off sound of a train—including whistle and bell—continues to stir memories.

On the Sabbath we attended Sunday School and church and did no work outside of necessary cooking and dishwashing. The town boasted two churches, Presbyterian and Congregational, and we attended the former. Sunday afternoons Dad made medical rounds, tending the sick, and I accompanied him; sometimes my mother went along. We rode in the buggy drawn by our faithful old horse Molly, and I had the job of tending Molly, seeing that she was tied, fed, and watered. I was fascinated by my father's care for the sick. On the drive home he recounted symptoms, causes, treatments, and at times, prognoses. He was a true family doctor who encompassed the entire family in his medical and emotionally supporting role and wept for the suffering. He carried the firmness of his faith to all, praying when he felt it would help. He treated patients with then known remedies, some of which were hotpacks, wool vests, flaxseed or potato poultices, physics, sedatives, and diets. I listened to my father explain illnesses, and how to help with God's healing. Nearly all chest conditions, if acute, were pneumonia, or if chronic, it was considered "consumption." His talks on the return home taught me about weaknesses and idiosyncrasies of people, and the price one often must pay for transgression of the laws of God and the conventions of society.

Sundays were not the only days my parents practiced their religion. It was a part of everyday life. Never was a meal partaken without asking the blessing; never a day begun or finished without thanking the Lord for lighting the way and giving wisdom to help others, and we acknowledged gratefulness for his blessings.

CHAPTER TWO
A TRIP TO COLORADO

I vividly recall the summer of 1917, at which time my mother and father decided to visit Dad's brother, Dr. Harry W. Graham and family, his wife Cora, and son Leonard, in Yuma, Colorado. We had a Ford touring car and we loaded it fore and aft. Some of the main highways were gravel and macadam, but many miles were dirt and mud, and ruts, when it rained. I remember the blistering, unmercifully hot sun beating down upon us as we drove through the flat prairies of Kansas. As we drove along we disturbed many a flock of prairie chickens and sage hens. Huge jack rabbits also loped along in front and to the side of our car, with black-tipped ears bobbing, showing no sign of fear. In early mornings we watched the prairie cocks flair their tail feathers, preen and dance. Hundreds of prairie dogs bobbed up out of their burrows, ran awhile, and dived in other holes. By many of the holes we saw a prairie, or ground owl, standing on the mound like a sentinel.

Many a time when the rains descended we rushed to fasten the side curtains. There were isinglass windows to peer through but to our discomfiture there were plenty of leaks to trickle or spout rain on us. Then came the mud ruts, and gumbo—the latter is stickier, like a mixture of glue and mud. Our wheels would sink down to the hub caps, and spin if we were on a high center. On such an occasion we had the fun of putting on chains, looking for tree limbs (with never a tree on the prairie) and stones where there were no stones using almost anything to place under the spinning rear wheels—where there was nothing but mud. Dad and I would get out and push the car in a rocking manner to gain traction, while Mom tried to steer.

In Colorado, we were caught in a drencher, stuck to the hubs, and the car seemed inextricable. We could either wait for help on a rarely traveled road, or walk to a farm house. One of the chains had broken, but I found wire and tried to wire it together, while Dad looked for some solid object to place under the wheel. One fact I learned that afternoon of battling around in the mud was that it is easier to accomplish your task when not concerned about soiling your clothes. I was trying to place a piece of bailing wire around the broken chain links when I slipped and fell in the mud-hole. The work became easier, as my thoughts were no longer on how to keep clean and I worked as I wallowed. The chains having been placed around the rear wheels we cranked up the engine and found we were riding on high center—the wheels had spun up to the hubs and the car was resting on the axles.

No rocking would budge the old crate. Dad returned from his search with a huge armload of sage brush, which he had found and chopped loose. We stuffed mounds of sage brush under the wheels and filled the deep ruts, Mom was at the steering wheel, while Dad cranked and sparked the engine up, choking it by pulling the wire protruding from the right of the radiator. The crank kicked back, but fortunately, Dad was not injured as it flew back out of his hand in a reverse twist. He then showed me how always to crank with one's hand cupped—with crank handle in hand and thumb never around the handle, as it could fracture a thumb, hand, or forearm.

The engine finally started and Dad and I rocked the car out of the ruts while piling sage brush under the wheels. I was one big mud ball, so Dad took me by the feet and pulled me through the buffalo grass until there was enough improvement to allow me to sit in the car. Dad had an extra five-gallon can of his mixture of gas and kerosene, so he filled the tank and away we rode, this time following the prairie floor and staying out of the rutted road. The racing motor had exacted heat and stress in the radiator and it soon began to steam and boil. Dad had filled the radiator from the water-filled ruts and found the small leak, which he repaired by putting some corn meal he had brought along into the radiator. To my surprise the hole stopped leaking. Dad commented that he did not know whether corn cobs, popped corn, or cornmeal pancakes would come flying out the exhaust pipe.

We rolled right along. Mom had retreated to the back seat to prepare peanut-butter and jelly sandwiches with homemade bread. I had washed off fairly well in the last water hole or rut and we felt like kings with our appetites appeased and our car functioning. We were in top spirits until we reached the outskirts of our destination—Yuma, Colorado—when we heard the sickening sound of air swish out of a rear tire. We stopped, jacked up the rear end, took off the tire, and took out the inner tube. We found a bent horse-shoe nail which he removed and Dad showed me how to patch the tube: we scratched around the hole, and used a special glue to affix the patch. We put the tube in the tire, and the tire on the rim. Then I pumped air in, and took the car off the jack, and again were on our way.

As we continued down the rutted road we drove through a herd of cattle coming down the trail in front of us headed for the railroad corral. The horses of the cowboys shied and reared up, putting on quite a show until we shut off the motor. Some of the cattle tested their heads and horns on the car but found they were attacking a rather hard-headed immovable "animal." One young bull tried to push us over. I honked once, pushing the old rubber-bulbed honker, and the bull backed off. But a cowboy suggested we not do it again as it might spook the herd into a stampede. The bull stood a few moments, then sidled off, but some of the cows continued to look at the car, until prodded along by the cow puncher.

At last we arrived at the house of Uncle Harry, Aunt Cora, and Cousin Leonard, battered and muddy, and worn; I'm sure we were a sight to behold. A few buckets of water in an old tin tub, a bit of soap, and we were shined up enough to put on a change of clothes. After talking until our eyelids were heavy, and our stomachs filled with lemonade and tidbits, we were off to bed. In the morning Dad and Uncle Harry were up unloading the car. The aroma of hot cakes, biscuits, and red-eye gravy, along with ham and eggs, was too inviting to remain in bed. I dressed and ran down to a wonderfully tasty breakfast.

The first day was planned for parental visits, and Dad was to see a few people for medical consultations, which his brother had arranged. The second morning we were to go hunting for rabbits, and prairie and sage hens for the evening meals. Cousin Leonard had a Paint pony, and he had a pretty Roan for me. He thought my longer legs would fit better to the horse he suggested. The first day he had planned for us to ride, get acquainted with my horse, and look around the ranch. He wanted to be sure I could ride well enough before we went hunting. He said I should learn how to handle the horse in all ways of fast maneuvering. He said it was more difficult hunting rabbits and prairie chickens on horseback; it might be necessary to hit them on the run. Leonard's favorite way was to ride bareback, but with me said I should use the western saddle. He had me put on a pair of his chaps, and the day was to be spent with him horseback riding. He was a splendid horseman, who appeared to have lived in the saddle, although he was only about nine years old. We rode two miles down to the back pasture where there were forty head of cattle. Our time was spent putting both the horses and ourselves through the paces; walking, galloping, trotting, and turning, using reins and our knees or legs. I soon discovered the horses needed no training; I was the one who needed the training. He showed me how to cut out a cow or a calf from the herd. Everything was new and interesting but my rear was tired and sore after four hours in the saddle. We rode home, and I told Leonard to go in the house and wash up for lunch and I would follow after watering my horse. I did not want to act as if I could not get out of the saddle. When Leonard went into the house, I slid out of the saddle and sat down on the grass while my horse looked at me. I felt bow-legged and my bottom was sore and felt like it was blistered. Walking was a task, but I finally made it. We had lunch and Leonard was ready to saddle up again and ride out to the range. I didn't want to refuse but there was no easy excuse. He thought I was kidding when I mentioned sitting around and reading for the afternoon. I ended up in the saddle, but convinced Leonard the scenery and flowers were so unusual and enjoyable I did not care either to trot or canter; only to walk the horse along and see the hills in the distance.

Leonard had taught me how to mount my pony, placing my left foot in the stirrup and quickly swinging my right leg over, settling into the saddle, and placing my right foot in the right stirrup. Aunt Cora and Mom had fixed peanut butter and jelly, and also cheese sandwiches. We put them in a brown paper sack, placed them in a saddlebag, and went up to the town's general store to get some dried fruit as Aunt Cora said she had used the last of her own for apple pie.

On the way to town by horseback we ran into a group of cowboys coming in for the rodeo. We stopped in front of the store, hooked the reins over the saddle pommel, dismounted, and flipped the bridle strap in half hitches over the hitching rail in front of the store. The cowboys asked the way to the rodeo corral, and Leonard pointed the way, which was only three miles up the one road or two miles straight across the prairie. They took the prairie route and we went into the store, to discover that we had forgotten what kind and how much dried fruit to get. The storekeeper had only dried apples and apricots so we took a half pound of each and placed them in the saddlebags.

As we rode back over the prairie and up the side of the hill, Leonard's horse reared up when a large badger rumbled across in front of the horse. With his horse rearing on its hind legs, the average horseman would have been thrown, but Leonard leaned forward to one side of the saddle horn, held the reins tight, and soon all was quiet. I was thankful it was not my horse cutting the capers, although Leonard acted as if it were a daily occurrence. We rode onto a large plain at the top of the hill, which I thought was a mountain. There the cowboys were busy cutting out the calves that were just past the newborn state, I believe. They bull-dogged them, lassoed and wrestled them down, tied their legs, and branded them on the left hip with (–G) Bar G, then swallow-forked the back of their right ears halfway down. The young bulls were de-bulled, then turned loose to run. The parts removed were saved in a bag. I never thought any more about this occurrence as I supposed the tissues would be probably used as fish bait or fed to the hogs. The next evening a new dish of food was on the table, called mountain oysters. I had some and thought they were excellent. This proved a most interesting afternoon. Eventually we turned toward home, cutting along the edge of a sugar-beet field, then down the path toward home. When we arrived we took off the saddles, watered, fed, and curried the horses, and put them in their stalls. After we had washed up we had a wonderful evening meal. We prepared that evening to go hunting the next morning and I was given a 410-gauge shotgun. Leonard took a 22-caliber rifle. We talked a little around the fireplace which contained a burning log, as evenings and nights were cold and went to bed under warm comforters where I dreamed of tomorrow.

We arose the next morning before dawn, had a snack, bridled and saddled the horses, and took off for the sagebrush plains. I found riding the horse easier by standing in the stirrups when it trotted, although I now had a sheepskin over the saddle. Reaching our destination we spread out and walked for awhile, later riding through brush and tumbleweeds where game was plentiful. We sat for a time, listening to the prairie cocks crow and watching them dance. We aimed and shot well enough for both of our families to have three meals—from five prairie hens, three sage hens, and five rabbits. We saw a few deer close by, and a herd of elk up the mountain. The sun came up blazing and beautiful, stirring the misty fog to rise from the earth. The blue sage was resplendent with pearls of dew in the morning sun. Some of the sage had a purple-orchid cast and some nearby appeared a pearly silver-gray. A pair of coyotes jumped up and were in no great hurry to trot out of gun range, stopping occasionally and looking back. We mounted our horses and rode deep-rutted hill trails until the sun was three quarters to the meridian, then turned and ambled back home. We stirred up a few prairie dogs, which barked and scolded before popping into their burrows. We took our time on return, winding around rustic trails. In the early afternoon we found a shady spot where the grass was green, and unbridled the horses to let them graze while we ate our sandwiches. We spent a while picking up strange and colorful rocks and stones. When the huge, blazing sun dropped to the western range and twilight was approaching we headed for home, where we again cared for the horses, cleaned and dressed our game, and placed it in a solution of salt water.

That night at supper the table comments varied from medical matters to philosophy, and about a troubled world filled with troubled people.

Mom noted to us that Leonard could play the cornet, and asked that he play. Leonard went to his room and took the shining cornet from its case, and Aunt Cora suggested "My Buddy." He played exceedingly well. My Aunt, however, disapproved of one of the songs where he played a double beat, which to me sounded better than the others. She told him to put the horn away, although we were enjoying his selection. Aunt Cora voiced her thoughts on a dour note, saying, "I do not know where he picks up that ragtime sound—I do not approve. The next thing we know he will be wanting to play in one of those vile late-hour dance hall bands."

"You bought the cornet, let him play what he wishes," said my mother. "It is very pleasing to the ear and will make so many people happy. He is talented to be playing so well at this age. You should be proud of him."

Aunt Cora then replied, "The pastor of the church has requested Leonard to play at services next Sunday, but I refuse to allow it, as I would perish if he broke out in that horrible ragtime. He somehow manages to 'accidentally' change decent songs into that brazen dance-hall swing. At his age, or any age, he will not play that type of noise. The bandmaster said he was a musical genius, but I am sorry we ever bought that horn, as it may be his undoing."

Leonard put the cornet away and whispered, "Let's get out of here, because Mom is warming up for a Sunday School lecture."

We slipped out the back way and ran down to the barn, got two ropes, and Leonard taught me how to make a lariat, which he called a lasso. We lassoed a tree stump from several distances, and then he taught me how to swing a circle lariat. He tied the rope into a slip knot and twirled the circle until it gradually became too large. He then jumped into the circle and raised and lowered it, circling from his outstretched arm over his head. We played with the lariat until it was safe to go back to the house.

By this time Dad and Uncle Harry had returned from Uncle Harry's office and were busy reminiscing. Mom and Aunt Cora spent the afternoon talking while sewing on a patch quilt. They later put the evening meal together and we could smell the fried rabbit and prairie chicken and the baking bread. We gathered around the table, Dad gave the blessing, and we never tasted such a feast. We had pickled watermelon rind, corn, potatoes, pickles of all kinds, jellies and preserves galore, along with the fried game and baked bread. After supper we all gathered the dishes, cleaned the table scraps for the dog and mixed some of the scraps with bran for the hogs and some for the chickens, ducks, geese, and guineas. Mom and Aunt Cora washed the dishes and we boys did the drying. We were told of our chores for the next day before we could play; Leonard and I were to get the milk and put it in the separator, and churn the butter and bottle the buttermilk. Mom and Aunt Cora were going to make cottage cheese and pies.

Evenings and nights were cold in Colorado but with the log fire in the fireplace it was quite pleasant. It was great fun to play the gramophone, sit around the fires, and roast marshmallows. We did not stay up late; "we went to bed with the chickens." As I was dozing off under the warm comforters, I thought of the new adventure awaiting me, as Leonard had promised to take me to the rodeo the next afternoon. Almost as soon as the sun rose, I was awake in anticipation. Leonard understood my excitement and said we would get on our horses after breakfast and go rock hunting on the way to the rodeo. We packed a few sandwiches and were on our way to the foothills. We looked for gold, but I would not have recognized it if we had seen it. We did find iron pyrite, or fools' gold, quartz crystals, other multicolored and attractive stones, and even some Indian arrowheads. Our big surprise was seeing a rattlesnake as we lifted up a large flat rock, and it was our good fortune that it did not strike. We put our treasure of rocks in our saddlebags and sat down under the shade of a tree to eat our sandwiches and rest a bit. After that we decided to head for the rodeo.

It was a hot day, and as we rode, I noticed that the prairie appeared blue from the shimmering heat veils near the horizon. At times, this blue appeared to be a lake. As we neared the corral where the rodeo was to take place the area was congested with trucks which had brought cattle of all kinds; bulls to rope and ride, a few steers, and calves for the roping and branding contests. There were many wild horses that had never been ridden. Contestants and animals had come in across the prairie from many different directions. Since there were few roads, one would simply take off across the prairie in the general direction of their destination.

The rodeo was to be in a large corral which had a circular raw-board fence with tiered rows of wooden planks for seats. On one side of the bench stands were four long stalls sectioned to allow a horse or cow into a fairly close fit—a shutter on the rear, and one on the front to drop down to hold the animal for the bronco-buster to mount.

The event was a wild and woolly roughhouse. The bull riders practically exploded out of the chute on the jumping, tossing, kicking and twisting animal. Each rider was timed to see how long he could remain on its back. The real threat after a fall was the goring horns of the animal. The fallen rider must protect himself the best way possible, and that is to run away from the snorting mad bull who may try to stomp or gore him. A clown sometimes entered the arena and tried to entice the bull to follow him instead of the thrown rider. The clown did his best to escape by jumping into a barrel, over a fence, or just run away fast.

Calf roping was an event which demonstrated the cowboy's skill. He may lasso the calf around the neck, dismount quickly from his horse, then throw the calf by hand, tying three legs together securely with a piggin string which he carries in his mouth until needed. Another method was to lasso the calf around the hind legs then toss and tie him in the shortest time possible. The rider's horse is trained to stop at the exact time to tighten the rope on the calf.

Next came the wild horse, or bronc riding with and without a saddle. The wild mustangs were actually corralled from a wild herd from the mountains and plains. These horses jump, twist, snort, and rear up on their hind legs with tremendous strength and fury. Bronco-busting is definitely only for the very hardy and daring. There were other contests of horsemanship, and finally the rodeo drew to a close, and we rode on home talking of the events of the day.

Not only had this rodeo been exciting and fun to watch, I learned much about the differences between geldings, mares, and stallions. I learned that each horse was trained for a specific duty: a cutting horse became adept at cutting out steers from herds, and rope horses were trained to keep lariats taut after roping animals. Leonard gave me a lesson on the responsibilities of the cowboy: he was responsible for a group of horses (seven to fourteen), keeping them fed, watered, groomed, and their tails kept shortened and trimmed. He was also to keep the hooves trimmed and shod according to what each horse was trained to do.

The high-heeled boots of the cowboys intrigued me and was told that the heels were sloped in so they would not catch in the stirrups, and if the rider fell off, he could dig his heels into the ground when he stood up to pull on the roped animal. His boots also protected his legs while in the saddle and afforded protection against snake bites. These versatile boots could also be used to haul water for animals if necessary. The leather chaps the cowboys wore protected the riders against the horns of cattle when they were herded.

All of this I had learned that day, and I was anxious to return to tell my parents of this new found knowledge and to relate the exciting happenings of this memorable day. Back at the house they listened to my tales with interest and said that this trip to the "wild west" had been well worth the time spent.

The next day we left our Colorado relatives with many affectionate goodbyes and our warm appreciation for a wonderful and memorable vacation. We were advised to take a different route home, which was a much better road, and only then did we realize that Dad had taken that awful road to Colorado because he thought it was shorter. The trip home was dreadfully hot and dusty and we drove hundreds of monotonous miles over the plains, but it at least was uneventful. After the flat, dry plains, it was good to see the beginning of the Flint Hills of Kansas with their beginning greening. The visit to Colorado was long ago, but it seems now as if it were yesterday.

CHAPTER THREE
MOVING TO THE CITY

My enjoyment of childhood was not abated, but became even more exciting in my innocence of the portent of what began to occur about the age of seven. In 1916 and 1917 came the rumblings of war with vicious propaganda, and the bands played "Johnny Get Your Gun," "We're Coming Over and it Won't be Over Till It's Over, Over, There," and "I'm a Yankee Doodle Dandy." Suddenly there were parades, marching bands, and lots of excitement. Along the streets of Highland, large flat bodied trucks, hay wagons, and other vehicles paraded slowly down the streets behind the blaring bands, beating drums, waving flags, and all the trappings of the propaganda for war; a war to "demolish the Kaiser." The slogans of the day were outrageous, bloodcurdling, and preposterous propaganda. Any man not arising to the occasion and getting aboard the vehicle was considered a slacker. Many men, including my father,were mesmerized by these "drums of war," with the waving flags and the synchronized sounds of marching feet. Men were urged to "join up."

My father stood with his father, who was a disabled veteran of the Civil War. Grandfather Graham sustained a lame leg and back, and a left eye was missing from his involvement in actual battles. I remember his making a statement to the effect that those courageous young men marching with light hearts and heavy determination had not the slightest idea of the horror and misery of war they would face. My father at this point said, "It is my duty and right to help and protect as many as I possibly can." My grandfather agreed. Perhaps, it was reflection on these words of my father that partially decided my life's course and later actions.

At the onset of the war, about 1917-1918, there were reports of endemic outbreaks of smallpox throughout the United States. As a result, it was mandatory that everyone be vaccinated against this dread disease. My father, along with the only other doctor in town, who was a veterinarian, and my mother, were busy inoculating the town and country folks for smallpox. All spare time was utilized by anyone not going to war, by busily knitting woolen khaki sweaters, making gun cleaning materials, gathering walnuts for gas masks, cutting bandages, making anything acceptable and utilizable for a ghastly war of which we actually knew very little except "God was on our side." My mother happened to ask one day, "Why did God leave the enemy and come to our side, as they have on their coins, 'Gott Mit uns,' and we have 'In God we trust.'" She was quite roundly chastised for considering that God could possibly be with the enemy too. It did plant a seed of doubt, however, about what I had previously heard. My father was soon off to Camp Funston and Fort Riley, Kansas, believing that he must carry out his duty to our nation. With the playing of the "Star Spangled Banner," today as then, continue to thrill to the ends of my hair. We participated, and we had the "Glory," but "What Price Glory?" as someone has asked. The treaty at Versailles left much to be desired and laid the ground work for World War II. The war continued on until 1918.

When I was almost nine years old and my father was returned from army duty, he decided to enlarge his practice and take advantage of broader opportunities offered in a city, such as utilization of the facilities of a hospital for his patients, especially for surgery, which he was qualified to perform. He felt also that my brother and I would gain a better education and my mother would be happier without farm work. He carefully pondered just which city, and decided that Kansas City, Missouri fit in with what he planned for the future. He carefully explained to the family the reasons for the move and the advantages we had to look forward to, so the move was not traumatic to me as it could have been had he not paved the way so well. Then Dad arranged for two young M.D.s to come to town to care for the community, and he bundled the family up to reside in Kansas City, Missouri in 1919. General medical and surgical practice was set up anew. He progressed remarkably well and also enjoyed teaching young doctors and yearly classes of nurses toward their degrees.

Adjusting to city life was not difficult for me. It was a new adventure which I found exciting. Initially I did have some problems from my peers in school. I attended Troost School in Kansas City, Missouri which was then located on the northwest corner of Sixtieth and Troost Avenue across the street from the Sixtieth Street Fire Station. I do not recall any inside lavatory facilities in the old red brick school. There was a six-holer, however, near the back of the school on the edge of the playground with the back toward the alley. The Board of Education must have bought up all the old catalogues from Montgomery Ward and Company, and Sears and Roebuck. To go to this school my mother considered that well dressed boys in the fourth and fifth grades should look similar to a character called "Buster Brown." She had me wear short woolen plaid socks of the Graham, Scott, or Wallace tartan, any of which could wear with authenticity. I also wore a large ascot tie, a wide brimmed hat, and short pants above the knee. The dress of the time however, where I went to school in Kansas City, was knee pants which bloused and buttoned either above or below the knee, and long black socks with button-up or laced shoes. The initiation to my city peers was like feeding a bit of fresh meat to the lions, and I was the bait. The hat disappeared with my first encounter and never saw it again, for which I was grateful.

My only training for self-defense thus far had been a bit of country wrestling which certainly did not prove sufficient. Day after day, week after week, I was either faster on my feet than my adversary, or was trounced. I learned a bit more about self-defense, however, when my brother John came home on furlough from Wentworth, where he was on the boxing team. He taught me some of the fundamentals of boxing which came in very conveniently for the new, strangely dressed boy in school. I refused to conform by a change in my clothes, except for the hat that I lost the first day. I was especially very proud of the plaid socks being of a family tartan like my paternal forefathers wore in Scotland.

Soon after coming to Kansas City, my mother bought me a new bicycle so I could carry and deliver the *Journal* newspaper which later became the *Journal Post* paper, and I received the sum of four dollars a week. My bike also aided in a more swift travel home in an effort to outdistance my adversaries. One day the head bully in the sixth grade, coached by the Chief in the seventh grade, caught me and teased me about my clothes. I took a fair battering until stepping back into the spokes of my new bicycle wheel, snapping off two spokes. I could do nothing then but fire back, and this I did with vigor. My adversary, Ed Donnelly appeared as surprised as I was. This was the first time I had ever retaliated, and I was more amazed than Ed that I whipped him. This proved to be the beginning of the end, as I had learned a few tricks, until the head honcho of the school was met.

While sitting in class one day in the sixth grade of the Troost School, a classmate, John Neff, handed me a note to pass on to another boy. The one I was to pass the note to was the head of the so-called "55 Street Gang," a group of young fellows banded together for a common purpose. They were not rowdies, only a group with similar thoughts. Steve was the head of the gang. He was not a bully, however, he had the established name as the best fighter in school. He was in the highest grade and I was in one grade lower. Steve was actually a fine young man whom I considered my friend. He was from a family of nine children. As soon as he received the note he turned red with anger and was obviously enraged. He told me he would meet me at the northwest corner of the fight ground on 59th Street and Troost Avenue. John Neff saw what was taking place and wrote a strong note to me not to tell Steve who wrote the note and he would explain at recess. I tried repeatedly, but in vain, to explain that I did not write the note, however, I refused to tell him who did write it.

Recess time came and John begged not to be revealed, but I explained that I was not willing to be a punching bag for that big Bruiser. John then explained that his mouth was filled with metal bands on his teeth and he would be ruined if I told. I tried every way to convince him to explain everything to Steve. The contents of the note was, "Hey Boob, where did you get the little Billy's haircut?" The fact was I had never paid any attention to the haircut and could care less about it. I found out one day that every two to three weeks Steve's dad would line the six boys up in the family, place a bowl on their head and proceed to cut and shave their heads below the edge of the bowl. I explained and told Steve I would not fight him as I was not the one who sent the note, and at the time knew nothing about it. Steve cooled a bit, however, the entire school had the propaganda quite disseminated. Obviously, this was a situation from which I could not diplomatically extricate myself. I then concentrated on how best to manage my defense. My brother had always advised me to attack in such circumstances, and to attack with ferocity and counter-attack before the opponent could get set.

My attack was being planned when the teacher called me to recite while at the height of psychogenic internal combustion. My first words were, "Yes Ma'am, Miss Good, attack hard and fast,"—then I caught myself, tried a fast verbal retreat and asked her to repeat the question. The issue was side stepped adequately, I think, as she probably thought I was day-dreaming again. The recitation helped, as it took my mind off the issue of battle for the time being. The final school bell rang at four o'clock, and there was no escape, as I knew this was something to be faced. One of Steve's gang was standing by my bicycle in the event I wanted to take that escape. We walked to the so-called battleground while my heart was pounding fiercely. It seemed as if the entire student population was there and a few adults. A large ring was marked off. Steve took off his shirt, so I followed suit. I made a last statement about not revealing the author of the note although he was there. My hope was for him to clear me, but he gave me no such help. Steve moved to center and I followed. We faced each other with fists held high and clinched tightly. Our faces were pale and my adversary looked mean. He told me I was scared and I said, "I sure am," and asked him to listen to reason. He replied that he would not listen to me. He flicked out a left jab and I immediately tore into him like a buzz-saw—afraid to stop: we both were surprised. His nose was bleeding, and he fell, not from my punch, but everyone thought so. However, he tripped over a ringside foot. The temporary halt was welcomed and I was too winded to attack again with such steam. I could tell, however, that my position had improved by Steve's expression and his nose was bleeding. Suddenly he bounded up and rushed me, and we both went down in a clinch. Up we came; he delayed a bit, rushed again, and I side-stepped and ducked right into a whopper. After the stars stopped flying, we both tagged each other. His gang was encouraging him, but my followers were tongue-tied. It was obvious then, that he was fighting for his honor and status, and I was fighting to get out, just hoping that darkness would fall. Oddly enough, although my face was swollen, I was no longer afraid, nor did I have any pain. He rushed again; we both caught each other, I gave him a left jab to the nose, and he caught me with a right cross to the head. We were obviously tired and out of breath, and I suggested we sit for three minutes, which we did. We were soon at it again, round after round. I discovered all the blood over us both was not entirely from his nose because mine was just bit leaky also. We battered away, both landing blows like two apes. I suddenly saw the look of fatigue or defeat in Steve's eyes. I could hardly hold my arms up and it was near dark; I put all my reserve steam into the battle. It appeared that he was nearly psyched out as well as worn out, and he could no longer hold his arms up to strike or for defense. I raised Steve's arm and he acknowledged he had plenty. I assured him it was a draw, however, I gained the plaudits, status, and esteem from our classmates. I then walked over to Steve and his now few followers, and asked, "What did this crazy fight prove? That same note was not written by me, and the one who wrote it meant no harm."

Steve replied, "Well, I guess it means you beat the hell out of me." I replied, "By no means, there is no win over friends." With this we shook hands and moved our sore, bloody, battered, and bruised bodies toward home. My fatigue was so great that it was too much drudgery to ride my bike home; besides I had the shakes.

At this miserable affair, there was a man watching who I found later was Sergeant Baker of the 63rd Police Station. He took me aside and asked if I wanted to make some money. I replied I had a job carrying papers. Then I was told I could be trained and earn over fifteen dollars a week within a year if I worked hard. He said all I had to do was box. My reply was, "absolutely not. Here I stand still half scared or shaking. Look at my eyes, I can barely see out of my very swollen and black left eye, my nose is battered and bloody. My arms and hands are blue and you are asking me to do this for pay—I need the money but there is no way I would ever do this knowingly."

Sergeant Baker replied, " You are entirely mistaken. You would have padded hands, use big thick boxing gloves and besides you would be trained several months in learning how to avoid getting hit, how to protect yourself. You will learn defense as well as how to box scientifically. The boxing time is limited to only a couple of minutes of three or rarely four rounds." He gave me his name and address of the police station. He said it works in well with my job carrying papers. I never told my parents of this. I continued to carry my papers and seasonally tended furnaces, hauled ashes, made gardens, and sold produce. I also trained daily, learning the art of boxing in the attic of the Country Club 63rd Street Police Station under Sergeant Myers and Sergeant Baker, and some local boxers. After about six months of vigorous training, I was given my first bout at which time I was classed as Fly Weight. I did not actually weigh enough and there was no such thing as a paper weight so my class was that of a fly weight.

I was very brave until I went to the Olympic Club and saw my opponent, who appeared not too unlike a gorilla. He had hair on his chest and appeared to be at least forty pounds more than my weight. The ring ropes were entered, and my heart was pounding into my ribs like a trip hammer. The referee gave his rules and admonitions. I dashed to the center of the ring, touched gloves, and immediately flashed a straight left sharp jab to the chin. My opponent fell, much to my surprise, and I gave a sigh of relief when the referee counted ten and said it was over. The following week, a bout was arranged in the Kansas City Athletic Club. This time was a bit more difficult; my left jab missed the intended spot and I collected a sledge hammer blow to the abdomen. This rather chilled me a bit, and I did everything but crawl out of the ring. Advice by the coach was then followed between rounds regarding using arms and elbows for abdominal protection and to flash the left jab constantly and never in-fight. I pedaled, weaved, dodged, and ducked until neither I nor my opponent could jab any longer. He dropped to his knees and I was dumbfounded. The bell rang; however, it was called a draw, and we had to box another round, making it four rounds. I wanted to stop, but I believed my coach who then told me my opponent was a smoker and was much more tired than I. He said, "look fresh and just hold the left jab high and in his face." I acted alert, pranced like a young colt, and amazed my opponent with a left jab and a right hook to his jaw. My arms dropped to my sides, feeling numb, each fist feeling as if they weighed a hundred pounds. Fortunately, my opponent dropped from sheer exhaustion before there were any further moves. I was given two dollars for so-called training expenses as I felt I still had not been trained enough.

Although I continued on with boxing for several years this took only a small portion of my high school years; there was a great deal of time to do other things. I have already mentioned being delivery boy for the *Journal Post*. This paper was the only competition that *Kansas City Star* ever had, and it became insolvent after some years, leaving the *Star* as Kansas City's only newspaper. I had to get up in the very early dawn, about four o'clock, go to the fire station at 60th Troost Avenue where the deliverer had left my papers to roll. After I rolled all of them, I made my rounds, rain or snow, hot or cold weather. I had my bike which my mother had bought me to make my rounds faster; however, there were many times when I had to walk my bike, and the papers, as the roads were too muddy and the ruts too deep. My route took me to and through the Forest Hill Cemetery where it was necessary to deliver a paper to the caretaker. My route then picked up directly on the other side, so I had to zig-zag through a few markers, many times whistling and pedaling with vigor. I then covered several more miles, looping back through another smaller, but older cemetery where the Daniel Boone family is buried at the southeast corner of the former Blue Hills Golf Course off 63rd Euclid. From there, it was practically all down hill on the way home where I would change my clothes, have breakfast, get my books, and go to school. I did receive the sum of $4.00 a week for this rigorous routine.

After about a year, I stopped the paper delivery and found other ways to make money. I helped some of the people nearby to make their gardens and sold produce from them. During winters I contracted with several neighbors to make their furnace fires or to stoke furnaces so that their homes would warm up before they arose. Then my Saturday job was to carry out the ashes which I shoveled from the furnaces.

Winter also brought fun when the snows came. My father and I built a long three track, double runner bobsled which could hold fifteen to twenty bundled classmates, ages around twelve to thirteen. Bobbing was great, either on long hills or on streets which had been blocked off for sledding. The long, steep hills were too icy for automobile travel, and there was never too much traffic on suburban streets anyway, so we were relatively safe. We occasionally hitched the bobsled behind a cooperative car for a good ride.

My first thrill of budding endocrinological burst was in holding tight to the bundled little girl, named Velma, in front of me who had long, golden curls. After the long and exciting sled rides, we all gathered at her parents home, Mr. and Mrs. Stanley Hill, where we were warmly welcomed with hot chocolate (then we called it "cocoa") with marshmallows and cookies. We were always rather sorry to see the snow melt away because we enjoyed those times so much.

As with every young person, some people and events had a profound effect upon me. Little did I dream that the pretty little girl who sat at the desk in front of mine at Troost school would have such a lasting effect on my life. Even though I had very little inclination or time to consider girls, her long golden curls particularly intrigued me, and could not resist the temptation to place the ends of those tresses into my ink well which was strategically placed just behind her. Much to my chagrin, she was then called upon by the teacher to recite and to go to the blackboard, revealing to our classmates and the teacher alike, her black-tipped dripping curls. The classmates, began to giggle and the teacher glared, wanting to know who did this. The girl, Velma, had a good idea but refused to tell on me. I was quite impressed, and this was the first of a long series of happenings which led eventually to her becoming my wife. I guess that my endocrines were faintly beginning to dawn and the paint job on the curls was a subconscious show of affection, as she was the daintiest girl in school. I have already mentioned the thrill and excitement of holding her while bob-sledding. We also had some contact when we took piano lessons together. My mother instilled music appreciation in me as a young boy by listening to the great arias, and she tried valiantly to mold me into a Paderewski. She decided that piano lessons were a must, and for eight years I practiced the piano. It seemed to me that exercises took up too much piano time, even the ones by Chopin. However, if the piano pieces were lively and melodic, I learned to play them well and enjoy them. Pieces such as "March Militaire," "Rustle of Spring," and Rachmaninoff's "Prelude in C Minor" still ring pleasantly in my ear. I remember being paired with that same golden-haired girl whom I have mentioned previously as if it were yesterday. We played duets together and at our final and impressive recital we played with two other students in a rousing eight-hand, two-piano rendition of "March Militaire." I have envied those fellows and my friends who could seemingly pick up any musical instrument and play it. I have friends who have never had a music lesson in their life, yet play beautifully. I wonder how they find the key board with the proper sharps and flats. For several years, I pounded out note after note then was lucky if I could play a composition of music from beginning to end without a blurp. My friend Herschel Oachs could beat out any classic or ragtime to make the toe wiggle and the legs fly into a dance and he never had a formal music lesson. I continued to pound out Chopin's exercises and the little ditties from *Etude* music magazine. Piano playing, however, eventually gave way to more exciting activities, when my mother finally decided I would never become a concert pianist.

We always managed to have some fun after my chores were finished. When I learned to shoot marbles, and how to handle a knife well, we had an area closed for a marble ring and mumblety-peg. We played hide and seek often, which was one of our favorite games. We also had a big bag swing that required a climb up a stepladder to jump on the bag and swing far out into space. We spent many an hour on this swing, enjoying flying through the air. Another activity which we found lots of fun was to have scooter races. We fashioned these scooters from an orange crate, a three-foot two by four board, and put old skates on the bottom. They were noisy, but great to race. I doubt if any modern ten-speed bike could have made us any happier.

Some of our activities would never have been approved by our parents. One morning when we were looking for something new and exciting, Louis Karges let me in on a secret: on the back of the outside privy at school there was a loose board which was on the girl's side. We planned a devilish trick for the next morning. We went to school early, armed with our bean-shooters, sauntered to the back of the privy, and removed that loose board, waiting for prey. Sure enough, there appeared before our eyes a big bottom sitting on the appropriate place—a perfect target. We took aim and let fly. There was an immediate whoop and holler and we took off in a flash. We never did discover who the victim was and we surely didn't inquire, but the next day the board was nailed on firmly.

Generally throughout grade school I liked all my teachers. They were thorough, kind, helpful, conscientious, and strict without being intolerable. They earned and received respect. Sixth and seventh grades were taught in the same room by the principal. I remember her well. She was ultra strict, austere, and unbending. She always wore dark or black clothing and black high button shoes. Her dark skirt draped down her slim, six-foot frame, above which she wore a pleated blouse with a high collar, which seemed to almost touch her ears and was usually of the same monotonous dark material. Her graying hair was piled in a tent-like, rolled knot on top of her head, which accentuated her height. Apparently she never entertained the thought of using any rouge to her face, as it was always a lifeless grayish white. Her teeth were dark and unattractive, which added to her general appearance of being forbidding. I remember she would tell us to brush our teeth with salt and soda paste, even though her teeth obviously were not a good example of care. I was not one of Miss Ida B. Good's admirers; my lack of admiration probably stemming from a bit of variance on how to arrive at the proper solutions to arithmetic problems.

I made many lasting friendships in grade school. There were Ranny and Lew Wenzel, who with their younger brother, Murray (eight years younger), lived in back of us on 57th Forest. Then there was George "Fats" Blender, a quiet and gentle boy, Ed Donnelly, and Eddie Swain—all good and close friends.

Summers were carefree for us, and my friends and I often waited on the steps outside the Wenzels' home for the huckster to drive by with his horse-drawn wagon filled with produce, shouting "cabbetches, cantaloupe, & watermelone." Sometimes we would parody his calls, but more often we would help him make a sale, for which we might get a plum or a few cherries. We also were happy to see the iceman, Benny Hayes, come by with his wagon. He would let us pick up the pieces of chipped ice on hot summer days and always promised to give me a job when I could swing 150 pounds of ice upon my shoulder, using the tongs.

We boys were always trying to think up different things to do and decided it was time to build a tree house. The great majority of boys have a phase of life where they must build a tree house and we were no exception. Ranny, Lew, and I found a large walnut tree in a glen between what is now 59th and 60th Streets and Tracy on the left side where the woods were fairly thick. First, the cross sticks were nailed securely to the tree for a ladder. The right area was chosen between four large limbs. By means of ropes and pulleys, boards were hoisted to the proper level, laid across the large limbs and nailed securely. The sides and roof followed. Holes were bored in all sides for spying and one in the floor for relief. We then nailed leafy branches over, under, and around the structure for a camouflage and a true hide-a way. In the event we were attacked by any marauder we had a bucket of mud balls, and if they failed or if the supply was exhausted, we had a bucket of water, bows and arrows, and a BB gun. If all failed, we then had a long rope well attached which we could throw down the escape hatch. We had candle light when necessary and a few cans of beans for feasting when we wished.

When we weren't occupied with chores or play, we would often dream up interesting things to do. Most boys are dreamers, I think, and it is one of the fun parts of living: a play world in which we would act out the part of some of our idols. It was fun to act out our dreams, especially on rainy days. One of our ideas was to dig a cave in Wenzel's backyard. The cave was dug eight to nine feet in all directions usually square, with a side recess. We covered the top with logs and made a trap-door entrance and a second escape hatch. Near the bottom of the cave we fashioned a side hole to be used as a fireplace. A hole was bored in the roof away from the logs to allow a chimney made of a round tin pipe. An open tin cap was fashioned over the vent and the tin chimney to prevent snow or rain from entering, but still allowed the smoke to vent and air to circulate. The logs on the top were covered with dirt and sod. At times the snow covered this, making it seem even more snug inside. It was real fun to bake potatoes coated in mud, and roast chestnuts, marshmallows, or "wieners" on a green stick over the fire we made in the vented cave. It was warm and cozy, even as we could hear the wind howling and blowing above us. This was indeed a dreamland of warmth and comfort. Recesses had been cut for the placement of candles for added light but at times we hung lanterns for light.

In the spring, the call of the outdoors with the early winds and rain was irresistible. This was the time to pitch a pup tent or make a lean-to, and ditch around them properly to keep the rain running away from our tent. The most delightful part was snuggling into a rolled up warm blanket while listening to the beating of the rain drops on the canvas tent sides and top. A springtime could never pass without getting our quota of frogs, tadpoles, or pollywogs, and crawdads.

My friend, Randolph "Ranny" Wenzel, later became captain of the football team in high school as a quarterback. His brother, Lew Wenzel, was somewhat of a rough and tumble artist, rugged and ready for practically anything at any time if it meant excitement. Ranny was usually more reserved and probably used better judgment, but Lew and I lived it up even in our dream worlds. He was a good boxer also. Their younger brother, Murray, was too far down the age line to join in much of our play. Lew and I would read Tom Sawyer and Huckleberry Finn and dream of similar adventures. I remember when we would tie a string on our toe and hang it out the window; then either Lew would come by or I would come by, and pull on the string which was our signal to get out and go to the graveyard and spook around there, the same as Tom Sawyer or Huckleberry Finn did. We had exploits based on many of the other books that we read, including *Tarzan*, and a few other interesting novels. We were very close friends all through our elementary and high school days. College and time separated us a bit, but we are close friends to this day.

We had a fine baseball team, but it was only scrub baseball; we played in the street until a car would come along. In those days, it was rather unusual for a car to come down the street. We thought we also had a very good football team among the neighborhood boys. Among them was Fats Blender, who weighed two hundred pounds as a sixth and seventh grader. Others were Dick Clark, who was usually in the backfield, Ranny and Lew Wenzel, Norman Green, Otis Gibson, Gene Allison, Louis Karges, George Eib, and his brother Harry Alvin Eib, Harrel Hill, who was a bit younger than we were, (Harrel was the young brother of my best girl, Velma). There was also Eddie Swain, who was later the battalion chief of our firefighters here in the city. Then there was Ed Donnelly, who later became quite an outstanding and well known basketball player. One of my greatest pleasures, and one which was a very positive influence on my life, was my involvement in the Boy Scout organization. At the age of twelve, I joined

Troop 44 at Troost School. Through diligence came the rewards of pleasure and the status I needed at that time. Friday nights were always for Boy Scout meetings where we learned the art of signaling by flags and the Morse code. We learned the basic meaning of good citizenship and the real enjoyment of camping and outdoor life. We learned the art of survival under varied circumstances, Indian lore, and how to build fires with no matches, using flint and steel or fire by friction. It was a real pleasure to learn, and to teach others the skills we had achieved. Anyone may peruse the Scout manual and realize the value of Scouting to a young man in his formative years. I remember well when we went on fourteen mile and twenty mile overnight hikes. In achieving the many merit badges, we learned much about plant life, insects, animal tracking, and so many other things, that I feel Scouting was an education in itself. Under a competent and good leader, the time spent in Scouting is invaluable, especially if the entire program is followed. I attained the ranks from Tenderfoot to Eagle in record time, but earning the many and various merit badges took study, work, and application. At the age of twelve, I attended Scout camp in Noel, Missouri. One summer I went to another Scout camp which was called The Dan Beard Camp in the East. Beard was one of the pioneers and early founders of the Boy Scout movement. He would emphasize Indian Lore and nature study.

The last two years in elementary grades were spent in a new school built between 59th and 60th Streets and Forest, one block east of the old school. Here we had indoor water and toilets, more room, and better facilities for teaching and learning. All my teachers were respected, kind, considerate, and knowledgeable, with ability to speak the English language in more than mono-syllables. The old teachers would be shocked to listen to the atrocious language and abominable distortion of our language that one now hears on television or radio. It is no wonder our nation rates low in the over-all grading of literacy. Many teachers today accept less than mediocrity in allowing students to go from grade to grade not knowing proper English, using illegible writing, and with no idea of how to spell.

There were many exciting events during these years of going through elementary school. One of them was in the year of 1920 when I was privileged to see the famed North American Air Ace of World War I, Captain Eddie Rickenbacker. He had a group of Army Air Corps aviators who went to various cities to fly people around their locale. The group was called the Lafayette Cocked Hat Escadrille. Their insignia was the cocked hat of Uncle Sam with a red, white, and blue starred ring. Their bi-winged planes landed in the old Richards field, which was actually a large cow pasture at that time, with no established runways. We went to see this hero, and I recall my mother saying that she wondered if Eddie Rickenbacker had ever met Colonel "Buddy" Manfred, Baron von Richthofen, often referred to as the "Red Baron." She did not mention the fact that he was a relative. Captain Rickenbacker gave great credit to Baron von Richthofen and complemented his skilled ability as an air ace. Actually, Captain Rickenbacker had to his official credit twenty-two German planes and four balloons, which he shot down in combat. He took me in his double cockpit bi-winged plane and we flew for a bit over thirty minutes. We had a very enlightened conversation which my mother particularly enjoyed. At that time, I had no idea that I would become acquainted with him twenty-five years later. He accompanied President Truman and me on one of our flights, and he later sent autographed copies of the books he had written of his experiences.

Summer evenings were often spent working as a delivery boy for drug stores. I would carry deliveries on my bicycle from six to ten. My pay was fifty cents a night and any tips I might be fortunate enough to garner. While working as a delivery boy I learned about the soda fountain. I gradually learned how to mix syrups, make a chocolate or other flavor of soda, milk shake, or malted milk, a black cow, root beer float and all the other sweet goodies. I finally learned adequately to be moved as a soda fountain dish washer and assistant fountain boy. I would take charge in the absence of the main boy in command of the fountains.

One of my best friends was Chuck Long and we were usually interested in the same enterprises. We thought we knew a bit about bees so the idea of bee keeping and honey business struck us. We procured a hive and were told to move it after dark as all the bees would be in the hive and sleeping. In the dark of the moon one night we decided to move the bees. We plugged the entrance with cloth. I took the back and Chuck took the front. We thought we heard the bees buzzing inside and decided that was the way they slept. Up went the hive and we were getting along okay until we came to a barbed wire fence. Chuck got caught astraddle the top wire and could not move. We managed to balance the hive on the top wire of the fence while I came around and unhooked Chuck's trousers. As he cleared the fence the top strand gave way and the bees began to pour out around the rag. Chuck yelled out, "these damned bees are hitting me in the ass. What will I do?" I said, "Don't drop it."—The box tilted, sliding the big brood box forward over the base board—now they were flying out the rear banging me from the belly button on down.

I whooped and howled trying to keep my body under control and not move suddenly as this would infuriate the bees more. I managed to lift the entire hive, set it down, align the brood box with the base and again stuff the entrance opening. My hands, abdomen and legs were burning, painful, throbbing and swelling; the bees were now crawling up under my trousers stinging my legs and getting in my hair and on my face. I walked away a few feet and laid down perfectly quiet. They soon left as I suppose they considered me dead. Chuck was running over the hill and down the valley getting his pants off and sitting in the cool mud of a creek bed. My eyes were swollen shut—Chuck drove home in the old Model T Ford and we both soaked in a bathtub of soda water. I became nauseated and vomited, we both developed throbbing headaches, however improved by morning. The old man and his grandson brought the bee hive over to our place however, we lost interest for several days. We finally moved the hive into our attic with the outlet through the air vent.

CHAPTER FOUR
HIGH SCHOOL

I was very fortunate in having excellent teachers throughout elementary and high school years. The emphasis having being placed upon proper speech, reading the proper books and writing with proper grammar. In grade school Miss Martha Burgess, Miss Lena Bruce, and Mrs. Dowdy were the most impressive and excellent on insisting on the proper parsing of sentences and the rules of grammar. I was well prepared for high school. Self discipline was primarily taught in my home and by strict coaches; Raymond Fisher in track and field and Harley Selvidge in football. All my teachers in Paseo High School were of excellent caliber; Mr. George M. Lortz in mathematics, Miss Ora A. Echles in history, Mr. Paul C. Constant for French, and Miss Ruth Mary Weeks in English, Mr. G.G. Carmen for Science and Chemistry, Miss Mary D. Lawrence in Civics and English and Muriel Moloney for Science.

I spent the first two years of high school at Westport High. At that particular time there were only four high schools in Kansas City: Manual, Northeast, Central, and Westport. I do not recall that there was much to rejoice about in my days at Westport. I found that Latin was not my favorite subject. Latin was more interesting when it was explained how it was considered a dead language yet was the basis for many of our languages of today. There were many word similarities in their derivation and meaning. Our language is heavily interspersed with unchanged Latin words. Latin would also be extremely helpful in learning other languages as well as following words of the church following the basic language. I did enjoy being in some of the plays that were given, but as usual, my most interesting times were in sports, history, and biology. I tried out for a tennis tournament there and was not in the least dismayed, but surprised that my defeats were at the hands of such stars as Junior Coen, Hal Surface, and John McDonald, all of whom were champions. Junior Coen was a Davis Cup, National and International champion, and similar heights were achieved by Hal Surface. Jack McDonald was an excellent player who, to this day, is one of my very closest friends.

In Westport, I also expended a great deal of effort in football, but for some reason or other, I could not convince the coach of my prowess. He simply could not see my potential as an All-American star. However, I did get the opportunity with the second team in my sophomore year to play in the last fifteen minutes of a game with Manual High School. My big moment had come! I was playing right end and a pass play was called. I caught the well placed ball and raced a few yards before it felt as if a ton of bricks fell on me. The startling part, however, was that while under the pile of twenty-one mountains of beef, someone held on to my jersey, and another tried to take the ball from me. At the same time, I was getting jackhammer blows in the face by someone's big fist. I held tightly on to the ball with one hand, but felt for the arm of the perpetrator of this dastardly deed with the other. I held on to his jersey until the cleated beef trusts moved off my back. It was then that I saw this very muscular and menacing character. He was from Manual, but I didn't know his name. A few choice words were passed, and a time and place was set for a settling of the argument by other means. However, as I neared the meeting place he had a number of his equally muscular friends with him. Two others started for me with clenched fists. I called no contest at this time under the circumstances and I am pooped out. I beat a retreat when seeing that I was so outnumbered.

I never thought anymore about this incident until the beginning of the third year when I began attending Paseo High, even though the building wasn't quite finished. Paseo and Southwest High Schools had just been built, and I was in the district to attend either one, so I chose Paseo. It was my first day there and while looking out the window of the third floor before class began, I saw this same character who beat me in the nose the year before in the football game. So I just "happened" to pick up something that was loose, a piece of desk I believe, and shouted, "Hey you Bum" and threw the missile down at him for a well aimed miss as he was climbing up the steps to school. He jumped back, looked up, and I looked down at him and said, "Do you remember me?" What I heard wasn't printable. He said, "I'll meet you right there at the steps." So I went back in the hall and we met each other on the second floor. We immediately started throwing fists. It just so happened that at this time, I was boxing in the welterweight division of the city and it was a pleasure to meet this character. We crashed as we met each other with all the force of two young bison. While we were battling it out a man came along and caught hold of us both by the collars of our shirts. He announced himself as being the vice-principal of the school, whose name was Mr. Harry Shephard. We tried to explain that we were just showing each other the finer points of boxing. He replied, "Well, it isn't exactly according to Marquis de Queensburg rules, so I am going to straighten you out. You and this young man will accompany me to the front office." We sat in the office and were given lectures by him and the principal, Mr. Stigall, on how a civilized citizen should act. We grinned and congratulated each other. I learned his name was Maurice "Mibbs" Golding. We then shook hands and remained firm friends from that time on. We never had another antagonistic word with each other. We sat in that office for two weeks and were told to memorize the words over the door to the principal's office. This was what we learned and never forgot :

REMEMBER WHO YOU ARE WHERE-EVER YOU GO, YOU REPRESENT, WHETHER YOU WANT TO OR NOT, YOURSELF, YOUR FAMILY, YOUR CLAN, YOUR NEIGHBORHOOD, YOUR CITY, YOUR COUNTRY, AND PASEO HIGH SCHOOL.

While at Paseo, the cinder track held my interest. When I say "cinder" track, this was literally so, as our running track was made of fine burned coal cinders. I understand this was to keep the track from getting muddy; also it made good traction for our spiked track shoes. I envisioned myself as a champion hurdler and I practiced every free minute. I ran, hurdled, ran, and hurdled. Coach Ray Fisher and Coach Harley Selvidge would preach, "Step over those low hurdles, never float." My track time was considered good. Then the day came for try-outs. I knew I had one man to beat—Jerry Hickey. On your mark—get-set—the pistol shot, and the five of us took off with a tremendous thrust. I felt as if I were going like the wind, but I saw only Jerry's back. I flew across the finish line, but the string had already been broken. Jerry was the winner and I was second. Jerry set a new record. I trotted around to congratulate Jerry, and in all good faith and innocence he said, "Say Wally, did I see you down there on the hurdle starting line?" Actually he was so far ahead of my second place, all I could say was, " I'm not exactly sure. I'll run the quarter mile better, I hope." In spite of this, I was always positive my hurdle time would be number one. I could never equal the time of Jerry Hickey, but I had some consolation in the fact that Jerry was city champion.

I did manage to stay on the track team in the hurdles, and our team got second place in the city, with Central beating us out for the first place by a fraction of a second in the half mile relay. Our mile-relay team was composed of Mark "Red" Smith, Frank Richardson, Ray McInerney, and me. The Central team had Tiffany, Wheelock, Allspaugh and Brannon. Brannon later became Chief of Police in Kansas City, Missouri. I believed I was a little better in track running the quarter mile, although I also ran the half mile relay in addition to the mile relay. Our high school mile relay team was invited to participate in the University of Kansas relays. This was an honor and we were happy to be a part of it. We all rode up in my old Model T Ford touring car to Lawrence, Kansas. It was unbelievable, but I had two flat tires in that old car on the way, and we arrived just in the nick of time to participate and win the high school mile relay class. The trip home was still another problem, as the patched holes in the tires could not survive being stuffed with cardboard as we had to do, and we limped home on the rim. This was a deflating end to an exhilarating day in Lawrence. Our spirits were still high, however, as we were holding the silver loving cup as a team trophy.

I had several different cars while I was going through high school as I began driving before fifteen years of age. They were all Model T Fords; ranging in price from five to twenty-five dollars. I bought one of the 1910 Model T chassis which I bought as junk for about ten dollars. I had it parked on the street in front of our house one evening when a driver in a Marmon car roared down the unpaved and rutted street of Troost at the tremendous speed of about thirty miles per hour, when it struck my car. I heard the noise and jumped out of the house to see the driver get out and weave over to see what damage he had done. He was obviously intoxicated and implored me not to notify the police. He then gave me fifty dollars and I was delighted. The chassis was hauled into our backyard, taken apart, and I sold it piece by piece for a total of thirty dollars. With the grand sum of eighty dollars, I then bought a Model T touring car. Velma and I drove in it as if we were royalty. I seemed to always have a Model T around (sometimes two of them), which I would fix up, taking the parts of one to make up the other into a running bit of machinery. I would have to crank up the cars to get them started, and there were times when I cranked for ten to fifteen minutes before they started up. I was often short of money, and had to have gasoline, so decided to improvise and make my own fuel. I had studied chemistry and made fuel from naphthalene, a bit of ether, and some alcohol, adding it to gasoline or kerosene. It was surprising how well the car ran on that concoction.

I needed to keep a car running to go to a job I got at the *Kansas City Star* newspaper. Some of my friends and I went together on Saturday nights to work from five o'clock to about six the next morning. We stuffed papers (this term means sliding the various sections into the papers). We did this on the belt line all night. For this we were paid five dollars, which at that time was a fairly large sum of money for us. Major Henry Fox was a most wonderful boss over us but he did demand that his work get out on time. He had been a colonel in the Judge Advocate General Department in the first World War. His two sons were good friends of mine, whom I admired and worked with. One son, Kenneth, became associate editor and editorial page editor of the *Kansas City Star* paper, and he was editor until he retired. I knew his other son better, as we were in Boy Scouts together. This was Henry H. Fox, Jr. who was a full colonel in the Judge Advocate Generals Department and later became a practicing attorney, then prosecuting attorney of Jackson County, Missouri, then became Judge of the Jackson County Court of the Western District in Kansas City; the same court that President Harry S. Truman presided over during his early years in politics. Judge Fox was, and is one of my very close friends. He has always been a generous, diplomatic person who has shown his friendship all through our lives together. His younger brother, Kenneth L. Fox became a full colonel in the United States Army also, and has been one of the outstanding editors on military matters of the *Kansas City Star* paper. As a matter of interest President Truman told me he also worked in the *Kansas City Star* mailing room as a young man the same as I, however several years earlier. I found this documented in the *Missouri Blue Book*.

High school days in the twenties and thirties were vastly different from the manner of student dress of today. The dress of today is more economical and certainly more practical. Jeans were unheard of as proper dress except in performing farm or garage duties. We did have variations in styles; the young men in one period would wear knickers called plus-fours with argyle plaid socks. A later fashion was Boston Bags which were ultra wide trousers legs the full length. This fad was followed by Bell Bottom trousers. Spats were always in vogue during winter or inclement weather or for the family reunion. To my good fortune, Velma's brother, Harrel, made the mistake of going with me in my Model T touring Ford. I had filled the gas tank with half kerosene, half low grade gasoline and a can of ether I borrowed from Dad's office then topped it off with two hands full of moth balls. I cranked up old Galloping Gertrude, increased the spark, and away we went. The road we took was filled with bumps and chuck holes. We were flying along at about twenty-five miles an hour when we struck a hidden rut, resulting in a sickening blast and the blubbering of air from the rent inner tube. This was not too surprising, and I was prepared with the jack, repair kit, and pump. All the tires were worn slick and thread bare in spots. The repair did not take long and away we sailed. Five miles flew by when a hog suddenly decided to cross the road. I jerked the steering wheel and successfully missed the hog, but struck a large rock on the side of the road. I was neither dismayed or surprised as it was the same tire which blew before. We again removed the tire and inner tube and found a different section was completely blown-out. I repaired the inner tube while Harrel searched for something to cover the hole. He returned with a piece of tire which we fit into the old tire after cutting it accordingly. All worked well, although we lumped along for another ten miles as if we had a square wheel. We heard a rather insidious, high, irregular, but familiar sizzing. Again we stopped, a bit disheartened, as here was another flat; the tire patch to cover the hole had knuckled out. We could do very little with the tire as its best days had been traveled long ago. We could have ridden along on the rim, but we thought we would walk up the road a piece and see what we could find. After walking two miles over a few hills, we went up to a farm house. The farmer listened to our tale of woe and said he had an old tire hanging on the side of an old Model T out in the barn. For fifty cents, we had another old, quite worn, but worthy enough tire. Back to the disaster, we fixed the tire and rolled on.

Excelsior Springs was crowded with people in a festive mood; a huge picnic was in progress and the band was playing in the pavilion. The day was hot, with the sun high and blazing, while many were seeking relief in the near-by swimming pool. The Hill family, including the branches of Norvell, Lucas, and Jeter, had congregated from Sam to Stanley. We were all very proud of cousin Philip Norvell as he was in the Harvard University School of Theology. Phil was quiet, reserved, brilliant, and very pleasant, as he is to this day. He now lives in Columbia, Missouri, where he and his wife, Pauline are friends of our daughter, Heather, and her husband, Dr. Jerry Foote. At the Hill family reunion we ate, danced, and frolicked, having a glorious time until dark. We stuffed ourselves with delicious food, had a prayer and started home. As luck would have it, we took a better highway back to Kansas City and never had anymore problems with my motor or the tires.

After the old touring car, we had what was called a Roadster that had a rumble seat in the back which we pulled up after the top was rolled down. This was really the forerunner of the convertible. To have a rumble seat was the height of sportiness, and I was extremely proud of it. Several of my friends rode with their girls in the rumble seat and the romance of riding out of doors in the moonlight paved the way for many a kiss. In fact, it was so tempting that my sweetie and I traded places when the moon was particularly inviting and we had our turn.

From about 1926 to 1928 while I was in high school, the rage of my age group and even older, was a dance known as the Charleston. I had a friend named K.O. Daniels who was an excellent dancer, and he suggested that we practice and perform on the stage, but first we tried to form an orchestra. My piano playing was very meager and poor, and he played the clarinet about the same way. He could also play the trumpet, but he was no better on that instrument. Someone else played the drums, and we tried performing with our "band." It was a dismal failure, but we could do dance routines such as tap dance, and a soft shoe dance and the Charleston. We decided that we were good enough at this to perform on the stage, so we worked out a routine and went to small theaters where dance contests were being held and where several of us young fellows, as well as the girls, could compete. We received some monetary compensation for our dancing, but the real thrill was hearing the applause. It was heady stuff, so we went to the better theaters in town such as the Newman, the Pantages, the Royal, the Orpheum, and the Garden Theaters where we were received with enthusiasm. We kept looking for better spots for our dancing, and when Major Bowes, the idol of aspiring performers held a contest in Kansas City, K.O. and I decided that would be our next step upward. This gave us the chance to shine and we received five and ten dollars for a performance. Finally there was a contest for city championship for performing the Charleston. K.O. and I agreed that we should try out for this pinnacle of all dance contests for us. We put our best into it, and to our surprise we won first place in the city.

Dance competition soon began to demand too much of us, however, so we turned to dancing just for fun—with girls. Then it was called ballroom dancing. We danced at such places as the Garrett, the Submarine, The El Torreon, and later at a huge dance palace that had been built, called the Pla-Mor, at about 35th and Main, which was reputedly the largest dance floor in the Midwest. What made it even more famous was the spring dance floor which was constructed in a way to cause less fatigue. Tireless dancing was an actuality, as the huge, glistening floor was supported by thousands of coil springs. On occasion, over three thousand people would glide, fox trot, waltz, twirl, and spin around the floor to the great band music. Some of the finest bands in the United States played there: Duke Ellington, Jimmy Dorsey, Clyde McCoy with his sugar blues theme, Cab Calloway with his 'Hi di Ho', Bennie Moten, and many others of "big band" fame. They didn't play just one or two nights; at times they played for months at a time. This beautiful dance hall could accommodate four thousand dancers under the huge, multi-mirrored, revolving ball in the middle of the starry ceiling, gently changing shades of color from light amber through the soft reds and blues. Many an afternoon matinée and evening were spent there in the romance of dance. Such beauty, harmony, elegance, and charm will never be forgotten, and it was under influences such as this that my romance began to blossom with that same little girl I had first met in grade school and we became very good dance partners, twirling midst a million heart throbs per twirl and we danced at every opportunity. Our favorite strains were "Josephine," "Sleepy Time Gal," "It's Three O'Clock in the Morning," "Stardust," and a multitude of others, orchestrated so beautifully by the big bands.

Dancing was the entertainment most of the young people then enjoyed. There were other dance floors we went to, such as one at Electric Park which was situated at about 47th and Paseo. It was actually a rather elegant amusement park with thousands of electric lights twinkling and sparkling at night. I remember that the climax of the evening at Electric Park was when a large and lovely fountain in the center of the park dramatically displayed beautiful girls rising on a platform in the middle of the fountain with water shooting up around them. Later, Fairyland Park at about 75th and Prospect Avenue offered dancers an enticement of a large outdoor dance floor with a roof, but with all sides open so that the fresh air came through to refresh the dancers. That was the only "air conditioning" in existence then. None of the dance places were rowdy, and there were no fights; everyone was there purely for the enjoyment of dancing and meeting friends. Much of the time we went stag, as there were groups of girls who went there and with whom we could dance. It was too costly usually to pay for two. Dancing in places like these gradually faded out over the years, however, and one by one they closed up. We sadly see the past areas of romance, enchantment,and beauty become the stalking ground for predators, spreading their tentacles of disruption, and preying upon decency. Beauty is lost, like our family groups, windows are smashed, and the hollow-eyed vacancies are covered by boards. Who did it? The unbridled, uninhibited angry groups of society whom we have tolerated!

Portions of the summers of my early and mid teens were spent attending to laying the foundation of my future, and I believed that part of that foundation should include some military service, even at that early age. Therefore I attended C.M.T.C. Camp in Fort Snelling, Minnesota. My parents had believed strongly in adequate military defense for our nation, and felt that our survival as a nation should be every citizen's concern, and that each should be held accountable in some manner for the welfare of our country. Since I had grown up with these ideas, it was only natural that I adopted some of these beliefs too. It was with great pride that I wore a military uniform and that I belonged to Company D2 of the 1st Infantry Division. Those were the days when we wore pegged trousers and wrap leggings. The machine gun we used was the water-cooled Browning, and the machine gun carts were drawn by a mule. I was squad leader and later platoon leader, with the rank of corporal and then sergeant. I remember spending many hours off-duty practicing taking the machine gun down and putting it together again from an assimilated block. I practiced in the woods so no one would see me until I had become proficient, as I wanted to make a good impression on our company commander whom we all admired. This was Lieutenant Cassidy, a recent West Point graduate with an impressive bearing, and who was a man of high caliber. Our company won the majority of accolades for, proficiency in drill and marksmanship. There was rigid discipline demanded of us in the Camp, and I liked it. This may have stemmed from the fact that my parents were both enthusiastic about military life, and I had been taught self discipline from the moment of understanding; never by force, but by explanation and hours of patient understanding, with logical reasoning.

I not only learned military science and tactics at Camp, but I also learned that the nights in Minnesota were very cold. I tried sleeping under my cot mattress instead of over it, but this was not much help. It would take until almost noon to get my body warmed up from the preceding night. On weekends, permission and facilities were arranged so that we could go swimming in Lake Nakomis. We would be taken to the lake about one o'clock in the afternoon, and with bathing suits on, we would dash out and jump into the lake as ordered. Suddenly submerging our warm bodies in the water, which seemed to be below zero, certainly awakened our senses. I believed occasionally that the commanders would have to retrieve my body by chipping it out of an ice block. The majority of my unit was from Texas, Arkansas, Oklahoma, and Missouri and one friend there, Elton Carpenter, from Little Rock, Arkansas, said, "I sure didn't know they were going to train us to be Eskimos." As a non-com, I could not gripe, but I learned that after the first gasp, I had better keep my body in motion.

During my years of high school, from about the age of thirteen through seventeen, I tried to crowd in as much as I possibly could, so along with working part time jobs, attending camp, going to school, participating in sports, and having a bit of entertainment, I also continued to be involved in boxing, as I had in the latter part of my grade school. I began coming home hours after school with my eyes frequently discolored and my nose a bit distorted. My parents knew I was doing all right in school and that I had part time jobs, but I wondered what they thought of this physical appearance which occurred too regularly. I didn't wonder long, however, as my father happened to read the sport page one day and saw that Wallace Graham was boxing for the welter-weight title. He set his jaw and looked at me for a full two minutes, then said, "Wallace, I want to see you in the library immediately." He told me of his basic disapproval of boxing. However, he said that I must fulfill my commitment. I told him the entire story then and requested that he never watch me box. The bout was nearing, and my opponent in the final was an Indian boy from Haskell Institute, Beaver Watson. I was warned to never in-fight, to be cool, side step, jab continually, roll with the punches, and jab at all costs with my left. I was also given all the customary warnings for boxing a very muscular and stocky opponent. After sparring through the first round successfully and my opponent missing most blows, I knew I could prove that in-fighting would be better, so I stepped in, flexed my body in a weaving motion, and received one blow on the top of my head, fell to my knees, and was up before any count began. I collected a few more or less destructive blows, but returned enough of my own to gain points until the final second when I flexed my body and our heads struck, his head butting my mid-forehead above the nose forming a large blood clot, swelling both eyes and discoloring them brilliant blue-black. I was awarded the decision on points, but my eyes were quickly closing. I could not attend graduating classes the following night because the mid-forehead blow had closed both eyes, and a short talk that I was to deliver was given by my friend. What a price glory! The diploma was sent by mail.

The summer before entering college I had applied for a job in the Consumer Ice Company to earn some extra money. I was accepted on the spot as one of the regular men was struck with a serious illness forcing his retirement. I saw Benny Hayes, our old ice man and he said, "Wally boy, can you handle a block of ice yet?" I said that I could sure learn real fast, so went about cutting 24, 50, 75, and 100 pound pieces of ice out of a 300 pound block with tongs and pick. The ice route was a real pleasure, as it kept me in excellent physical condition and gave me the opportunity to talk with all the fine customers. I carried these blocks of ice up to the second and third floors in some of the homes, and I can assure you that if you do this you are bound to be in good condition. The ice wagon was horse drawn by two horses, and at the end of a long day I was to care for the horses too. After a week, I decided that I would hire a helper, so paid one dollar a day to a man to remove the harnesses, feed, curry, and stall the horses every evening. The ice route allotted was in an expanding old neighborhood where I was acquainted and the customer load had doubled. There were nearly a hundred tiny tots on my ice route and they loved to have their pictures taken astride a horse so I cheerfully cooperated. This made them happy and I got more customers, but I soon found I was in the "free" photography business. One day I was called to see the boss of the ice routes. It was with a feeling of trepidation that presented myself, as I felt he was going to reprimand me for the photography while on duty. I was asked where I got the idea, and I explained this may be the first step in dispelling for fear of horses in the children. I explained that I was also very cautious and watchful every minute the children were on the large, very gentle horses. My fears were eased when the boss, in a booming voice, stated he was very proud, as this was great advertisement and we should have more enterprising young men in the organization.

Throughout high school, all the activities of which I have written were stimulating, and romance was delightful, but I knew that in college and medical school these would be limited, as I had an overpowering sense of obligation and responsibility toward reaching my goals in life. I knew that if I were to be accepted into medical, my college academic work would have to be well above average. I knew that to reach my goal of being a doctor it would require long years of study and concerted effort which could hardly be shared without emotional strain, inhibitory restraints, and unfair cloistering of life. Therefore, the majority of my actions were harnessed by the governing and overwhelming desire to direct all endeavors toward my goals and principles, but at no time was there ever a ruthless desire to obligate or infringe upon any individual for self-gain.

I bid adieu to my parents and Velma, who had decided to attend the Junior College in Kansas City. At that time, the Junior College was situated at 11th and Locust and was reputed to have the second highest academic standing of Junior Colleges in the United States. I knew that in spite of this separation, I intended seeing her at intervals. However, each of us had our own paths to follow.

CHAPTER FIVE
THE UNIVERSITY AND MEDICAL COLLEGE WITH INTERNSHIP

Both my grades and letters of recommendation had been accepted for undergraduate studies at Missouri University at Columbia, Missouri. As I stood at the base of the columns on the campus of this awesome place, *The University*, my blood coursed warmly through my body as if girding for a fight, and I felt a sensation of lordliness; yet there was also the realization that this person was a small David facing a Goliath. I was thrilled, however to be an integral part of this institution of higher learning and prayed that I would gain strength and vital knowledge from the many men and women who were dedicated to imparting the intellectualism of the day and age, and the past. I reasoned that this was a gigantic stepping stone to prepare and guide me toward the goal of my anticipated world of Medicine. The summer before entering, I had read several interesting books which further stimulated me to the necessity of learning and understanding the trial along the world of the humanities and to medicine. Two of the books which left a lasting impression upon me were *Arrowsmith*, by Sinclair Lewis, and *The Magnificent Obsession* by Lloyd Douglas. Douglas was a Lutheran minister whom I later had the honor of meeting, and I enjoyed his other literary works.

Thinking more realistically, I began to recall the advice from my older brother John, who had told me what to avoid, how to act, and advised me about the customs. Although my thoughts were not impervious to the charms of the young ladies, there was a clash of emotions within me as I pondered pros and cons. Basically, I had to keep in mind that ahead of me was a long road of learning to master. To accomplish this, it was necessary not to become heavily involved with any force which might ultimately lead to too much diversion and deviation from my main goal.

All these thoughts and dreams were in my mind as I gazed about the campus. I recall now, as one of my high school instructors said after he had read one of my essays, "If you will just digress a bit from your dream world, and use your creativity, you might build a reality some day, Mr. Graham."

My life began at Missouri University at Columbia, Missouri with the lines of students in alphabetical rows for matriculation; the wearing of the freshman beanie (or cap), and rear stimulation by the sophomores as we sang a school chant. Visits were made by fraternity chanticleers extolling the virtues of life under the aegis of Greek symbols—all advantageous to the groping neophyte. The opening day of classes finally arrived with the assignments of study and lectures. I was very disappointed that there were so many students in the classes, but bent every effort to do well. I also became involved in football, boxing, and track, as long as they did not interfere too much with study. Anton Stankowski was a fine freshman football coach and he was a hard driving, tough, task-master whom we all respected. After training and being cannon fodder for the varsity, I was awarded the numeral sweater.

My sophomore year at the University began with considerably less enthusiasm than the first, but I was still imbued with the learning process. The University of Missouri seemed to be a separate city of its own. There is much history in this university as in most state universities. The school and campus were expanding during the years I attended. There was the quadrangle of older buildings, all of brick construction, from the Jesse Hall for administration to the other buildings including those for geology, math, English, journalism, and engineering.

These buildings were all in one large square around the famous six columns and was called the red campus. To this campus, connected by Rollins Street and lined by library and book store, was the white campus which began with the tower of the Student Union and included all the sciences and being so-called because the buildings were all of white stone. The chemistry building, now called Schlundt Hall, was there. The botany, zoology, and anatomy buildings were yet not completely finished and now many more have been added. Fraternity row included Beta Theta Pi, Beta Sigma Phi, Kappa Alpha, Sigma Chi, Phi Gamma Delta, Sigma Nu, and others. "Greek Town" was the area encompassing the majority of both fraternities and sororities. There seemed to always be an inner turbulence or restlessness within me while attending the university. Sports seemed to quell the unrest to a degree, but I had a very strong desire to visit other countries and to meet people in far away places. It was quite obvious and mandatory that before any adventure or exotic travel, I needed a good basic educational foundation. I wanted to learn the history of nations and peoples and I knew it was essential that I concentrate on a prescribed course, but for some unknown reason it was difficult to harness and bridle myself. I had to attain my degrees before I could yield to my inner yearning. With this attainment I could then give attention and full expression to my own individual dreams and fantasies. In other words, I actually wanted to expand to higher aspirations without first achieving a solid technical foundation. With the inner turbulence there, it was difficult to keep myself reined tight until the appropriate time to break out. I knew I could develop and find my mission and destiny in life after having attained my scholastic goals. There was a strong desire to learn geography and history, as well as the anatomy of the human body. I began to realize the reason for chemistry and physics, and to apply these extrinsic principles to the intrinsic function of the human body with all of its cellular and intra-cellular activity. Yes, my first two collegiate years were turbulent, enjoyable, and finally controlled to the basic realization that a broad education was absolutely mandatory, even though study and concentration were at times difficult when I was wont to dream.

Chemistry, formulas, and atoms were learned easily by the method of Professor Dr. Schlundt, with the diagrammatic methods he used with wires and balls for atoms, and demonstrating their affinity, one to the other. Comparative anatomy was another world of similarities in the creation of all forms of life, with the ultimate, being that of man. Then I saw the basic embryonic life and anatomical structure of man which was very similar to the pig and other animals. This study of comparative life with its biophysical origin and development began to lift the curtain that concealed the secrets of the development of man. At this time, it seemed to me that the adventurer, like the physician, must be a special breed of man. He must be an explorer with a definite aim in life. At this time in my collegiate career and in reading the history of explorers there was one outstanding observation. The most immortal findings in the course of history have been produced by the physician more than any other man. It is a fact documented from the medical journeys of Democedes of Croton who searched far and wide over 2500 years ago for the advancement of man. At this point it would be enjoyable to write a separate dissertation on the physician explorer, with adventures of world import. My method of writing being as heterodoxical as it is, my pen tends to wander, although trying to stay within the confines of my early collegiate days.

In some classes there were incidents which engendered considerable disparity in the method of grading. My roommate at one phase of our early collegiate years was Charles Long and we had some classes together. I was positive that Chuck knew the material quite well, and in my estimation were in equal status in this one class. My grade was uniformly high and his was routinely low. At the time of an examination we were handed blue-books to write in the answers to the examination questions. This one time, however, we exchanged blue books where he had my number and I had his. We wrote the exam and when the grades were returned my number had the usual high grade and his, that I had actually written, had the usual inferior grade. I thereupon went to the Dean and requested the blue books. After considerable words were passed, the books were produced. The disparity was noted, the papers re-examined and the outcome was that we both had high grades. I was roundly chastised but I considered our actions perfectly justifiable. The outcome was that I won the battle, but nearly lost the war.

Fraternity life, in my estimation, was a valuable part of collegiate living for many young men. Much depends upon the maturity of the men and goals of the organization. It is an important step in many aspects such as group encouragement to study, mutual cooperation among members in the fraternity house, and teaching the neophytes social graces at the table. This last duty was taken over by the upperclassmen (usually the sophomores) over the freshmen; for instance the upperclassmen made it known that the knife placement should not be like that of oars on the boat. If they were placed so, those at the table would act as if they were rowing a boat and sing the song, "Row, Row, Row Your Boat" and telling them emphatically that the knife should be placed at the top side of the plate. They said, "Sit straight, not stiff; keep your head out of the plate, or it may be pushed into the food face first." They further admonished that hands were to remain in the lap or on the edge of the table, unless in the process of eating. Slouching or slumping and tipping the chair or the table was unforgivable. In general they advised that silverware was to be used from outside in toward the plate and not to grasp the utensil as if handling a shovel or pitch fork, or one was liable to be stabbed. This advice was for the social betterment of the members of a well run fraternity house. Also fraternity life teaches respect of others' property, yet sharing at will. Correction was never to be made in an obsequious manner. The so-called pledge father was chosen for his discretionary and inoffensive manner in fraternity training of neophytes. Academic and scholastic honors are still of primary concern in the majority of fraternities, as well as sororities, and one must have a worthy grade level or he is deleted by the group. Athletic excellence and other university attainments are also encouraged and lauded. Pride was instilled in all for keeping the house in general good condition. Special decorations and hospitality were accorded to visiting members from other colleges and universities. Homecoming and gala events for athletic and scholastic endeavors were enthusiastically shared. The organization was a true family of brothers. A house mother lived in and helped to hold the even tenor of the house and to see that everything was kept in the proper perspective. As a rule, she was taken out for dinner by two members on Sunday evenings or was accompanied to church services.

Special programs at the university were fostered by the school's performing arts program, which was enjoyable and informative. Artists from many areas of the world performed. I recall hearing and seeing the renowned pianist, Ignace Paderewski, Weiner and Douchet, celebrated French two-piano artists, Yasha Yushny, the leader of the Bluebird Russian Revue, Conchita Supervia, the great Spanish soprano, Paul Althouse, tenor superb, a world famous Australian soprano, other opera stars, and a host of great artists who delighted the student body. At the end of my second year at Missouri University, I went home for summer vacation, having no idea that I would not return there as a student.

On returning home, before I could take the bags to my room, Mother notified me that I had arrived just in time. The lawn mower was in the garage, the grass was "nearly knee high," and the lawn was to be finished before Father got home. She handed me a sandwich and told me to hurry. I was mowing the grass and was about finished when one of my close friends and high school teammate, Jerry Hickey, drove into the driveway. At Paseo High School, he had run the hurdles so far ahead of me he hardly remembered I was the one he saw on the starting line. He had the city and state record time for this race. We exchanged the usual warm greetings, and he immediately began with, "Come on, Wally, we're going to school." He then asked me to go to Warrensburg, Missouri to attend Central Missouri State College with him and said that we could both have athletic scholarships there and that he was on his way there now. I said, "Jerry, it was my impression you had an athletic scholarship to the University of Kansas," and explained that I had just returned from Missouri University within the past two hours and had no intention of going to any school this summer. Jerry then explained that several of our former teammates were all going to this school too, and he knew we would all like it there. Jerry said this was a better place than where I had been, and he proved to be a good salesman. Both of us then finished mowing the yard, and I informed my mother I would like leaving right away for Warrensburg with Jerry if it was alright with her and Dad. She called my father and informed him. I received their blessings, so we put my bags in the car, and away we drove.

We drove into the town of Warrensburg, saw the very pleasant surroundings and located a place to live immediately across the street from a very well-planned and attractive campus. We stayed at the home of Mr. and Mrs. Lou Russell, a lovely and understanding couple. Jerry and

I had no difficulty in securing rooms for ourselves and holding four other rooms for former teammates who Jerry told me were to follow. The next morning was the day to matriculate for the summer session, and I thought it would be a good idea to obtain a few more hours in advanced chemistry and physics through the summer. The following morning dawned and we were awakened by a thunderbolt of laughter, chatter, and guffaws. We were then rudely rolled out of bed by none other than Tiny Anderson, a six-foot, four inch, two hundred forty pound character, Mibbs Golding, another muscular behemoth, Marty Coppaken, Rudolph and Adolph Gangle, Marcus Smith, and Harold Kirkpatrick. The house was filled with star athletes from various areas where we had either played with or against one another and knew each other quite well. There was always a camaraderie and good clean fellowship between athletes which, to me, was a most enjoyable type of friendship. This probably stems from a certain hardship of strict dietary rules, hard training, and the self discipline of a spartan body building effort to be the best for yourself, the team, and the school you represent. Many interesting incidents occurred as we spent the next years together. My past studies had encompassed a great number of hours in the field of biology and I was asked by the professor of biology, Professor George W. Stevens, to substitute for him on several occasions. He was an excellent teacher with a superb background, and was a former member of an expedition to the Arctic and North Pole. He was a tall, kind man who had a profound flash-back-store of memories. The years were beginning to reveal the inroads of physiological change in him. He would repeat himself, telling the same stories multiple times. The cerebral changes wrought by the effects of arteriosclerosis were becoming more manifest. On one occasion he and his wife drove to Kansas City to shop; he was to meet her at a certain corner at a specific time. Unfortunately, he returned home to Warrensburg, forgetting Mrs. Stevens. His children reminded him that he had taken their mother with him. Meanwhile, Mrs. Stevens had called the home, worried about why the professor had not met her at the stipulated time. Professor and Mrs. Stevens had no children of their own; however, they adopted nine children, all of whom were very fine examples of perfect home-life and training.

Our group was invited to the Sigma Tau Gamma fraternity house during the rush week. We were dined and treated like aristocracy, and the advantages of fraternity life were extolled. We were feted both collectively, and later individually. The fraternity lettermen, champion debaters, and other campus notables were met. After a week or so of feasting and learning of the virtues of the Greek way, I began to notice a trend to group separation and even separation of individuals in the group. After the rush period was over, some were requested to join the fraternity organization. We were also told that we must live in the fraternity house. It was at this point, that we realized our paths would be divergent. The bonds of close friendship in the Russell House were firm, however, having been tested by time, toil, and tribulations through the preceding years. We were as close as any blood-brother could be. The fraternity vote, as a rule, must be unanimous—some of our group had signed on the "dotted line" with the belief we would be together as a unit. When we were later advised there would be some deletions and we would have mandatory fraternity house living, our reactions were as one, and we declined the honor. We continued living in the Russell House immediately across the street from the campus. It was then that we were classified as the "Barbs." As far as we were concerned, all students were on an equal basis, and our group became even closer.

I became good friends with a great number of students on campus, and had a faculty of remembering names and truly enjoyed getting to know everyone I possibly could. I had no political axe to grind as I never considered any political office. I mingled with the various campus groups, and found it very interesting to learn about the way of life many had pursued. In my adult life, I had not known people who lived on farms and small towns, and I found their stories of life on the farm very interesting. I remember particularly students from the town of Hermann, Missouri where the majority of the citizens of the town were of German descent and still spoke German among themselves. They told me of their wine festivals; October Fest, Mai Fest, and other occasions where fun and dancing and eating were entered into with great verve and enjoyment.

I had never lived in such a friendly, wholesome atmosphere where friendships arose and were spontaneously shared, and where there was always a spirit of cooperation. As I muse on my days at this college, there is a warm glow as I recall my association with the members of the faculty under whom I studied. Their personalities, educational accomplishments, and way of imparting knowledge served as an inspiration above didactic textbooks. They taught, and the students were inspired to greater heights of learning. In chemistry, study was greatly enhanced by the methods of Dr. Earl Foster, one of the most respected professors there. He was a most pleasant man; dynamic, yet soft spoken, was quite positive, and could be forceful in a pleasant manner. He was tall, had a ruddy complexion, and sharp blue eyes that comprehended the thought and reaction of his students at a glance. He was kind and fair, and had a natural, built-in smile, as the corners of his mouth were set in this pleasant cast.

Dr. Wilson C. Morris, the professor of physics and chemistry, was my ideal of a human dynamo, both mentally and physically. His many aphorisms were sharp, meaningful, and to the point. Professor Stevens, the head of the biology department, and I had a close friendship and a most agreeable, happy, and respected interrelationship. Professor Maude C. Nattinger, the associate professor of biology, was a superbly understanding and knowledgeable lady. She knew how to portray and thoroughly project her subject in a professional and concise manner. Professor Anna Marie Todd was a lady of great intelligence and memory, who was very understanding and helpful in solving many problems inherent to young, college students. Professor Annie G. Harris, who taught languages, was one of the most erudite of professors, who understood the special language needs of the pre-medical students and would help after hours if it was necessary. Professor H.G. Bass in history, Dr. F.W. Calvert in sociology, and Dr. James H. Scarborough, professor of mathematics, were all fine and intelligent gentlemen.

Professor L. Martin was the master of English and Shakespeare. He could deliver the most interesting lectures on Shakespeare which were brought out so beautifully in explanatory phrases with the intricacies of tragedy, pathos, happiness, and love and all the psychological input. This was one class where not a student would ever nod in slumber. One such lecture was on the thirteen different types of jealousy shown by Othello. Professor Martin was the well dressed, beautifully soft spoken intellectual who knew the psychology of college students and would present the Shakespearian plays and dramas accordingly. He was an inspiration to every student.

The entire faculty was understanding and each member was generous in giving extra time to help those who wanted and needed the added push. In this institution with dedicated professors, the goodness and brilliance was evident from the President, Dr. Eldo L. Hendricks, to Dr. Walter E. Morrow, the faculty Dean, to the physical education department of Coach "Tad" Reid, Clarence Whiteman, the physical education director, and Professor Caskey Settle, also in physical education through the excellent librarians, with Dr. Ward Edwards, through all departments and personnel too numerous to extol at this time. There was a great spirit of friendship and happiness in this wonderful school. In all, I feel it was a privilege to have attended. I did not have classes under all of the above named faculty members, but I enjoyed getting to know them in close association. I could reminisce ad infinitum regarding the faculty of this college. In my experience, there was never a more enjoyable group of knowledgeable professors.

I was particularly interested in the sciences, and was quite enthused about biology class under Dr. Stevens. To stimulate his students into studying zoology more zealously, he offered extra credits for large collections of insects and other such bugs that we could study. I gathered them with keen enthusiasm until I had shoe boxes filled with all types of entomological specimens. Most of them I had prepared, mounted, and named for an exhibition in the biology department. However, I also had a large box of live specimens. A bit of misfortune occurred, however, in our quarters: on leaving my room on the second floor and going down the carpeted stairs, I tripped midway down and fell—butterflies, moths, beetles, arachnids, and bugs galore jumped, crawled, ran, hopped, and flew in every direction throughout the house. With help, we gathered the majority of them. One of my dear roommates then spread the word to the housemother and father that I was collecting lice, cockroaches, bedbugs, and vermin of all kinds, and they all got loose in the house. After considerable explanation, Mr. and Mrs. Russell were moderately convinced that most specimens were no longer living and generally they were properly mounted except the harmless specimens from the one box and they had been returned to their proper placement. The entomological lecture and demonstration was later a success and was appreciated by the classes.

This is only one of the many lively interludes which occurred in the Russell household. They were, however, very understanding and tolerant of this unpredictable group of young men. They did not serve meals, so as a group from the Russell house, we went to the dining table of Mrs. Munkers, who apparently had been adapted to feeding farm hands, and was well versed in the various dietary regimen for our activities. One minor annoyance at the dining table, but occasionally humorous, was secondary to an anatomical defect carried by "Tiny" Andy Anderson. By a freak accident during a football game, the flexor tendon of the middle finger on the right hand had been severed. He had never bothered to have the defect repaired and lost the power of voluntary flexion, causing the finger to be continuously extended. Consequently, if he did not hold the finger flexed with the adjacent fingers, it would point directly forward. The problem then was that when he reached for the various foods such as soup, whipped potatoes, and other tasties, this obstreperous finger would invariably be plunged into the previously appetizing food. This predicament was finally remedied by forcing this massive hulk to be the last served, keeping all the food out of his reach unless it was too hot for consumption or touch; the latter resulting in a few blisters. "Tiny Andy" was always cheerful, fun loving, and quite gregarious, as well as being a gourmand. In contradistinction there was our champion swimmer, Louis "Pooey" Silverman. Pooey was a philosophical type, serious and intellectually oriented, however, he thoroughly enjoyed a bit of "horse play." Pooey was of "block-buster build", being five feet, five inches in height, and was one hundred seventy-five pounds of bone, muscle, and brain. He had captured practically every swimming record established for distance. To this day (as we have closely continued our friendship) I know that he continues to compete in swimming events, and has recently placed near the top in the Olympics for those past the age of sixty.

Those of us in the Russell House rarely dated girls, as we were not the most financially affluent, coupled with the fact that to keep abreast of our studies, athletics, and work, it was about all we could manage. With the close of the day we were tired, and there was not much time for other extra-curricular activities. "Tiny Andy", to the best of my knowledge, never dated until the end of the college year, when he managed to get a date with one of the college queens. He was getting ready for his date and was singing in a contagiously uproarious manner while bathing in the tub. He was in a hurry, as the time of his rendezvous was approaching. During the body rinsing process the back of the bathtub being adjacent to the door, someone silently opened the door. The singing reaching an operatic crescendo when suddenly and dramatically it changed into a bestial-like roar, which shivered the timbers of the house. Some unknown scoundrel with devilish intent, had emptied a bottle of black ink into the tub of bath water. All of the innocents were amazed and ostensibly shocked that such a catastrophe should befall our beloved compadre. We all did, however, help in the cleansing rinse-down process, but deleted the areas about and in the ears. We told him we telephoned his queen that he had been unavoidably detained. We had told his girl that he had a fetish about cleaning his ears and we requested that she examine and remark about his ears and how nice they were. She entered into the occasion beautifully, however, barely avoided an acrimonious explosion when her eyes met the auricular appendages. Our hero questioned her if anything was unusual. His lovely then stated that he should either grow hair over the ears or try to wash out the earthy covering—That did it! Later Tiny confessed he "darn near bawled." When he discovered the trick we had played, he laughed, washed his ears, and the evening was a success. Tiny was on the receiving end of other tricks his friends played, but he suffered them in good humor.

It was in my tenure as assistant to Dr. Stevens to schedule a biology or nature-study hike. The trek was arranged for the next day following the noon lunch and the study was to take a two hour period; one hour to supplant the classroom, and the second hour to take the place of the laboratory hour. One of Tiny's dear friends was extracting croton oil in the laboratory and was writing on its various usages. One of the physiological effects of this oil is that if a drop were ingested it would result in a dynamic purge. A test was made to ascertain the strength of the substance. Thereupon, this friend had a fiendish thought. He knew Tiny loved banana cream pie so he placed two drops of the croton oil on a piece of luscious cream pie which was avidly devoured by our friend, Tiny, who then accompanied the class on the nature study hike. While studying nature he had a sudden sick, pallid, facial expression followed by a rapid dash in retreat behind a large oak tree. He was asked if he needed help—his reply was "Hell No!" One perceiving and knowledgeable friend found the distressed Mr. Anderson and hastened to help. This unexpected exigency had not been anticipated, consequently Northern tissue or White Cloud was not readily available. A few greeneries with leaves growing in groups of three, were found and handed to the hapless and near prostrate body. The interlude can be imagined, however the epilogue later involved soothing lotions, as the application of the greenery happened to be the very offending poison ivy. It also was realized later by his dismayed friend, that this amount of croton oil could have proved quite dangerous.

Another attempt to be hilarious was when the chemistry-physics devotees were experimenting on the natural gases; not only the various components of vegetation gases, but also animal gases from protein destruction, including human physiological reactivity. "Tiny Andy" was again chosen as the proper and deserving subject for the experiment. The propitious moment and place was chosen, a candle was lit and placed in proper proximity, and without quoting Chaucer directly, I note that "a mighty blast" was echoed, only to be superseded by a howl of anguish. Tiny guessed that Jerry was guilty of tricking him and was roundly admonished by choice Anglo-Saxon "verbology." We all came running to the bathroom to find Tiny sitting in the bathtub with the cold water running full force. Soothing lotions were again applied along with platitudes extolling his endeavors to be a part of a great experiment. The only reply was "if this project is to be written up, leave my name out."

With levity aside, I diligently attended to my studies, and the horseplay I have mentioned helped to relieve the tenseness of studying earnestly and consistently to learn, and to obtain the necessary high grade level for acceptance into medical school. Finally, in May, the end of my undergraduate days was upon me, and as I walked upon the rostrum to receive my Bachelor of Arts degree, I had mixed feelings. I wanted to begin the new path toward my career, and yet it was with a feeling of sadness that I was to leave these many friends and the warmth of the entire Warrensburg era in my life.

Just before graduation, everyone on the campus was entering into a type of carnival atmosphere in the upcoming election for honorary nonacademic titles. One of the campus highlights of the year was the nomination and election of "Most Popular Man", and "The Campus Queen" of the University. The competition and feeling ran at high pitch, involving specific allegiances, as each fraternity and sorority wanted to produce a winner from among their group. The big hullabaloo began with parades, screamers, streamers, and gala events. The campus glittered with student activity, and the parading of signs extolled the virtues of the various candidates. Friendship, laughter, and camaraderie were all inherent to this event, and included not only the students but the townspeople and faculty. We were all caught up in the excitement of the event. Each candidate had the election machinery well geared by the party officers. Louis P. Silverman was my campaign manager as candidate for this— to represent the "Barbs." He had the astute, observant, and political *savior-faire* of one schooled in the politics of true hegemony. He knew the value of personal appeal through inspiring the lieutenants with behind the scene subtleties. He was quite aware of the coalition of the Greek societies, however, he was even able to garner votes for his candidate from their members. My managers held to the premise that there were no organizational ties behind the Barbs. Their campaign fostered the fact there were many popular young men and women; however, one who rode on an open ticket, one who held no rancor between one group and another, and was open and above board, was the one to choose. My campaign managers stressed the fact that a Greek organization would naturally be a block vote and that the candidate would be a pawn of that group, whether they had a rightful place on the throne or not. However, my opponent, Perry Gibbs, was a member of Sigma Tau Gamma fraternity and was a prince of good fellows. I considered him a good friend and is to this day. He was always friendly, considerate, and well understood the situation of the campus. I was touted as being unfettered and unattached because my allegiance and loyalty had been proclaimed as being to no one group, and that my friendships were not bound in any manner by race, creed, color, or religion. They made this fact known throughout the campus, and it evidently made a great impact, as I was elected "Most Popular Man." I personally questioned why I was elected, and the workers on my behalf attested to the above reasons as to the outcome of the election for me. I appreciated the diligence on my behalf of Pooey Silverman, Jerry Hickey, Marcus Smith, Tiny Anderson, and Martin Coppaken.

The non-academic collegiate honors were: The May Queen was Maralee Stiles, the Beauty Queen was Margaret Russell, the Honorary Queen and

Captain of Headquarters Company of the Missouri National Guard, was Mirza Thomas-Smith. The Most Popular Girl was Marilue Hall, and I was named The Most Popular Man. The festivities that followed the election were those of one gala event after another. We were presented as our titles indicated at the grand May *fete*. There was dancing and the presentation of plays, and the entire pageantry was a culmination of my collegiate years, which added a very touching, yet happy finale to a beautiful chapter of my life.

To gain admission into medical school has always been considered as being difficult. Consequently, application is usually made to several. Since my grades were high, I believed acceptance would not be exceedingly difficult but applied to four different medical schools and was first accepted by a northern mid-western school, so promptly sent the necessary fee. The second and third school acceptances arrived with my father receiving the notification and acceptance. It is now recalled the month of my acceptance, however I did go to the college which accepted me first and was impressed with the students. Some of them took me to their fraternity house, the Phi Rho Sigma medical fraternity, and were very helpful. My sleeping quarters were to be on the third or perhaps the fourth floor. Being a freshman, my bunk was to be on the top tier of four bunks. The two or three days I was there was yet relatively summer time, however the wind was freezing cold and continuously whipping in off the huge lake near which the house was situated. I shivered through two days and nights, and the third night ushered in a snow storm in early September. There were only open windows in the dormitory and the snow came breezing in covering our bunks. I feared all my teeth would be chipped off during attacks of shivering chills. The next morning, after loosening up the cold stiff joints, I called my father and he told me of an admission fee he had sent to another school which had accepted me. On hearing this I decided to leave this Eskimo land. The cold nights and windy days actually would not have deterred me if I found it to be a necessity, but when given another choice, it was difficult for me to understand why I should be concerned about shivering through the years there when it would be more comfortable to stay in the Midwest.

Though it was paradoxical, the school I went to finally was in Omaha, Nebraska, where it was very cold in the winter also. This was Creighton University School of Medicine, where I had also applied, because a former dear friend of mine with whom I used to box and wrestle had gone into the priesthood and was located there. He would work-out with me if I would listen to his teaching and learn the various parables. We had a great friendship. He had been a Creighton graduate and would at every opportunity extol the virtues and greatness of Creighton University and the many outstanding and famous men of medicine who were on the faculty such as Dean Herman Von Schulte, Doctors Fred J. Schwertley, Adolph Sachs, Charles M. Wilhelmj, Victor E. Levine, and Maurice C. Howard who was later a major consultant to the Presidential family. After finding lodging at ten o'clock that morning, two well-groomed young men, Emery Bordeau and Joseph Prince, introduced themselves. After passing the time of day, they facilitated my enrollment. My new found friends took me to the proper offices.

Entry into medical school was a great thrill of life and at enrollment I actually felt a great sense of exaltation and real adventure of mental buoyance which seemed to make all tribulations and problems vanish; I felt there were no more obstacles to getting down to the final study for a great career. My entire environment had changed and now with this elevated academia I felt like the entry into man's estate. Here I am rubbing shoulders with brilliant students chosen who come from far and wide, as well as near, and work with scholars who have won distinction in the profession.

Following enrollment, we proceeded to the Phi Rho Sigma fraternity house which was a coincidence, as it was the same national medical fraternity to which I had been invited at the other medical school. All the advantages of fraternity living were explained, such as the value of group study and regular lectures by upperclassmen in each subject. This all sounded very appealing to me. The question of the medical school neophyte is whether one may gain and attain more from study and application by oneself or with a group. In the quandary of whether to align myself with a fraternal organization, I studied the array of members and learned that ninety percent of the faculty belonged to the Phi Rho Sigma Fraternity. In this group of course there was no hazing; as in medical school the students are too mature for such ridiculous antics. It is my opinion that hazing is an affront and a humility to anyone, no matter at what age. A member was chosen for a medical fraternity because of scholastic attainments and general personal desirability. The group attitude of study sessions and lectures by the fraternal upperclassmen, and the direct personal devotion for the well-being of the underclassmen were factors in my fraternal acceptance. The academic level was the highest among all other similar fraternities and from those not belonging to organized groups for study. The attitude of every member of this fraternity was that of kindly, cheerful, but serious interest. I accepted their invitation to join and felt that this move was my first well planned and beneficial step in medical school. I was profoundly impressed with our initiation ceremony. The various participants were both active members and faculty who were all superb actors who articulated their portrayal of each part in a wonderful manner. The ceremony portrayed medical history, revealing the roles of Hippocrates, Aesculapius, Galen, Paracelsus, and even the role of Mephistopheles as the Satanic tempter. The lights were dimmed for the play, and each character was in the complete authentic costumes of the historical times. The philosophy of the Greek physicians was revealed as following the ideals of the Hippocratic oath. The play then reflected on the Arabic attitude of shunning surgery as violating the body by scalpel in favor of the utilization of cautery. Also the Arabs were noted in the play as favoring counter-irritants, both for physiological and psychological benefit. The era of Galen was depicted as the time when the art of medicine progressed through the Renaissance, with the actual in-depth study of the human body. Also brought out were the incomparable dissections and explorations of anatomy by Vesalius. Paracelsus or Theophrastus Bombastus von Hohenheim was portrayed as being the "Prince of Quacks, iconoclast, and dealer in nostrums of unfounded questionable values." The factor of sin and temptation was portrayed in-depth by the actual presence of Mephistopheles and the desecration of the Hippocratic oath and principles of ethics. The theme then was the advancement to the humanistic way of life and the medical doctor as being impressed with the ideals of sanctity by his every thought and action. He was to maintain dignity, yet be realistic, and he was to present a good appearance. He was to continue reading, studying, and searching for advancement and wisdom. When the initiation was over, every new member was deeply impressed. I personally shall never forget it.

Medical school was hard concentrated study, however I enjoyed every class as I knew this was the final stretch. Every word was needed regardless of how long it took to grasp. Much of the tension, the striving for honors in ancillary subjects and the severe competition was now gone. The major elimination of many splendid students who would have made excellent doctors was made in the collegiate pre-medical years. Medical schools and the number they have ability to accept is fractional to the great number of good students who apply for admittance. Our system of choice in my estimation is quite archaic in resolving the final word to the judgment of three men. It is difficult to find an appropriate improvement on this system which follows general examinations of aptitude.

Pre-medical stipulated studies are fine. However the formation of a good doctor should include studies in the humanities and certainly teach them how to write legibly. We are getting farther away from general care of the individual and tending more to super-specialization. Many of us are of the opinion that before one is to specialize he should be a good internist. He should know the body as a whole person and not as a single disease entity. Specialization tends to produce the so-called "doctor with tunnel vision." He sees only the disease but not the real suffering individual who may have other ancillary or basic illness which may or may not bear upon the seemingly most predominant ailment.

Our medical curriculum of four years was divided into sections. The first two years' studies were of basic medical science; it is the study of normals, composed of very intensive application to anatomy. We also had thorough dissection of a cadaver, which in itself is intricate and detailed to the most finite point. We learned every tissue in detail; the origin and insertion of every muscle, the course and relationship of every blood vessel, lymph channel, nerve and nerve plexuses with action and function, every bone of the body, and every organ. Other studies included the microscopic cellular study of normal cells, histology, human physiology, embryology, physiology, genetics, neurology, psychiatry, and basic ethics. The second year is that of other intensive studies such as pathology, microbiology, parasitology, immunology, pharmacology, materia medica, neurology, epidemiology, cardiology, and special studies in anatomy and physiology. There are also lectures in medical history, ethics, elementary history taking, and physical examination.

In my estimation and analytical judgment, medical education is one continuous, concerted effort in study and dedication. The tremendous amount of material in the various subjects demands long, tedious hours of concentration and later application. When the days, weeks, months, and years are finally ended, we find the welter of unknowns continuing to loom ahead like a vast waterway with the thrown pebbles of knowledge causing ripples, and we must continue to cast the pebbles or the waterway will remain placid. We look then to other landscapes and farther horizons where the brilliance of the changing landscapes of medical possibilities will forever loom for the physicians in his quest for excellence. With this perpetual quest for knowledge, one must also hold fast to ideals and continue the fundamental beliefs in the potential goodness and dignity of man. Good physicians, we learn, should have the intuitiveness to see patients as individuals with sensitivities. We cannot look upon them as a disease entity, but must transpose ourselves to see the patient as he sees himself. Every word of hope, with sincere kindness and positive thought and action, is needed to assuage the fears of the patients and to instill confidence in your ability to help them. We were taught not only the art of medicine, but the ethics and history of medicine from its primitive inception to the present. Much of this was imparted by our very astute physiologist, research scientist, and historian, Dr. Charles M. Wilhelmj.

There were times, usually on a Saturday, after having completed a long day that we would seek some diversion. A few of us would drive down to a warm and cozy inn named for the owner, Louise. Louise and her husband, Tony Salerno, were two very warm and charming people. There was always a bit of light wine or soft drinks, and the spaghetti and meat balls were super delicious. The various Italian foods tickled the palate and warmed the gastric pouch of many a tired and hungry student, as well as some of the selective gourmets. Louise always had time to sit and talk with us or to listen to our trials and tribulations, and she would encourage us through the worries of examinations. Here we exchanged thoughts, compared notes, and enjoyed a few hours in genuine camaraderie.

My roommates and fraternity brothers, Don T. Weir, Stanton Lovre, Bus Sorenson who was a brilliant concert pianist, Frank Brown, Joe Kafka, the house steward, and Clarence Kurth, our fraternity anatomist, and I spent hours lecturing and quizzing one another. We would also use little sayings or poems to help us memorize various anatomical parts such as the actual branches of the descending aorta, bones of the hand, skull, feet, grouping of the nerve plexuses and other parts. The following is one of these aids to memorizing the branches of the descending aorta in the chest, *"Pleasure by easy money is scholastic suicide"*: P-Pericardial, B-Bronchial, E-Esophageal, M-Mediastinal, I-Intercostal, S-Subcostal, S-Superior Phrenic.

There were of course, periods of discouragement. I recall one evening following a particularly difficult examination in neurology when my bench partner, Kenneth Fujii, from Hawaii, Paul Suski, from Seattle, Washington, and I were consoling ourselves when Ken spoke up: "Believe me Wally, I was really depressed and scared when I read those questions. I prayed to your Christ, my Buddha, Allah, and every God I ever heard of to give me enough knowledge to pass this difficult examination." The examination was rough, and we later learned it was advanced beyond our present stage, for a purpose. We had the understanding at that time that if we failed one course we would be dropped from school and there was to be no recourse. I recall vividly how very worried I was, and wrote to my parents that I was afraid I had failed the test. I received replies by telephone and by telegram from my father during a time of depression and self pity. In it he stated, "Regardless of the outcome of the examination, you should continue to apply yourself, attend to your duties to God, and keep in mind that if you want to be an M.D. you will be, even if it becomes necessary to learn in a foreign land somewhere." He further reminded me that in foreign lands the people are children of God, and their illnesses and misfortunes need tending wherever they were. This morale bolstering came at the propitious moment. The grades were posted, and to my great relief, I received a passing grade. However, I felt the comfort of my father's deep understanding and support even more than before his reassurance.

On entering the third or junior year, I was aware of a definite change of attitude not only with my colleagues but with the Professors and the studies. This is the year of application or the beginning of study combined with clinical aspects. Here we see the patients and are governed as well as taught in classroom, clinic, and bed-side in the hospitals. We now are in the period of application and putting together the studies and lectures of the first two years. The first year having been an extension in the study of the normal, the second year is that of the abnormal or disease otherwise called the pathological state. Now the third year is the beginning amalgamation and answering of our problems by proper treatment—all under strict supervision of both the resident doctors and the chief staff doctors. The third year of medicine was the beginning of clinical clerkship, hospital ward work, and rounds. That year was to me, analogous to the metamorphic emergence of the moth from the cocoon. This was the first clinical year when we had actual patients under professorial tutelage. We did have a few days of holiday through this third clinical year when my thoughts were directed to my girl back home. There were letters and telephone calls. On available days, regardless of rain,—storm, cyclone, or blizzard, I drove from Omaha to Kansas City to see her. She had completed her college courses and was in the school of nursing to attain the degree of Registered Nurse in June from the Saint Mary's Hospital School of Nursing. The courting was limited, but we were both convinced that life would be bleak and dreary without the completion of our long and harmonious duet, to be culminated in unity for life. I had already been accepted for externship in the Massachusetts General Hospital for the summer of 1935, to be completed on the 12th of September. We were united in wedlock the 15th of September, 1935, and left for Omaha where I would complete my last year of medical school. Velma Ruth Hill became Velma Ruth Graham, and she continued nursing duties as an R.N. in Omaha, Nebraska.

The time span between didactic and clinical years of application seemed interminable until it had been abridged. Once reached, the time interval seemed like a flash. The great step of scholastic attainments, juxtaposed with the gentleness of love and marriage exerted its impact upon me with dramatic acuity. On reflection, it seemed like the unfolding and realization of a true drama of romance which had been accentuated through the inexorable brevity of time. Marriage actually afforded many advantages. There was a dramatic change of my lifestyle: for instance I no further had loss of study time due to trips to and from Omaha and Kansas City with repeated exposure to the hazards of driving in my antique Ford. Some of those trips were more thrilling than I desired. On many occasions there were swirling snow storms, and on one occasion a sudden onset of blinding blizzard struck, with flying vortices of huge flakes obliterating all evidence of the front of the car and the highway ahead. It was dangerous to stop, and probably more perilous to continue. A sudden blast of wind caught the well worn top on my old roadster, and it was ripped across and flapped madly in the gale-like winds. After many unsuccessful attempts to harness the flying black canopy, I held it with one hand and drove with the other, practically creeping. Fortunately, red reflecting markers had been placed along the highway adequately so that I could see them occasionally. The time was late, and darkness fell like a black mask, being lifted only by swirling snow in the lights. I realized that this was a very dangerous trip on the old highway, which was not too well traveled. I chose this route because it was the most direct, although the road was macadam, not concrete, and made it even more difficult to see. My slow progress seemed interminable, and for nearly one hundred miles there was no lessening of the storm. The cold was intense, and although my tip-holding hand was gloved, it was fixed, flexed, and devoid of feeling in its frozen grasp. Managing as well as possible, and praying for a station to be open in the small town of Clarinda, Iowa, at the cross highways, I finally reached this point and saw with utter dismay that the station was blanketed over and closed. My thoughts were challenged on whether to stay or continue. My antagonists were the blinding snow, freezing cold, the black of night, and no outlook for warmth for another 75 miles to Council Bluffs. There was also the possibility of running out of gas and the not too remote possibility of freezing. I tried sitting on my nearly frozen hand but this didn't afford much heat. The ferocity of the blizzard abated somewhat with the increasing frigidity, and by the time Council Bluffs was approached dawn was breaking over the white roofs. A frozen, chilly, and very uncomfortable morning ushered in the day. On reflecting, I wondered if I would do this again, and decided I probably would take the chance; as I had driven many times in storms at night with rain, hail, sleet, snow, or drastic weather changes and these challenges were met without thought of possible outcome. In contradistinction, I enjoy the breaking and pacifying effect of dawn and sunshine. My body had been attuned to stress but I was grateful for return without insurmountable incident, and the comfort of a warm house. Following a warm shower, thirty minutes of rest, a warm breakfast, and a reviewing scan of the day's schedule, I was off to the clinics and lectures.

Extending into the fourth year of medical school, the clinical training was superbly taught by the actual practicing physicians and by the chief clinical professor. Excellent scientific disciplines and clinical instructions were given and stressed individually; not in large group studies or mass lectures. Each student was assigned special case studies and the professor would personally oversee, direct, and teach the fine points of diagnosis by sight, history, touch and insight on every patient. This was designed to bring out the diagnostic acumen in each student. As senior students, we would then carry on the same analytical process in full explanation to the professor. Every clinical or hospital day was a day of rugged discipline and examination. This year was the actual "jewel in the toad's head." I found that time was never a factor; the professors to whom I was assigned were dedicated to the art, practice, and teaching of medical and surgical skills. This fourth and final year of medicine consisted of both the didactic class lectures by a splendid medical faculty and clinicals. Among the faculty were such figures as Dr. Maurice C. Howard, Ernest Sacs, Ernest and Robert Kelly, the neurologists, Victor E. Levine, M.D., Professor of Biological Chemistry and Nutrition, John Phillip Cogley, M.D., instructor in surgery, James Kelly, the Roentgenologist, Fred J. Schwertley, Professor of Anatomy, Eugene F. Noonan, M.D., Professor of Anatomy, Charles M. Wilhelmj, M.D., Professor of Physiology with Nancy Catania, M.D. as assistant professor. The last year in medical school included another round of surgical anatomy, special lectures in medical and surgical diagnosis, psychiatry, etcetera, correlated with the clinical work at the hospital. Clinical training was most excellent. Each professor took special interest and time in teaching the integral parts of the art of clinical medicine.

In our medical fraternity house, a graduate M.D. and resident would give us night lectures on diagnosis and patient care. One of our most outstanding lecturers was Clarence J. Kurth, now an attending M.D. in the Menninger Clinic, Topeka, Kansas. He would also review anatomy and physiology, and have question and answer periods. Since ninety percent of the faculty were members of our fraternity, there was no difficulty in having a round-robin of lectures, revealing their diagnostic acumen to the avidly respectful and listening group. During the last year in medical school, Velma was a plucky heroine. The winters in Omaha are quite severe; at times reaching 20° to 30° below zero and there were heavy snows not too unlike the Klondike for relatively short intervals. Velma would be doing nursing duties at the hospital and regularly walking to and from the hospital morning and evening. Often times she would find it necessary to stop at a store or an apartment to get a moment's warmth before proceeding. She was on night duty, so our time together was rather sparse.

It has been said that no one ever fails out of medicine the third or fourth year, but this is not entirely true. The student, regardless of the year, was fully accountable for his grade averages as well as his student and extra curricular activities. If the college deans believed the individual student would not be a good representative and competent medical doctor, he or she was dropped, regardless of the year. Actually, we were kept studying and alert at all times and to the very end until graduation with the coveted M.D. degree. In surgery, residents taught us only basic techniques such as the method of surgical scrubbing, the use of different instruments, operating room conduct, and techniques of patient care and pre- and post-surgical care. A relatively small amount of time was spent in the laboratory, unless being involved in a research project. In medicine and the sub-specialties the continual questioning, drilling, and lecturing kept one studying constantly to keep abreast.

I did not feel very intellectually strong in neurology, and the majority of us in the fraternity felt this was our weakest subject. To improve ourselves, we took special tutoring from a brilliant neurologist, Dr. William Kelley, who was the son of the head of the department who was later head of the same department himself. Those of us who took this special class were Don Wier, Stan Lovre, Bus Sorenson, and I. It always seemed that I learned more from pictures than I did from words. Consequently, in off hours I studied various pictures of the tracts and pathways of the nerves. I don't believe I had a photographic mind, but I was always able to recall every detail of the pictures I studied. I can vividly recall to this date that the rubio-thalamic pathway was in red. We had broad examination which meant nothing really, except to tell Dr. Kelley what we knew or didn't know. So on about our fifth tutoring lesson, he, gave us an examination. Oddly enough, it was on special tracts which was far ahead of where we had ordinarily studied. Much to my amazement most of the questions asked were on what I had studied in the pictures, as I had thought they were the most interesting. Dr. Kelley then asked me how in the world I knew such advanced neurology. I told him frankly that I didn't know much about neurology, and he assumed then that I was simply inordinately modest and labeled me as a genius in neurology. It was very embarrassing to me when he constantly referred to the fact that I knew so much about the course. I tried to explain to him but utterly failed in getting my point across. Consequently, I dropped out of the course and paid for the course for one of the other fellows, who then would come home and was kind enough to teach all he had learned each day. The word also happened to get to the head professor about how good I was in neurology. I was completely embarrassed; however, when the grades came out I was given a very generous grade. I was very glad when the school year finally ended. Dr. Kelley was amazed that I did not make a specialty of neurology. I made no comment.

I had made many good friends through my medical school years, and still recall the relationships with genuine warmth. However, most of us went our separate ways, and contact with them was limited. However, my old bench partner, Ken Fujii, who was also a good friend, and a fine person, a splendid M.D. with great sense of humor, has been to visit us on occasion and we have remained good friends. He now lives in Hawaii, where he has retired from a very fine practice in medicine, and has a son whom he named Creighton.

The winding down of four very pleasant but arduous years came to all of us in the class as we were preparing to enter a new and separate phase of our professional lives as interns and residents. I had been accepted for a rotating internship in the Kansas City General Hospital and was anxious to begin. Graduation day was the climactic placement of the wreath of victory over four years of constant and concentrated study. It was a beautiful day, and quite a spectacle as we appeared, dressed in our various colored robes with the green stripes of medicine blending with the colors of our alma mater, and our tassled mortar boards. We marched proudly into the University stadium to the chords of the appropriate music and heard the commencement address, which in itself, was a great send-off. Also those of us who had had military training received the rank of 1st Lieutenant, and transfer from our previous arm of service into the medical corps. I was particularly proud of my parents and my wife as they shared my happiness and I recalled their staunch support throughout the years.

CHAPTER SIX
POST GRADUATE STUDY & RESIDENCY, EUROPE, VIENNA

Following graduation, I asked the military when they wanted me and was told I would be in the service soon enough—they would contact me. With other duties completed and the cherished degree in hand, the next step was to take the State Board Examinations, allowing me to practice according to the state laws. This set of examinations was also to affirm the fact that we, as recent graduates, were adept in the basic sciences, as well as being well versed in the art and science of medicine and surgery. These examinations were taken in the state capitol building in Topeka, Kansas and when they were completed our group felt reasonably sure we had passed the examinations and proceeded to our respective hospitals for the beginning of the first year of internship.

It is usually not a good practice to place all the eggs in one basket; and by the same token, good internships were not easy to find. However, I only applied to one place. From the experience I had by first hand observation and letters from other interns and residents in various large hospitals throughout the United States, I chose the Kansas City General Hospital.

This hospital was not chosen because it was my home, but because it was overflowing with a wealth of material. It was very well attended and supervised by practicing physicians and surgeons of outstanding ability. The attending staff was in rotation, each spending a stipulated number of months each year.

Another factor was that the interns were carefully selected for scholastic attainment and industry, integrity, and references from professors of the college from whence the application came. Interns had to do most of the work, because there were no residents. Interns were on call and responsible for assignment day and night, with staff supervision and direction. I remember that while in the final part of my last year in school I received an answer to my request and application to this hospital and thought my heart would pound through my rib cage as I opened the letter, for this had been my only application. There were the magic words of acceptance and I was overjoyed.

The day arrived when I traveled the clouds to the great hospital of my expectations. Velma had been asked to be assistant surgery supervisor at Saint Mary's Hospital in Kansas City, the first married nurse they employed. As she went to Saint Mary's, I entered Kansas City General, the large red brick building on Hospital Hill trimmed with white stone and topped with gargoyle rain spouts from every four-cornered turret. The front marble steps were deeply worn by the sick and weary and by hospital personnel who trudged up through these portals of hope. On entering the hospital and looking over the large doorway above the steps, the following quotations from Shakespeare's "Merchant of Venice," was etched in stone below the State of Missouri crest:

"THE QUALITY OF MERCY IS NOT STRAINED.
IT DROPPETH AS THE GENTLE RAIN FROM HEAVEN
UPON THE PLACE BENEATH. IT IS TWICE BLESSED,
IT BLESSES HIM THAT GIVES AND HIM THAT TAKES."
1872----------GENERAL HOSPITAL----------1905

The superintendent, Dr. Harvey Jennett, a quiet kindly gentleman, gave me the honor of a private tour. The hospital reeked with the smells and aura of antiquity,which to me was like a beautiful bouquet. The tinkling bell calling doctors, rang through the many wards where a multitude of humanity was lying ill. Nurses, aides, and technicians were hurrying about their tasks, and interns in white busily attended their duties. We went through ward after ward, all filled though there were a few single or double rooms for specific care. Gowned and masked, we went through the building of isolation for ills of contagion. We then went into the clinic and on to the emergency area adjacent to the ambulance area. Here were the acutely ill or recently injured, awaiting their turn to be seen by the busy interns and nurses.

I recall that the last place was the top floor opening into a large room lined with beds similar to a scene as in army barracks. The day was hot, and being close to the roof, the room had the atmosphere of an attic, clammy with heat. There were two large electric fans, idle at the time, and a cooler of water. I was not dismayed nor disturbed when Dr. Jennett stated that the heat wouldn't matter to us as we would get accustomed to these quarters, everyone would be so tired when he got to the quarters after duties that he wouldn't mind the heat. I later found these words prophetic. Even so, I felt fortunate to have such a place, and was grateful for the fans. The idle corner cobwebs were like the strings of a harp as they glistened in the sunshine, beaming through the large windows. The view was grandiose, as the hospital was on the highest hill in town. It overlooked the main part of the city to the Missouri River, which idled along its muddy course on the other side of the tall buildings separating Northtown from the main city. To the west I saw the trains moving to and from the Union Station. Here over the roof points of the station also were gargoyles from which flocks of pigeons launched themselves into the clear sky, floating and sailing down for a bit of spilled grain from an overloaded rail car. The sun was like a hot golden shaft, and appeared to bounce from the open and grotesque mouths of the gargoyles to the train rails below.

Dr. Jennett explained in detail the duties and obligations of the interns to the institution and the many patients under our care. He reminded me of rules and regulations regarding the hospital, and then enumerated the services. We were accountable twenty-four hours a day and night unless otherwise designated. Emergency service included being ready to ride the ambulance to any area of necessity. Dr. Jennett said "I hope you like it, Dr. Graham." He appeared rather dumbstruck when I replied, "To my eyes this is the most beautiful site in many a moon." His reply was, "Um-mm," along with a quizzical and possibly unbelieving glance. We proceeded down the stairs to the library, filled with the hundreds of old and new books. Time was limited, so the grand tour of the General Hospital was finished. Two of the interns who had already been there a year told me that they were continually busy and had excellent supervision by staff doctors who were always willing to oversee, advise and teach, and were always on call for suggestions.

Our duties began almost immediately. The intern group of twenty-five enthusiastic young M.D.s was given orientation lectures and assignments, for which we were grateful, and considered it an honor and privilege to have the assignment.

I learned that several rooms were available for the interns apart from the large work-like room. A drawing was held, and I drew a room as well as a fine roommate, Hubert Lee Allen, Jr. whose home was also in Kansas City. He had his medical training at Tulane University in New Orleans. "Hub", as he was called, was the nephew of Phog Allen, the famous basketball coach at the University of Kansas. Hub was a tall, slender, erect, debonaire young man. He was a person of action, yet was kind, attentive, and immediately inspired confidence in his patients. Hub and I were great friends, probably because we both worked long hours and shared our problems, heartaches, and patients. Hub was planning his residency in eye surgery. We were both in a rotating internship, so we traded services. He took my obstetrics and I took his few months in surgery, making us both happy. Hub had no desire to be with the hard-driving, sharp-tongued square-jawed chief of surgery, Dr. James G. Montgomery. I enjoyed this great surgeon, who had been an Olympian athlete in track. He demanded practically everything but the intern's life blood. He expected him to be on duty practically twenty-four and be attentive, as well as know every detail about the surgical patients. It was my unusual distinction to have never had a tongue-lashing from this admirable man, and we worked well together. He would call us at all hours inquiring about blood counts, blood pressure, and vital statistics. His voice was strong at four in the morning as at four in the afternoon. I learned many lessons from this fine teacher. It was also my good fortune to assist other excellent surgeons, among whom were Claude Hunt and Ralph Ringo Coffey.

We made knowledge from autopsies, learning the why of illness and exodus. Dr. Victor Buhler, our pathologist, gave detailed reports. Later we not only assisted but performed postmortems under his capable guidance.

The interns held their first meeting and it was my honor to be elected president of the house staff, and was to be spokesman for our group. One duty was to see that we had an egg in the morning instead of a frankfurter. Mission accomplished. We had an exceptionally fine group of interns, all honor students. We practically stumbled over the Phi Beta Kappas, Alpha Omega Alphas, Phi Kappa Phis and other honor society keys. The only unusual fact was that every intern was such a personable, fine man who had no "hang ups", and who was always willing to do extra duties regardless of fatigue. James French, of our class, went on to become chief of pathology in the College of Medicine in the University of Michigan. Every intern became well know in his specialty.

We had many adventures during this year. We rode ambulances during our rotation of services, and I remember that one call for the ambulance was for a woman who had been shot. I dashed to the seat in the ambulance and it roared out into the night, siren shrieking and blasting through the chilly air. The ambulance was weaving around trolley cars, autos, and pedestrians until we reached the designated area. Medical bag in hand, and with the driver, Nick Costello, leading the way up a long flight of stairs. I heard the quiet of the night doubly split by two loud blasts from a shotgun. It seems as if the gunman had not yet completed his task, as he unloaded both barrels into a man as Nick opened the door. We stepped to one side and announced we were the doctor and hospital ambulance driver. The man holding the gun was wild-eyed and cursing, pointing the gun carelessly while he fumbled in his pockets for more shells. Costello, struck and subdued him. There were two victims, a man with his left shoulder mangled and a woman with her right leg and thigh blown away. The man who had the gun was pleading to be allowed to kill himself as the police came upon the scene. Both wounded were placed into the ambulance with whimpers and a few moans. Such scenes were not rarities. We interns had charge, and saved the majority of lives.

One of my calls toward twilight hours (rush time in traffic), was to a house of questionable repute. A young man was apparently making the rounds for collection. As he opened the door another man was standing in a chair with a shotgun in his hands. One blast practically tore the left shoulder and the upper pulmonary lobe from the collector's body. The entire night was spent with continuous transfusions, using two units of blood, acacia (a volume expander used at the time) and repeated fluids with electrolytes, plus surgically removing shell waddings and devitalized tissues. The victim later regained his health and lived an exemplary life. He acquired several grocery stores and was a pillar of strength in church and his community.

My ambulance duty was filled with many similar stories. Our city was open and notorious in the mid-thirties. I was reprimanded by a staff member of a nearby hospital because my picture was in a detective magazine. The picture was taken, unbeknown to me, while I was administering care to a gunman who had been shot and thrown from a car in gangland fashion.

Frequently, an emergency call would come in, only to have a house doctor hurry out for a call that turned out to be a minor incident, not an emergency. I recall one such on a busy Saturday evening. The call was from a woman crying that her little son, Sammy, had cut himself, and screamed over the phone. "He is bleeding to death and blood is everywhere." When we asked her to bring him in, she responded that there was no way she could rush him to the hospital. I ran to the ambulance with the driver, Kelly, at the helm, and tore out, roaring through the streets to the city limits, and when we arrived I dismounted with bag in hand and ran to the door, met the mother, and asked where the wounded boy was lying. The mother looked around a bit, then remembered she had sent him off to the grocery store. She said he would be back in a minute. She said her mother was really the one who wanted me to see. She knew we would not come out to see her mother who was ill, but not an emergency. I was ushered into the room and saw the elderly woman in bed, who readily diagnosed her own condition as a bit of constipation. Examination revealed normal peristaltic bowel sounds and there had been no nausea or vomiting. Careful examination revealed she had no intestinal obstruction or any serious disease. I proceeded to administer a somewhat drastic purge which would give her prolonged beneficial results. I then listened to the story of the one who made the call. I asked her if she had a chronic backache, to which she answered in the affirmative. I administered another drastic purge to the boy's mother who had made the call. Sammy came home soon and I examined the primary excuse for the emergency call. It was a small cut on the hand that needed no suture. I cleansed and sterilized the area accompanied by vociferous howling, and while Kelly held the screamer I placed a band-aid on the cut, I returned to the mother and grandmother who both wanted sleeping pills, administered adequate dosage to insure sound rest for both and returned to the hospital emergency room.

My partner, Hub Allen, followed me on duty at midnight and related his calls to me the following day. He told of a frightened male voice, which called the E. R. frantically requesting immediate help. There was a question of two women in a family possibly dying. On further questioning the man on the telephone stated that both women were unconscious and smelled dead. The ambulance went out to the house and Hub found the two women sleeping peacefully, but soundly. Both had filled their beds with defecation. Hub immediately sensed the situation, as I had given him a complete report when I left duty. He demanded that the neighbors' relatives be called at three-thirty that afternoon. He advised a good soap bath for both, and prescribed coffee and a bit of quinine water every few minutes, then call in the results when Dr. Graham was on duty. The backache of the mother and the constipation of the grandmother were cured for the first time, they said; but they were embarrassed by the horrid mess they had made. I advised by phone that only emergency calls could be made, as they had misrepresented the primary call, and that any future call would be jeopardized by their falsification.

Ambulances rides were wild, and hazardous, but we all came out of emergency service with no disaster, with one exception: one of our intern group, Dr. Gordon Oldham, was injured in an accident while riding the ambulance call—this cost him a finger and a kidney. The average night's rest was four to six hours for all interns in this busy city hospital. To the best of my recollection we kept good dispositions and were rarely, if ever, brusque or sharp with patients.

The year of internship proved a great maturing process, from the first call-bell on 1 July until the last bell, 30 June, the next year. Our sleeping quarters were adequate, if not built for style or comfort. None of us seemed to mind, as by the time we could reach our quarters we were ready to drop. Everyone expended his energy on the wards with his patients. When forced to retire he welcomes the bed. The winter was cold and summer hot. The only air-conditioning was an occasional breeze from the open windows or the three revolving ceiling fans. We were recipients of good training and were considered professional workers without pay. This is quite a contrast to the remuneration of today, as interns and residents receive wages with fringe benefits.

Our patients were mainly the indigent, elderly, and those suffering from diseases who had run the gamut of costly hospitals and doctors; those who had often abandoned hope, and who were in the terminal phase of life; or those who thought they were near the point of exodus. We cared for those with trauma necessitating shock treatment and our best wound care possible. We did not do the laboratory work as this was allotted to technicians. We were expected to know vital signs, laboratory details, blood work, detailed history, and physical findings in assigned patients by the time for ward rounds, which were conducted by the attending staff doctor. We would have already ordered, and, or read, the EKG, gastric analysis, and other data. A factor in learning was study at the autopsy table. Here we learned the nature and actions of disease by sight and touch, and learned of possible mistakes of others. Emphasis was on obtaining an autopsy permit for every death. A prize of fifty dollars was given at the end of the year to the intern having the greatest percentage of autopsies—that year it was won by two interns who shared the prize given by the Melody-McGilley Funeral Home. Dr. Hubert Lee Allen and I shared the honor of being declared the winners, as we both obtained permits for one hundred percent of the patients who had died in our service.

Telephone switchboard operators at General were pleasant and cooperative with the house staff doctors. They were helpful and shielded us from calls from multiple relatives of patients. Each doctor had so many calls it would have been impossible to see many patients if he had to answer the phone so much. These understanding girls kept us from everything except emergency calls, and could always find us, as they knew our haunts. Among the operators was Faye Schultz who, later was coordinator of medical staff affairs and then assistant director at Menorah Hospital, Rosemary Connor, who was chief switchboard operator, Laura Whalen who was executive secretary to the administrator, and Madge Freeman and Freda Rabinowitz.

Married life was difficult for Velma and me, for she was on duty in surgery at Saint Mary's. If I had any free time to see her she was on duty and if she had any free time, I was on duty. We did phone frequently so that we did not feel completely apart. Never was there a grumble or note of dissatisfaction from either of us, as we felt our responsibilities keenly.

The final day of my internship arrived on 30 June 1936. The departing interns acquainted the fledging M.D.s with their duties, made rounds and introduced patients with their medical problems and therapy. As in many departures of old friends, there was a note of sadness upon leaving fine colleagues and such nurses as Rosie Price in pediatrics, and Miss Florence in orthopedics.

Even while bidding adieus to my General Hospital friends I was anticipating my next trip, which was a residency in Vienna, Austria at the famous Allgemeines Hospital. Even though I was anxious to go to Europe the thought of over a year without my wife loomed, and I confessed to my dad that I wasn't sure I could be gone that long without her. Without hesitation he said, "Why, I expected her to go, too." That was my dad with his understanding and kindness. He rose to the occasion with no thought of stress on the family budget.

We began to prepare for the trip and Dad and Mom decided to drive us to New York to board the S.S. *Washington* on 27 July 1937. On the drive East, we stopped by to see Dad's brother; Wallace Scott Graham, in Lancaster, Ohio, and to visit with his sister, Ella Henry in Earlville, New York. I had contacted my friend, Elton Carpenter, then living in New York, and we all went to the dock together, where the *Washington* was steaming up, awaiting its passengers. Elton, was my friend from army camp in Fort Snelling. He was in New York at that time, having been awarded a scholarship to Columbia University. Our luggage was put aboard, we all bade farewells, and up the gangplank we went. Most gathered at the rails to wave to families and friends who in turn were wishing *bon voyage*.

Finally the gangplank was pulled away and the side rails locked. The docks vibrated as the ship pulled away behind tugboat, puffing and hooting midst the bellow of a foghorn. Circling over and around the ship were beautiful white sea gulls, floating and gliding through the air with their plaintive mewing, swooping down for an occasional floating morsel. We pushed on, passing the Statue of Liberty, doubly inspiring as we went by realizing she was our symbol of liberty and land, and that we would again see her as we returned, welcoming us back. As tugboats, relieved of their burden, chugged back to the docks, the bow of our ship was plowing along through the ocean at about twenty knots, spitting a green furrow with white crests while the stern was kicking up mounds of foam like a giant Mississippi sternwheeler. The three smokestacks, amidship, trailed a dark carbon smoke from the bowels of the ship as we hit a gentle ocean roll. The battery of buildings gradually disappeared in the haze and spray, and as we looked out over this vast, deep ocean, realizing that we would see nothing outside the ship but water for five days, I reflected on the vastness of this body and that eighty percent of the world's surface is water. I mused on—that water is the compound that constituted the environment where all life began.

We decided to look around the deck and acquaint ourselves with fellow passengers. Standing closest were two young gentlemen who seemed anxious to become acquainted. They introduced themselves as Eric and George Schubauer, German citizens, who had been working in the United States at our Norden Bomb Works, and were on their way home. Conversation veered toward the background of most people in the United States, who I told them was English, Scotch, Irish, and German. I mentioned as a point of interest, that we once came within one vote of voting for German as our native language. We spoke of the heritage of Germany and other European nations, as coming from Gauls; Celts, Norsemen, Romans, Mongols, Turks, Magyars, and a host of others. Eric and George questioned me on my background and I informed them that on my paternal side, were three clans from Scotland: the Scott, Wallace, and Graham. On my maternal side the Veneman, Reiser [also spelled Reser], and von Richthofen families. George grasped this trend, and wanted to know what part of Germany they were from. I pleaded ignorance of the site of my forebearers in their country and tried to impress them that I did not know, other than they came from Indiana and Kansas. I must mention at this point, that I had been briefed by the army that on this trip I was to be alert as to any information about persons, events, or things of use to our country, and to report them on return. As our ocean voyage continued, I had reason to suspect that these young men might be of interest to us.

We went to our stateroom and prepared to go to the dining room, as we entered the latter we heard an orchestra and everything was gaily decorated. It was a spacious room, beautifully arranged. Dinner was commensurate with the decor. We became acquainted with other passengers, and enjoyed pleasant conversation. The evening was happy, and when the orchestra played songs of countries represented by the travelers, inhibitions disappeared and we all entered into the spirit of the occasion by performing dances of our countries. A young girl became enthused with the sound of an Irish song, and performed an energetic jig. A couple, apparently from Austria, danced a beautiful Viennese waltz to the melodic strains of the Emperor Waltz. Others joined in a Slavic folk dance, and Velma and I and other Americans did a fox trot. Finally the Greek music brought out everyone who felt like joining arms and doing the dances so typical of that country, the Chcemeko and Surto. In Greece only men dance, but some of the women on board joined. This desire to enter into the happiness of the dance contributed to a conviviality that made the first evening memorable.

At the close of the evening, we decided to walk on the deck. The breeze was refreshing, but there was no moon or stars, nothing but the Stygian blackness. We were grateful it was not necessary to depend on a navigator to be guided by a silvery caravan of stars nowhere to be seen. The Greek argonauts with all their skill, would need more than the sextant to direct this modern liner through waters on a night like this. We reflected on the daring of earlier adventurers such as Vikings, Columbus, and Marco Polo. We became tired and welcomed retiring, as our day had been filled.

We were awakened in early morning hours with a bit of a roll. Velma was not enthusiastic about breakfast, but I enjoyed it. She settled for tea and toast. Our voyage was progressing uneventfully, even though the sea was described as "oily," disturbing to the uneasy stomachs on board. Most of us ate the excellent cuisine with no difficulty, and enjoyed deck games, sunned, walked the decks, and generally had a relaxing vacation.

We made a few friends who were interesting, and we found that Eric and George were becoming more attached to us. They seemed intelligent and interesting men, but were constantly inquiring about our country and questioning me about military matters or strategic placements. I pleaded ignorance, as I became more concerned about them. As we sailed along the coast of France, my suspicions began to solidify as I noted their taking photos. Later I would report to the authorities. It was exciting to put into LeHavre and we were told we could visit the city and return no later than forty-eight hours, but to check in twenty-four hours.

The second largest seaport on the Normandy coast, LeHavre is built about the mouth of the Seine River. Huge mortar locks guarded this port, which was heavily fortified. We sailed into the bay where a pilot and guide tug led our ship to the dock. The morning was warm and languid—the longshoremen and dock workers were all lying around, showing little interest in our docking. After considerable time, which seemed needless to us, we were secured and allowed to disembark.

We walked along the streets with Eric and George, both of whom were quite outspoken and loud in denunciation of France and its policies. Leon Blum was premier. He was allowing the Communist party to drive France into a socialistic state and labor was belittling capitalism. The cost of living was spiraling, while wages were increased beyond tolerance by governmental finances. Apparently, French labor had only one thought and that was to do as little as possible for the most return. Most workers were idle and shops closed for three day weekends. Strikes were specially prevalent in industries essential to defense. Our ship, although a passenger type, carried a large load of copper and other materials meant for munitions. The ship had docked mainly to unload the material. The French stevedores, allegedly leftists, were having a meeting, which delayed the unloading, as well as departure. Sailors from our ship had heated arguments with the French stevedores. Our sailors declared the French workers Communists who would not help their own country. More words, and flying fists ensued. After four days of delay, with nothing unloaded, our ship was forced to leave the dock with the material still on board and it had to be returned to the United States.

George and Eric harangued the stevedores and encouraged them not to unload. They told the French that Germany would soon be smashing the hell out of them while they were still gloating over their strike. The ship left for Hamburg, and Eric and George continued to take pictures of the French harbor and coastline, which they undoubtedly presented to German Intelligence.

The few troops we saw in the French Army were as depressing a group of men in uniform as we had ever seen. They were a shabby spectacle of sloppiness representing a once great nation. What had happened to the sharply dressed *poilu* of a few years back? Where was the officer with the polish and shine of the old army? Some of the soldiers weaved about as if intoxicated or extremely fatigued. These soldiers could not have been a representative group of the French Army. Our experience and observation during the few days in France saddened us. The French boasted of the great power of the Maginot Line, while our traveling companions scoffed and said how Germany would capture all France while the French were dancing in night clubs and laughing over financial spoils from tourists.

Leaving LeHavre, we sailed along the coastal lanes of the Normandy coast up the Channel, through the Dover straits, past Boulogne and Calais, then Dunkerque. We never ever dreamed of the later stand of the brave British and Allied forces to be etched in history within the next few years when three hundred fifty thousand Allied forces, nearly surrounded by German forces, were rescued by a thousand French and British ships, large and small. We sailed on past Belgium, Holland, and Germany, past Bremerhaven, by the tiny isles of Scharhorn and Neywerk into the bay of the Elbe, and then Cuxhaven. We were fifty-five miles north of Hamburg. From the port to Hamburg the countryside was bustling. Lines of U-Boats nestled obliquely along many docks. Ships and U-Boats were in the making, and the smell of tar, hot metals, paint, and salty sea was mingled with sounds of pounding on metal. There was a rat-a-tat-tat of multiple steel riveters and blue-orange fires with sparks flying from welders' torches. Drydocks were cluttered with yet to be finished hulls.

Debarking in Hamburg was at hand. We were impressed by the industriousness in Germany. It was apparent that the entire nation was preparing for war. All Germany was involved in a concerted effort to achieve strength. Hamburg, we learned, was one of the world's largest coffee markets and one of the busiest ports of the world. It was also a great shipbuilding center.

As our ship was guided and pushed to the pier and the anchor dropped, George appeared on the scene saying, "It is great to be back in the fatherland. See the difference?" I replied that one would be both blind and deaf not to see and hear the difference. Then I asked how long so many workers had been this busy. Eric replied that workers were always busy, happy, and proud. George interjected that workers were only so happy and energetic since the Fuehrer had put all idle hands to work. "We would see," he said, "what they would do for the Fuehrer and the fatherland." He said they had to defend themselves against enemies and for the Danzig corridor. He told me the Fuehrer wanted peace and wanted all people to work to become prosperous.

The moment we reached the border we knew we were in a different atmosphere, with awareness of discipline, definable in word and action. All officials were in some uniform. The customs officials were expedient, thorough, direct, and militaristic. Regimentation was obvious as officials barked out over the loudspeaker where they wanted the carry-on luggage and where all other baggage would be, according to the letter of the last name. All passengers would be in line in columns of two, and in alphabetical order. Anyone deviating from the order would be taken last. Questions followed examination of our passports and occasionally a few words in German were inserted to note our reaction and if we understood; *"Waren irhen Mutter oder Vater in Duetschland geboren?"* The question was well understood, as anyone born in Deutschland is considered a citizen, regardless of subsequent citizenry. The question was superfluous as names and places of birth were in the proper place. It was interesting to attempt to psychoanalyze the agents; some tried to please and create a favorable impression. Another could not hide his chilly attitude of self-importance, exercising it to fullest extent. This latter individual peered repeatedly through the passport and repeated the name, "Velma Ruth." The question arose as to whether she was of Jewish heritage. She stated she was named for an aunt who was the wife of a Baptist minister. He thought a bit, but handed back her passport. We were repeatedly asked if we carried tobacco, lipstick, or silk—Neither of us smoked, and we said we were students who could not afford such luxuries. Final clearance was given, although guarded suspicion was present. After questionnaires in triplicate about our background, friends, and relatives, the air cleared and we proceeded to the Bahnhof for a train to Berlin.

Wallace Harry Graham

Trains in Europe were built for the class-conscious, and one paid accordingly. In third and fourth class one might find himself sitting next to a farmer with his pig, chicken, or other small farm animals. A train car may be dropped off on a siding to wait for hours on another engine or train. The first-class train car was compartmentalized, with sliding doors. Trains in Germany were divided into categories according to speed. The F. D. or Fernschnell was the fast express or through train running on the main line, with only first and second-class carriages. The D train was not as fast, was generally more comfortable, and carried three classes. The D was also an express, stopping only for larger cities, and traveled at least one hundred miles between stops. The Eilzuge was fairly fast but was not an express,and carried only second and third-class. Fourth-class was only for local runs. We took the Fernschnell, or Berlin Express, from Hamburg to Berlin.

Rolling into the Berlin Bahnhof we were anticipating the many duties confronting us. We decided to walk a bit and see Berlin, which is the largest city in Germany. Here, as elsewhere in Germany, platoons, squads, or individual soldiers were on the streets. They seemed continuously on the march in their hob-nailed boots. The brown-shirted Storm Troopers were practically always within sight. It seemed as if everyone of all ages, from children to the elderly, was in uniform. The German philosophy is to never do anything half way and this trait, although remarkable, may be either good or evil. We visited the Kaiser Frederick Museum where we viewed many of the paintings by Rembrandt, Holbein, and Vermeer. Berlin radiated power. Perhaps it was because of the presence of troops and the crashing of hob-nailed boots on the cobblestones. The city's beauty was apparent in a massive, cold manner. We passed the huge government buildings daily, noting the *Zeughaus* (the huge arsenal), the *Reichstagsgebaude* (Parliament), the Bismarck memorial, the huge old Rathaus, and the Staatsoper on Unter den Linden Strasse.

Berlin denoted massiveness to me; like the capital of an empire. It seemed stolid, yet attractive and imperial. Buildings appeared monstrous, from the Reichstag with its high gilded dome to the Reichkanzlerei. The tree-lined Sieges Allee extended to the Platz der Republik, and numerous statues of Brandenburg kings were along the way. We walked along Unter den Linden, a very wide street, divided in the center by a promenade lined with linden trees. Many a conquering hero, nobility, and the otherwise famous had passed along this street, over which is the imposing Brandenburg Tor. This gate supported the famous four bronze horses, stolen by Napoleon and taken to Paris, but in later years it was regained.

Velma and I were impressed by all the people, particularly those forty years of age and younger. Most of the men appeared to us to be arrogant, handsome, slim, yet muscular, and walked erectly, as if with a goal and purpose. Their eyes were like steel, which looked with disdain on those believed below their status. At first I looked at them with a measure of disgust but my outward attitude changed when I thought it would not be to our advantage to meet fire with fire or arrogance with disgust, so we smiled blandly and accomplished more. We hailed a taxi, and the ride was short, direct, cheap, and the driver refused a gratuity. It is true that a small gratuity had been refused in Paris, but that was followed by a loud ruckus demanding a greater gratuity and only by a near physical battle were we finally left unhampered. The Dutsche taxi man was friendly but inquisitive.

Berlin was a clean city. We first stayed in the Kaiserhof—excellent in all respects, reasonably priced, with splendid meals and service. Our bags were meticulously inspected when we left our room. This had been anticipated but nothing was ever stolen at any time, regardless of value.

We learned that dark-haired, brown-eyed Germans were usually from the Rhineland or Bavarian areas, whereas the others were usually blond and blue-eyed. We wondered whether Hitler considered them second-rate citizens in his Nordic mania, even though he was dark-haired and brown-eyed. It is amazing that he did not bleach his dark brown hair. We both remarked that we had never seen so many young, vigorous, handsome people. The young men all appeared as if they had the world in their hands. Most women were buxom, Nordic types, with blonde hair, rosy complexions, and blue eyes.

We entered the train station and placed our bags on a small wheeled tender, when suddenly two stony-faced, blond, muscular soldiers snapped to our sides, both well over six foot, appearing even taller with their military, domed headgear. They asked for our visas and a glint of friendship was apparent in their blue eyes. They made every effort to help us to the Berlin Express. With some wurst and a bit of hard but tasty bread from a vendor, the world appeared generally more cheerful. On the train we were directed to our compartment through the sliding doors, where we sat across from two silently observing men who returned our greeting with only a nod.

With the train's high, piercing whistle and a lunge or two, away we went, down the rails. Looking through the window we saw that everyone along the way appeared busy, going someplace in a hurry or carrying bundles by cart, bicycle, or other conveyance. We were wearing tweeds and people asked if we were Anglicans. When we said we were Americans the air cleared a bit, and many told of an "onkel" in Detroit or elsewhere. Along the way we saw great numbers of young boys in dark uniforms, not unlike our Boy Scouts, but wearing *lederhosen*. They were carrying sticks like guns and marching in a military manner. There were large groups of healthy and strong looking young women with their golden tresses in braids and rosy cheeks gleaming in the sun. They, too, were marching in uniform. Remember, that was early 1937. Soldiers were everywhere. Uniforms, flags, Nazi insignia, brass bands, parades, drills, trucks filled with rigid troops moved almost endlessly by. Trains were loaded with artillery pieces, tanks, and explosives. Everyone appeared busy—walking, working, driving bicycles, motorcycles, or cars. There was no loitering and no pandering.

Against a backdrop of political turmoil in 1937, Velma and I journeyed from Germany on to Czechoslovakia, and stayed in Prague for a few days. Prague is known as the city of spires, as there are so many of them pointing to the heavens. Although most foreign nationals were under surveillance, we felt we could go about easily. But upon entering Czechoslovakia the intelligence pickup was instantaneous. We were interrogated twice but found it rather awkward, as we could not speak Czech. We did, however, find the people friendly and hospitable, especially when they realized we were from the United States. The only exceptions were those with either fear of or amicable feelings toward Germany, since 1937 was a period of apprehension over the question of the Sudetenland where most of the people were of German heritage. Many Czechs were afraid to voice their sentiments. All this did not deter us from sightseeing in this beautiful city of antiquity, built on both sides of Moldau with bridges spanning the city's two parts. The Old Town square is on the east bank of the river, and is the historic center of Prague. Here is the famous Tyn Church, whose tall spires can be seen from the entire city. There is also the Old Town Hall, built in 1381. I wish we had had more time in this interesting city where old Gothic met modernity. From viewing the old significance, it was started by command of emperor Charles IV in 1344 built by Matthew of Arras, a Frenchman. Construction was carried on later by Peter Parler, a German. A most interesting history abounds in this great edifice. Intrigue and mystery could be written if the dusty corners could reveal their secrets. There was one wooden door with a large bronze ring in the Wenceslas chapel where the Czechs murdered their young King Wenceslas in 929 A.D. The bronze ring hangs today as it did when the murdered king grasped it in his dying moments after having been stabbed by his brother because the king was thought to be a religious fanatic. Rudolph II, the Habsburg Emperor, lies in a crypt of the cathedral.

As our train pulled away from the Wilson station, we began looking forward to our arrival in Vienna, only about a hundred-twenty-five miles away. Our train ran through miles of plains where fields of grain were being harvested by the peasants. There were as many as six to ten women picking up loose grain, while others pitched shafts of straw or hay to the high wagon atop which the only man was sitting at the front like a king, driving the horses and lazily arranging the hay. We were amazed at the use of every piece of available land in crops of some kind. Land was precious in Europe because of the density of population. As I recall, we were amazed when we returned to the United States to see the vast areas of land not used.

En route we again passed through Germany, stopping in Dresden, capital of Saxony, which was among the most beautiful cities in the world. There were no great manufacturing plants, no smoke, no smog. Theaters, museums, and cultural institutions were the finest. Dresden was the headquarters of Luftkreig Air District III from whence the anti-aircraft artillery batteries controlled protective measures such as flak-regiments for Dresden and surrounding area. This city was also the communications center for the nation. In World War I there had been an ammunition plant or arsenal in the northern district out of the city limits, but became only military garrison with barracks and parade ground. Being built in underground rock northeast of the city was a large command bunker of military importance.

It is easily understood why Dresden was called the Paris of Central Europe. As the capital of Saxony, the city was a masterpiece of architecture. As we walked through the castle of Frederick the Great we saw in the inner court the long earthen areas used by knights for jousting after being mounted on their horses by lifts. Some mounted their steeds by steps. They would dash at each other in full armor, spears or long lances aimed at each other. We saw the mid marks where they clashed, trying to dislodge or unhorse their adversaries. Many of the knights' suits of armor were encased behind glass within the castle; the armored coverings for horses and the ribbon colors of each knight also were on the lane. The castle covered a huge area, and it took over half a day to see the interesting rooms retained exactly as in the days of King Frederick.

The great Zwinger Museum of Art was one of the prime attractions in Dresden, and housed a priceless collection of paintings, including *Sistine Madonna* by Raphael, which was large and dramatically occupied one end of a room. This famous painting was viewed by all in silence, admiration, and awe. Dresden was a most attractive city for the Madonna, as the city was devoted to art. There was also a collection of jewelry in the Zwinger, which had formerly been worn by the aristocracy. It was shown in the Green Vault. There was a collection of items with exquisite detail in gold, silver, and precious stones. Ivory and jeweled scabbards there had been collected by the King of Saxony, who also brought the Madonna to

Dresden from Piacenza. The Gemaldegalerie in the Zwinger Palace was the finest museum in Germany if not the world. Here we saw Giorgione's *Sleeping Venus*, Rembrandt's *Samson*, other masterpieces. Also on display were pieces of Dresden china commissioned by Frederick the Great and Augustus the Strong. This fine porcelain, known as Dresden, actually was made in Meissen, not far from Dresden, and is known the world over.

The beautiful Hofkirche was another architectural sight. The Frauenkirche and most of the beautiful buildings were baroque. Dresden had that unmistakable gracious charm, aided by a great river, the Elbe, as it flowed majestically through the beautiful city. The river was the most beautiful promenade in Europe.

After such an interesting journey of sightseeing we were at last ready to go on into Vienna. I was excited at the prospect of entering a new phase of my education under the direction of some of the famous doctors in the world.

On arrival in Vienna, we established ourselves in a pension on the corner of Alserstrasse and Garnison-Gasse. It was on the fourth floor, and special arrangements were necessary to arrange for a bath, the key to the elevator, water, and utilities. The military garrison was one block from our pension. The Allgemeines Krankenhaus (General Hospital) was one block away, on Alserstrasse, across the street from the church where Ludwig von Beethoven played the organ on Sundays.

In midsummer we found the weather quite pleasant, due partly to the proximity of the mountains. The drinking water, which flowed down from the mountains was clear and cold, and most welcome. Vienna and its environs was a most interesting city. It had been a city of happy people who enjoyed open air, mountains, skiing, opera, hiking, vacations, weekends, and holidays.

Until the onset of World War II, many generations of doctors were trained in Vienna, as it was a mecca for medicine and surgery. There were large hospitals with superb medical staff doctors who were gracious in teaching other physicians. The Allgemeines hospital was the largest on the continent, occupying over fifty acres with grounds. Surgery and pathology were of the highest caliber, and I felt fortunate to have the opportunity to be there. The professor of surgery, Professor Dr. Hans Finster, was expecting my arrival and I was introduced to others in surgery and pathology, including Dozent Chorinnini, Professor Dr. Werner for gynecological, surgery, Dr. Fuchs, and Dr. Deutsche.

At the onset, our qualifications were authenticated and we were examined. Following this we spent some time in pathology and cadaver surgery. We then became assistant and eventually reached full hospitantship.

My duties were to maintain a surgical hospitantship, gain surgical expertise and obtain training in pathology, as well as keep abreast on political movements. Surgical duties were many. The first three months I spent in pathology performing autopsies, and performing surgery on cadavers under professorial guidance. It was law in Vienna that for everyone who died a complete postmortem was mandatory. In surgical deaths, it was our duty to state every finding and give a report on why the persons expired, and if they could have been saved. The attending surgeon or first assistant was always present, and explained all past surgical procedures on the patient. Every tissue was meticulously examined, the organs weighed, analyzed, measured, sectioned, stained, and blocked for microscopic study. We were not allowed any error; the slightest mistake was tantamount to a sin. Punishment was to complete charting and cleanup through the night, without help of the dozent. Our term in pathology ended only after a final postmortem, during which we were blindfolded, and the tissues handled and examined by touch and weight. We then gave our lecture, estimating body weight and age, naming the involved tissues, with textures, diagnosis, and cause of death.

Forensic pathology was an interesting challenge, this being the study of trauma or sudden and often unexplained death. Autopsies were performed usually by the dozents or hospitants (staff physicians and residents). On occasion there were lectures by Herr Professor or Dozent Chorinnini. There were always sharp quiz sessions, with sectioning of tissues following. Postmortem examinations were performed in the museum, actually an extension of the main hospital, named for the famous Viennese pathologist of the mid-nineteenth century, Karl Freiherr von Rokantansky. I have seen there the preserved tissues of many of the Viennese greats, among them Beethoven, whose remains are in this great institution of pathology. The graduate doctors who had been through at least twelve months of internship or residency were tested in written examinations, and if they passed were accepted into the classes. This process was followed by a second assistantship with surgery and constant quizzing. Then on to first assistantship for a specific number of procedures. The professor thereafter assisted the hospitant as many times as he deemed necessary. He then moved back and observed while he provided a more experienced hospitant to assist the so-called student surgeon. Major work and direction was then performed in wards at the bedside, exacting fluid balances and other essentials. We then went to the pathology laboratory and examined tissue removed, under or with direction of the Dozent or professor. Time and hours were meaningless to the hospitant. Rest was important, but faculty and staff were relentless and strict. One needed only to have physical stamina and mental ability, along with dexterity and the will to succeed. Knowledge of the patient and all systems was mandatory and was expected to be completed.

These were the years in which gastric surgery was in its infancy in the United States, and gastric resections were considered exceedingly dangerous. The opposite was occurring in Vienna. Patients survived the surgery here at that time by the renowned surgeon, Professor Doctor Hans Finsterer, and it was my privilege to assist him. Finsterer had his own techniques, and I remember his saying that we treated the gastric and duodenal ulcers in the United States with constant medication and by interminable dietary regimes. He further stated that the majority of people in Vienna ate what they could manage regardless of illness, so it behooved the doctors to eliminate the ulcer-bearing area of the stomach so they could continue to eat their harsh diet. One of the factors in his success was that he used largely local anesthetic for this surgery. The patient was administered hypnotics, followed by inhalation of nitrous oxide gas. He then injected the abdominal site for the incision with local anesthesia, made the incision into the abdominal cavity, lifted the stomach forward, then injected a specific amount of local anesthesia into the splanchnic group of nerves posterior to the stomach that lie on either side of the vertebrae. This maneuver blocked the impulses to the brain and prevented shock. He proceeded to resect the area of the ulcer with the gastric-producing section of the gastric pouch and performed his modification of the technique of Hoffmeister, another famous gastric surgeon from Bonn, Germany. The operation was called a gastro-jejunostomy. This is the fixation of a by-pass from the gastric pouch to the first part of the jejunum, which is the first emerging part of the small intestine from behind the stomach. He did this with speed and great skill. Patients responded within a very few minutes following the operation, and on the following morning they would stand at attention at the sides of their beds when the Herr Professor Dr. made his rounds.

All subdivisions of surgery in the specialties were performed with absolute discipline and skill. Both the German and Viennese professors were exceedingly capable, obviously enjoyed teaching, and were gentlemen of the highest type. They were self-disciplined, and sternly expected the same from students. I found every one of the professors meticulous and willing to repeat details of interest and importance to all of us who requested or needed information. We could receive lectures in either English or German depending upon our adeptness. If one could speak the language of the country, he could gain more understanding of the people.

Dr. Werner lectured in gynecological surgery, and for general surgery we were under the direction of Drs. Fuchs and Deutsche. It was a wonderful experience for a young doctor because of the immensity of the available pathology and excellence of the professors. Most patients appreciated and welcomed complete and intricate examinations by the young surgeons, with never a complaint.

The central point of activity for foreign doctors of medicine and surgery studying in Vienna was the Café Edison, which housed the American Medical Association of Vienna. This café was in an ideal location on the second floor of a building at the corner across the street from the Allgemeines Krankenhaus, on Alsterstrasse #9, one block from our pension. The American Medical Association of Vienna was sponsored by the city of Vienna under guidance of the university. It was first formed in 1903. It served as a bank to exchange foreign currency, as a meeting place for members, and as a dining establishment where Americans could obtain ham and eggs or some other back-home meals. Classes were arranged there, and it served as headquarters for personal and professional activities. Some classes were held there, after which we could go to the hospital. It was a good place to study especially before the advent of the American Boards.

The café was demolished during the war, but it is my understanding that it has been rebuilt and now is managed by a gracious lady, Gnädige Frau Anna Engel, who has a prodigious memory of past members. This great café and the American Medical Association of Vienna was re-established through the efforts of Dr. M. Arthur Kline.

After the courses and records of individual doctors had been verified, whether completed in months or years, they performed operations designated by the Herr Professor Doctor, and under his direction. If the requirements were met when courses were finished, they were examined in all subjects, and if successful the degree of Master of Surgery was bestowed. One section of my exam was taken blindfolded as mentioned. The body had been opened for complete postmortem. It was necessary to state the approximate age and describe every tissue and organ in detail including location, and with examination by palpation this included weight, as compared to normal weight. Bones were split in half, and after palpation and description we could order it sectioned in any manner by the Diener. With the blindfolds removed we would then again describe in detail the histologic and pathologic status. I remember that one of my patients had a Krukenberg tumor, a malignant tumor arising from the gastrointestinal tract and simultaneously from one or both ovaries. After these examinations were over, we all gathered at the Café Edison to talk over problems during the courses and discuss what we planned to do next. We had made good friends, and of course we all hoped to meet again. Most of us were from the United States.

During that era before World War II, Vienna was reputed to be the best place in the world for the study of medicine, pathology, and surgery. During and following World War II, tremendous strides were made in the United States and throughout the world, particularly in large cities. After the final examinations I received my Master of Surgery. It was none too soon, for two days after receiving it, while we were still there, Hitler marched into Vienna with his troops and armored vehicles, changing the character of the city for decades to come.

Even though study and clinical work at the hospital took most of my time, we still managed to become acquainted with the many facets of Vienna. Though the city was in an economic depression, as was a great part of Europe, the people of this once-gay city could still enjoy outdoor life, the coffee houses, their beloved opera, their beer halls and kellers, and many could still attend the *kinos* (movie houses). We rarely attended movies, but when we did we usually saw a brief news item, many times of an American in the United States doing something ridiculous. Perhaps this was the influence of the Nazis, who were trying to discredit us to the Austrian people. During intermission at the movie, attendants routinely sprayed up and down the aisles with a scented flea powder. We could all feel the fleas hop on or off our legs. I don't recall small dogs being taken to the theater by patrons, but there were many fleas. It became routine among Americans to undress at night over a sheet so as to watch the fleas jump off and try to kill them. It became a joke, but their presence was most uncomfortable.

The Kellers were the old, picturesquely furnished wine cellars, filled with steins, heavy furniture, and large casks. There were recesses in the walls which held small pieces of statuary. The Rathaus was a large stone building, being the city hall and keller combined. In the lower floor of the Rathaus was a large room like a wine cellar where doctors had an area set apart so we could talk over the cases of the day, sing songs, or just converse.

On weekends many Viennese saddled themselves with a "rucksac" or knapsack filled with cheese, wurst, bread, and perhaps other tidbits. Off they went to the Wienerwald (Vienna forest} and nearby mountains to walk and enjoy, the exercise and fresh air. Occasionally we joined the exodus and participated in this wholesome pastime. I donned my *lederhosen* for these hikes. They are short, heavy leather pants held up by typical Tyrolean suspenders. *Lederhosen* are comfortable and sturdy and worn many years: some fathers pass theirs to their sons, after a lifetime. Velma donned her embroidered blouse, skirt, and Tyrolean sweater and we were ready. Taking the train to the end of the line we hiked through the clean, green forest and up the *racz* (mountain). As we walked up the low-lying mountains, there was respite along the way in stopping by one of the little way-stations or inns perched along the paths. There one could purchase wine, milk (including *sauermilch*), beer or soda, and snacks, including cheese, wurst, or heavy-crusted rolls for the hungry hiker who had not brought his own. Benches and long wooden tables were outside the little stations where we could eat and sip while admiring the trees around us and breathing the crisp air tinged with fragrance of pine. I remember how delighted we were on one of these hikes to find among a craggy area the famous mountain flower so highly prized, the edelweiss. I proudly stuck the flower in my hat and joined new acquaintances in singing the lilting song, "Edelweiss", as we picked our way up the mountain. After these long hikes we came home tired, but relaxed and happy.

On looking at the map of Vienna, one notes a wide street like an irregular hoop, which encircles the central part of the city. The entire circle is known to the Viennese people as the "Ring." The history of the wall goes back to Ottokar, the powerful king of Bohemia who changed his residence from Prague to Vienna and constructed a fortified wall around the city which he had enlarged partly with an extensive addition to Saint Stephan's cathedral. This pleased the Viennese so much that they were willing to retain Ottokar as their permanent ruler. Ottokar had not had the blessing of the Pope to invade the Danubian lands, including Vienna, so approximately twenty-five years following the invasion and completion of the wall, the Pope took action. Papal electors named Rudolph of Habsburg ruler of the Holy Roman Empire. This dislodged Ottokar. The wall held against the siege of the Turks, but in their retreat they left a few sacks of coffee behind. The Viennese liked the coffee so much that coffee houses began to evolve until this city became famous for its coffee houses. With advent of gunpowder, the wall became worthless as a fortification. Later it was used as a promenade for city people, but finally it was demolished and the wide area on the outside of the former wall was incorporated into the ring. Along this ring a series of impressive buildings were built such as the Rathaus, the University, Parliament, two museums, the Palace of Justice, and in part the Imperial Palace. Among other buildings of interest on the ring was the historical museum where displayed on the second floor was the banner of Mohammed and the cord used in the strangling of Kara Mustapha on his attempt to conquer Vienna. To add to the impressiveness of this Ringstrasse are the little parks fringing the ring.

The Danube does not flow through Vienna, but there is a Danube canal through the middle of the city: the river being five miles north of the city. Even though the great Viennese composer, Johann Strauss, immortalized the Danube, I have never seen it blue even when observing it on many occasions at different seasons. The river is wide and swift, but is always a dull gray. It is not as extensively traveled as the Rhine, Elbe, Seine, Thames, Tiber or Volga, but the Danube has carried the history of Europe on its waters from Wurttemburg through Germany, Austria, Hungary, Romania, the Carpathians, and finally to the Black Sea.

Vienna had a history of being a center of culture, of producing many composers including Beethoven, Schubert, and Brahms. The large opera house on the Ringstrasse was the mecca for many a famous singer and for lovers of music. For a small price, people with little means could attend and enjoy the opera even though standing in the balcony. I remember that we went quite early to purchase an opera ticket, but when we arrived there was a long line. We took our place and waited for what seemed an interminable time, and finally decided to go down the block to get a snack. When we returned, expecting to go to the end of the line, we were surprised to find that our space of a few feet was as we had left it. It did not occur to people in line that they could have taken those spaces. We found this an admirable trait among the people of Vienna. This was only one indication of their honesty, as they were people of integrity in business dealings also.

The Straatsoper was a national institution, performers being paid by the state, and after a while they were pensioned for life. Most of the Viennese people we came in contact with, from waiters to professors, loved music and could sing arias of the operas. The most outstanding voices and symphony orchestras in the world could be heard in this famous opera house, for small cost. On our first attendance we heard Verdi's *Aida*, and the voices were magnificent in this melodic story of the captive Ethiopian slave girl whose love for an Egyptian captain, Rhadames, ended so tragically. We purchased the cheapest tickets in the balcony and received the score so we could follow the story and arias. During intermissions we were surprised when many people brought out paper sacks from which they began munching black bread, cheese, and even hard-boiled eggs, which they noisily cracked on the seats before peeling. Even more surprising was a scene in the lobby, where we saw an elegantly clad lady purchasing a hot wurst from a vendor which she unceremoniously dipped in mustard and proceeded to munch in an inelegant manner. We found this not unusual, for many others just as formally clothed enjoyed the wurst in the same manner. Vendors did a brisk business, and also sold hot chestnuts and spicy pumpkin slices, redolent with cinnamon and nutmeg. It was not unseemly for members of the audience to peer at one another intently through binoculars. This was accepted practice, which added a bit of interest to the evening. During intermission it was interesting to watch people promenade in the marble-floored foyers, bowing or nodding to acquaintances, and stopping to discuss the opera. Some men were in white tie and tails, appearing uncomfortable trying to keep their jowls free from the irritating white collar.

Viennese celebrated many different days, so there was always a holiday. One new to us was Krampus Day, an important day, respected by all. Krampus, other wise known as the devil, came on the eve of 6 December, with horns and tail and in full scarlet regalia, visiting every household. Each family was to leave a small bundle of faggots or switches by the outer door. These bits of thin boughs were ostensibly to be used on children who had misbehaved throughout the year. Krampus opened the bundle, asked parents and children about any naughty deed, and if there were any, made frightening gestures with light strokes. Krampus began his punishment. But suddenly Bishop Saint Nicholas appeared on the scene. Dressed as we know Santa Claus, Saint Nicholas exonerated the children and drove Krampus away. Saint Nicholas was kind and took the word of the children that they would be good the forthcoming year. Krampus often had helpers, appearing as dragons, gargoyles, and vampires. Saint Nicholas, with his shepherd's hook was always successful in saving the children and driving Krampus away. Saint Nicholas then distributed candy and sweets, after which he left to catch Krampus in other places. Following this was singing, eating of kuchen and other sweets, dancing and everyone celebrated.

It was unusual to have more than one or two evenings a week to enjoy the Viennese environs, but when I did, we enjoyed an evening at the beer gardens, summer institutions in all Germanic countries. The garden was more like an outdoor café. Guests contributed a small sum as an admission cover charge or gratuity to the Herr Ober. There was always an orchestra, playing both in the afternoon and evenings, and music was uniformly excellent. It was said that orchestras in many of the gardens would make any city famous. Programs were operas, operettas, and occasionally more contemporary tunes—always in good taste, fitting the atmosphere. One could have coffee or "*chocolade mit schlag*" or "*ohne schlag*" (with or without whipped cream).

There were many vineyards on the slopes of the Vienna Woods around the city, and in the Heuriger season when spring wines were flowing, many of the villagers on the outskirts of Vienna celebrated the new wine with gaiety. Outside the cottages were wreaths of grape vines designating the Heuriger. Visitors to the villages knew they were welcome to drink the wine and join in celebration. One of these villages was Grinzing, famous for its Heuriger season where the strong wine flowed freely. We went to one of these cafés in Grinzing and had a thoroughly enjoyable time. It was in a beautiful setting under a large and spreading chestnut tree. Guests sat at tables and listened to the German band, which played vigorously and with relish. At this café comedians pranced around and entertained the guests. The high spirit of the musicians spread to the guests, and there was a general feeling of *"gemutlichkeit"* which the new wine enhanced. Participants were dressed in typical Viennese costumes of bright dirndles and skirts on the girls, while the men wore *lederhosen* and Tyrolean hats with brim decorations and feathers. Guests joined with entertainers in furnishing amusement for all—everyone joining in singing and dancing. Guests usually gathered about seven in the evening with dignity and decorum, until the wine began to unleash restraints. If a group from a foreign country were recognized, the band would strike up the appropriate national songs. In this manner the *"Auslander"* (foreigner) became the focus of attention. Laughter and jokes permeated the setting. Rough-housing, vulgarities, or quarreling were not present. In an evening at a Heuriger all were friends. Away from the city, people seemed free from the cares, worries, and wars that were talked of in the coffee houses of inner Vienna.

There was so much to savor in Vienna, and professionally and culturally we could have remained longer and it would have been even more of an enriching experience. However, after several months of surgery and surgical pathology in Vienna, I was to be sent to the University of Budapest for surgical examination, then placed in a hospital under a professorial surgeon for continued operative technique. Following this experience I was to return to Vienna to the Polyclinic, where I could study gynecological or thoracic surgery or continue in general abdominal surgery. We packed our bags and went through the formalities of obtaining our necessary visas. We bade our adieus, taxied to the railway station, and took the evening train to Budapest.

CHAPTER SEVEN
LIFE IN HUNGARY, SURGERY,
AND RETURN TO HITLERIAN CONQUEST

Budapest is one of the most beautiful and unique of European cities, however, although lovely and gay it is also melancholy. There are many destitute as often found in large populated cities where one may be more lonely than in a small village. Many of the forlorn and romantic found the bridges over the swift Danube irresistible to their desire for freedom from life. There are six bridges spanning the Danube which is the swiftest river in all Europe. Most men would leap from the large suspension bridge built by Tiernay and Clark, two British engineers. This bridge is flanked on either side by huge stone lions. According to official record not one woman among the long list of suicides was found to have leaped from this bridge from 1926 to 1937. Many women, however, leaped from the Elizabeth Bridge or the Margaret Bridge upstream. The more fanatic and extroversial would leap from the Franz Josef which was of great height and suspended from four very tall columns upon which a large bronze figure of a Tural bird known as the Eagle which is legendary as the great Eagle which led the Magyars and their tribes from their inception or basic home in the heart of Asia to the great Balkan Valleys known as Hungary. The bridge farthest to the South is a railroad bridge—there is more noise and industry fluctuating here. Some prefer this area to mask the sound of the splash to the last minute involuntary scream because of change of heart or mind. This is the bridge most commonly used for self destruction according to statistics.

I have learned from medical colleagues from Budapest that in World War II every bridge previously described was totally destroyed by the Germans and the Russians. The great majority of both cities Buda and Pest was totally destroyed. Budapest has however, been completely rebuilt and the bridges replaced as well as building one more bridge named Arpad Bridge which was completed in 1950. This is the longest span of the eight bridges across the Danube River. Prince Aquad was the great tribal leader of the Magyars during the conquest of the country in the ninth century A.D. This bridge was greatly needed to connect Uipest to Obuda so the people would have ready access to Marigold Island.

Hungary is the land of the Magyars, whose language has no actual similarity to another. However, there may be a few possible similarities to the language of the Finns, though the basis of this has never been found or proven, to the best of my knowledge. It is in this most unusual, interesting, historical, and beautiful country that one may see at a glance the changes in human characteristics brought about to a great extent by the migratory and invading tribes over the centuries. In western Hungary, one continues to note the Germanic influence, where blondes and blue eyes are not a rarity.

The Rumanian influence is noted by variations in the language, as Hungary is the only area in which one detects an abridgment of Latin. The Rumanian people have their origin from the Roman conquerors during the Holy Roman Empire under the Emperor Trajan, whose Roman Legionnaires established this area as their permanent home following their defeat of the tribes of Cacians. The Magyars, or true Hungarians, were a different people from the east. The true Magyars followed the invasion of the Huns. The Huns were short, stocky, dark skinned, black haired, rugged horsemen with slanted eyes, and were the terrorists of all they encountered, and who were under the leadership of Attila. The so-called Huns were not Hungarians, although there may have been a connection. The period of the Huns was from 375 AD until 451 AD. Then the Huns were destroyed by another warring tribe, the Avares, who lived by the booty gathered by their raiding and organized cruelties in 796 AD. This deviation to touch upon the historical past is to more vividly understand the variation in peoples, their attitudes, and physiological aspects, as well as their sociological differences.

As we delved deeper into Hungary, and particularly the smaller towns and cities to the east, we detected the more typical Hungarian or Magyar. The early Magyars were great horsemen, and lived as nomads, frequently raiding other tribes, taking the vanquished peoples' gold, treasures, and many women. Their leader, King Stephen, married a Bavarian princess. He then established his throne in the capital city of Buda. The city of Buda is situated on high hills and overlooks the Danube River separating Pest from Buda which is directly across the river. Many rulers have invaded Hungary, and the influence of intermarriage can be seen in the various sections of Hungary. An interesting note is that all Hungarians use the family name first. The famous pianist, Franz Liszt, would be designated as Liszt, Franz. My mentor in the town of Szolnok was Sabo, Sandor, and in Szeged, Hungary, the hospital chief was Professor Dr. Hedry, Miklos.

Hungary was occupied by the Turks and ruled by the Turkish Pasha for one hundred fifty years. The rulers reigned from Buda, the capital. The Hungarians are a very proud people, and as a whole, quite vivacious, earthy, fun loving, colorful, and voluble. Their characters are also vividly epitomized in their music and the famous Czardas dance. Gypsy bands and orchestras abound in the majority of areas of public gatherings in hotels, cafés, and other areas of amusement. The music is beautiful, at times, sad, melancholy, and heartrending, while other times it is wild and fast; always played with the two violins, bass violin, cymbalorn, and zither. The cymbalorn is probably a type of early piano played with two soft padded sticks. This type of music is in contradistinction to the beautiful Hungarian Rhapsodies.

Many of the Gypsies and the Magyars have similar physical characteristics, with their swarthy skin, black eyes and hair, as well as the very slight eyelid tilt, suggestive of the influence of the Mongols. In my opinion some of the most attractive women in the world are from Hungary. These peoples are a whisper between the East and West, or Europe and the Orient. This is vividly apparent in the city of Buda and Pest distinguishing the two civilizations meeting and coalescing in a more beautiful and cohesive world.

Buda is a most enchanting section of the city pointing to the huge fortress at the top of the hill, and is the hub of the many spokes of cobblestoned streets spread like a wheel, and leading to the iron gates and huge steps to the fortress of castle-like proportions. Cannons and pyramids of stacked cannon balls are appropriately placed. These obsolete munitions of defense were used against the city by the Turks in their siege of Buda, as well as against the Viennese. The batteries are relics of the contenders, the Austrians and Turks, as well as Austrians and Hungarians. The Royal Palace is also auspicious, and one of yesterday's architectural beauties.

The markedly unique, interesting, and unusually different atmosphere of this divided city could be told in many pages. This duel city should be seen and lived in to enjoy its exciting life. There are six bridges spanning the Danube from Pest to Buda. The tumbling waters of the Danube are particularly swift through this area, and many a depressed soul has been enticed by the wild waters below as they became tired of living. The largest and probably the most outstanding of the bridges is the suspension bridge, Saint Margaret, guarded by massive stone lions on either side. A large suspension bridge, the Elizabeth Bridge, leads from Pest over the Danube to Buda. Pest is the more modern section of Budapest and the most alive, certainly the most exciting, and teeming with night life. Buda is the older section, and permeated with historical significance. The magnificent structures along the Danube are startling in their architectural beauty, and the House of Parliament is unmatched in its individuality. For one to know Hungary and the Magyars, it is essential to know something about their tempestuous history. Their past and present tribulations are necessary to realize the way of life with the motivations and reasons.

Hungary suffered under the Trianon Treaty following four years of exhaustive war with tremendous loss of manpower due to casualties. There was internal strife followed by two revolutions, then the invading Rumanians looted the country until it was practically sterile. Dissolution of the monarchy led to nearly complete dismemberment of the country and the threat of rising Bolshevism. At this point hatreds blossomed and were fostered against the instigators of the revolutionary movements, especially Kun and his followers, and the impact upon the regime of Karolyi. Karolyi Huszar, President in 1929, was at the helm of a country wracked and torn with complete distrust of all government officials. Through all this upheaval and tragedy, the Hungarians maintained their dignity and pride. However, as a continual reminder of the travesty of the Trianon Treaty of Versailles, the Hungarian flag had been continually flown at half mast symbolizing a state of mourning from their loss of territory after World War I. On the door of many of the homes and apartments was a metallic print depicting Hungary before the war, and superimposed upon this map was Hungary after the war, surrounded by a crown of thorns and drops of blood. Under this picture were the words, "*Nem, Nem, Soha*," which meant "No, No, Never, will we ever forget"—the injustices done to our country by the unjust terms of the Trianon Treaty. Pictures in full color of this same theme were sometimes imprinted on the knapsacks the children used for carrying their books. Some of the pictures were even more graphic—revealing the Hungarian soldiers, along with the Hungarian flag, which was being ground into the mud and trenches, and the Hungarian soldiers being slain by the British, with the British flag being flown high as the conquerors of Hungary. All of this is the type of propaganda which deepened the ingrained hatred, and fostered deep, resentful feelings against the countries they blamed for their loss. Hitler was capitalizing on the Hungarian dissatisfaction, and flooded the country with more propaganda, engendering more hatred, suspicion, and fear among many, but attracted many fanatical followers.

Treaties of commercial enterprise were made between Gyula Gömbos, the Hungarian Minister, President, and leader of ten Right Radicals, and Herman Goering, and later with Hitler. Gömbos was definitely anti-Semitic and feared Germany, however, Hitler was suspicious of the Hungarian policy. Hitler would not assure Hungary of regaining any lost territory except a section from Czechoslovakia. Gömbos died in October 1936, thereupon the regent Horthy, Miklos appointed Kálmán Darányi a relative conservative. Hungary wished to bask in the power of Germany, however, was very fearful in so doing. Germany disliked Darányi, and the regent Horthy replaced him with Bela Imredy. Hungary being generally unarmed, hoped to influence the West and Britain. However, their appeal for land restoration fell upon deaf ears. They were left to the mercy of Hitler who was quite agitated with them, but he needed Hungary for collaboration. Imredy was also anti-Semitic, and was instrumental in having anti-Semitic laws passed.

Kanya, the foreign minister, was dismissed in favor of a Count Istvan Csaky, who was in strong agreement with the Rome-Berlin Axis, and a follower of Hitler. Imredy, although anti-Semitic, was found to have a remote Jewish ancestry, and he resigned in February 1939, being replaced by Teleki, who took a strong position to prevent Hungary from having any confrontation with the West. Czechoslovakia was dismembered, and Hungary was given Ruthenia in March, 1939. Teleki was in favor of a coalition with Yugoslavia, and continually pushed for this accord. He wanted the two nations to form a bloc to resist the efforts of Germany to involve them in any conflict against the West. A Hungarian-Yugoslavian treaty was signed 12 December 1940. The treaty soon collapsed when Hitler demanded their help, and although they refused armed aid, Hitler's armies marched through Hungary unopposed. Hungary declared that Yugoslavia no longer existed; Croatia declared her independence on 11 April, and Hungary occupied some of the previously lost territory. Teleki took his own life and was replaced by Bardossy, who was forced into military participation with Germany. Germany quickly induced Hungarian participation after bombing the Hungarian city of Kassa. The average Hungarian feared the participation of the United States and although a forceful commitment had been made, the country with Horthy believed it was all a lost cause.

The train from Budapest to Eastern Hungary, Szolnok and Debrecen, crosses the Tisza River at Szolnok. The river is the most narrow at this point than any other place and too, the most easily fordable. This part of the Tisza was used by the Romans, at the time of the Roman Empire, as a crossing point for their armies on the march. The cross was then from Pannonia to Dacia. This was also a cross trading center, North meeting South and East meeting West. Szolnok was established on the right bank of the river, lying in a crescent following the river curve at this point. It was interesting to see the spouting of the warm, radioactive waters spouting like fountains from the ground. In the wintry season, like that one present, the springs bubble and spout tall spires of steam and hot water, from a depth of over three thousand feet and with a temperature of 134° Fahrenheit. One spring alone, produces one hundred sixty gallons of radioactive alkaline water per minute. The water is potable and reported to be effective in the treatment of gastric ailments. Directly across the river from Szolnok two very interesting areas are distinguished as the Jaszag and the Nagykunsag, known in historical times as Jazygia and the Jazygians were originally Indo-Iranian having been driven West by the Mongols as they swarmed across Asia. It is said that the main town in this area is Jaszbereny; it was the headquarters of Attila, the chief of the Huns. Another point of historical interest is the Lehel's Horn which is a minutely carved elephant tusk which belonged to one of the Magyar chiefs. The Horn is in the Jazygian museum in the town of Jaszbereny. The age dates from approximately the year 1025.

It had been advised and arranged that my duties should carry me to certain areas in Hungary where there were surgeons who were University professors of outstanding ability and where I might see and work with those who had some differences in technique and types of operative procedures. Arrangements were made for me to attend the University of Budapest where examinations were taken under the chief of surgery who was Professor Dr. Kiss (pronounced Kish). Following my clearance and acceptance, I was sent to Szolnok, Hungary, to the Saint Joseph Kozkorhaz Hospital, under the direction of Dr. Szabo for a period of three months. Szolnok is east from Budapest and half way to Debrecen near the eastern boundary of Romania.

On arriving in Szolnok, we took the *fiakre* (horsedrawn buggy) from the station. This conveyance reminded me of Russian villages where the sleighs are pulled by horses with high hoops over their back. On these hoops were tiny tinkling bells melodizing beautifully as the horse trotted along. The driver held the reins loosely, as the horse knew the exact destination. The driver perched his heavy boots on the front guard; the boots curled up at the toes from many a winter's rain and snow, and caked with a bit of barnyard mud from several winters back. He was a picture of health, with ruddy cheeks, and a karakul hat sitting at a jaunty angle on his head. The huge black and wide moustache made me think he would fit well on horseback riding with Kubla Kahn or Attila the Hun. His teeth were white in contrast to his moustache as he bellowed out equine commands. The steam leaving his lips formed clouds into the cold morning. We were well bundled with a heavy blanket and snuggled into the seat as the horse jogged along. The man was gallant in his helpfulness. His deep laughter seemingly boomed with vibrations enough to cause the newly formed icicles to fall from the tree boughs as we clattered along the snow covered cobblestoned *utca* (street). The snow was falling slowly, drifting down like tiny feathers from heaven and was light enough to allow the horse to be sure of hoof. We now realized this was a really beautiful pre-Christmas morn. Artesian wells were noticed all along the route, the steam spouting ten to twenty feet high from small openings in the earth. The crisp needle-like grass sparkled like crystalline green emerald spikes surrounding these occasional spouting artesian streams.

Szolnok is a most delightful town which was once part of the Holy Roman Empire and was one of their famous spas for warm water baths from the constant flowing artesian waters. The Romans installed lead pipes to channel these waters which were still functioning as efficiently as when first installed. These were similar to the ones in Bath, England, which were also put in by the Romans.

There were times when the quiet beauty of snow had a restful and subduing effect, yet the soft cool winds were exhilarating. The dry flakes of snow were whirled about and blown over our blanket. We were taken to the Hotel, Tisza Szalloes Gyogyfurdo in Szolnok. After showing passports to the hotel manager and establishing ourselves, we were told the routine of the extras; extras included the lift (elevator), the key, a bath,warm water, linens, towels, and soap. Breakfast, room care, and shoes polished were included as one item.

The evening was spent getting acquainted, eating, and supping with a few Hungarian Army officers and townspeople. We danced to the music of the Segoyha attempting the famous Chardas dance and singing Magyar tunes. We conversed in German, broken bits of Maygar, and some English and had an absolutely grand time the entire evening. On awakening the following morning and looking out the window, we saw a picturesque snow-covered village. We had a breakfast of tea and *polichenka* (type of rolled pancake similar to a crepe), then a slice of something we could not recognize, covered with paprika and a wee bit of spec, which I later learned was a bit of raw bacon fat. The room was cold but the bed was the warmest and most "snuggly" ever, with a mountainous, billowing, feather-filled covering nearly a foot in depth. Breakfast was served in bed—an indulgence to which we were not accustomed.

Our gifts to each other were meager-a tiny porcelain Hungarian flask which we have to this date, also a half pound of chocolates I had managed to buy the evening before. The tidbits were saved for nibbling later. Up we bounded to move our circulation along, bathed, dressed, and went below to the lobby. We admired the decorations, glanced at the papers, and arranged for an afternoon sleigh ride. The driver who met us at the station was there with his horse which was beautifully harnessed and outfitted with tinkling, tiny bells. We got into the sleigh and the driver blanketed us, covering our legs with a black hair cow-hide. The snow had deepened through the night, yet the artesian waters were spouting steam and hot water through the earth and snow. Bela, the driver, had been humming along almost in tune with the beat of the horses' hoofs: then he burst into full voice as we neared our hotel. We had learned much about the village and its peoples, the army garrison, and the many village activities from this learned driver who loved to explain and enlarge upon many interesting facts. We were told about the *körzö*, which is the promenade in every Hungarian village or city. This is the town walk usually in mid town or city, and is like a park or beautiful garden surrounded by a large, paved, oval circle, or straightway.

In the towns where we have stayed or lived in Europe, there was always a beautiful area set aside for strolling, usually in a park or flowered section, and the walk way was built or paved like an oval track. This area was called the *körzö*. We took many walks along and around the *körzö* and they shall never be forgotten as they were thoroughly enjoyable. Everyone greeted one another. However, the Magyars were very class-conscious, and specific days were set aside for the promenade along the *körzö* for each class: the "elegants" on one day, the peasants on another, and the middle class on another day. Generally, the average Magyar feels that he is in a geographical pincer, being squeezed between opposing forces.

Strict and proper social etiquette was adhered to by all Hungarians regardless of social standing. The men stood at attention in greeting and in salutation to one another, heels were clicked, the hat doffed, and a polite nod or bow was made, with either a hand-shake for the gentlemen or "Kiss die hand" for a lady. The finest clothes were worn on these appropriate days.

The people of every city and town in Hungary were the truly the most interesting in all Europe. In their faces we found overtones of the Orient, reaching back to the days of the Mongolian hordes of Kubla Kahn, Attila, and others. The Orient is mixed with the Occident here whether in Buda or Pest, Szolnok, Debrecen, or Pecs. We noticed the sensuousness of the Far East, like the dreamy scent of musk flowing through the portals of history and stamped upon their visages. There was the influence of the Tartars in the wide set eyes and the rather swarthy skin tints over high cheek bones. The Turkish influence is seen in the sharp aquiline nose, and the black hair and eyes. The years of the great Austro-Hungarian empire left their mark in an occasional blond, blue eyed specimen of the Prussians and Germans.

We enjoyed the Hungarians, those sensitive people with their proud mannerisms and very proper social bearing. We admired their manifestation of national pride and spirit. Living with the Heller family in Szolnok was particularly a pleasure, as they were such wholesome, kind and generous people. Alternate Saturdays, and Sunday we could sleep late, and on one cold rainy morning after sleeping late, with the wind shaking the shutters and the rain splattering on the moss covered roof we found it was very difficult to get out from between the huge billowy soft layers of goose-feathered blankets. However, warmth from the tall porcelain triangular-stove in the corner of the room was offered as a reward. I remember yet the white and shining stove, with beautiful flowers of yellow, red and white, decorating the tiles.

The hissing and honking of a gander or two around our window let us know the sun was trying to break through the gray clouds. The kitchen aromas tickled our cold noses with the delectable fragrance of roasting goose with a faint touch of garlic, herbs, and a whisper of onion.

We finally bounded out of the cozy bed, opened the shutters and discovered the rain had stopped and the street was ablaze with sunshine. The outer window box was filled with pink flowers, dazzling in the sun and recently moistened with drops of rain nodding gently in the slight breeze. Mutter Heller heard our movements and told us she had a "*kleinesschnitken*", a big surprise for the afternoon dinner. We opened the door a bit to see what the outside fuss was about; the old gander was hissing, trying to tell us one of his finest fat ones from his harem was missing. Now we understood the delightful kitchen aroma and the consternation of the old gander. We finished dressing and washing, and heard new sounds as the geese were honking because the "*katonak*" were coming, meaning the Hungarian soldiers were marching and the cadence of beating drums disturbed them.

Mutter Heller called Sandor and Imera, and appeared worried, shaking her head in sadness. She tried to tell us about the Hussars who were their protectors. She then talked of the Rakoczy and the music it made. She said we should forget Katonak, and think of the delicious Hungarian goose, cabbage, pastries, "*kaposztasretes*" that we would soon be enjoying.

The sound of heavy, spiked boots on the cobblestones grew faint and the drumbeats became muffled. Mutter Heller looked at us, trying to stir a smile—saying we must be happy while we could and we knew what she had in mind, but she busied herself in the kitchen then.

Imera poured the light Tokay Hungarian wine, Sandor broke the huge roll of heavily crusted bread, and cut the cheese, and we finished our "*schnltchen*." The women, Mutter Heller, and Elizabeth, busied about basting the huge goose, and dropped the dumpling batter into the bubbling goose broth. After our snack, and to whet our appetite for the feast in the offing, we decided to take a long, vigorous walk. As we walked, we thought and talked of the probable future for the Heller family, and knew we had to try to get them to leave Hungary before the Nazi plague befell them. We asked, begged, and cajoled in trying to persuade them there was a better life if they would only allow us to help. Our pleading suggestions met with a sad shrug and words interpreted as "this is our plight, come what may." With this complete rejection, we changed the subject and entered into the preparation of dinner.

My days were spent in the Saint Joseph Kozkorhaz (hospital) which was actually a surgical proving ground, with excellent instruction. On an average day there were about five to ten major surgical procedures. I performed about a hundred of these entirely on my own, except for observation by the Chief followed by technical discussions on the procedure. Patients were of unique interest, and included many types; agrarian peasants, wounded soldiers who had been returned from participating in the Spanish rebellion, and a good cross section of Hungarian folk. I was grateful for the previous good medical education and excellent clinical work I had experienced, both with surgical instructors and with my father, whom I assisted on many occasions in surgery.

The medical personnel, the nurses, and all hospital officials there were always very strict, serious, and socially proper with one another. There was one day, however, when that social ice barrier cracked somewhat. I looked younger than my years and wanted to appear a bit more mature as chief surgical hospitant. My thought was to grow a moustache. This, in itself, was no great feat. However, the hair coloring of this lip adornment was most unusual—as it grew in, different colors of hair appeared—red, gold, brown, blond, and black. On this particular morning I decided this was no asset, so attempted to color it all one shade. There was no dye, but I found that black shoe polish worked wonderfully well, and even allowed two stiff lateral points to be shaped. On arriving at the hospital I noticed everyone was smiling and unusually friendly. I was pleased to know that the barrier was lessening, and that formality was not so rigid. Everyone spoke and not only did they smile, but they laughed and were more informal and cheery than I had seen at any previous time. After my clothes were changed for surgery and the pre-operatives and their charts were reviewed, I proceeded to the surgical scrub room where there was a large mirror. I could scarcely recognize myself: the black shoe polish had melted with the warm moisture, my moustache had faded and wilted down into a Fu-Manchu, like a drooping or dripping moustache. The black shoe coloring was drooling down over my mouth and chin. This episode ended my one and only attempt to have a moustache.

The evenings were spent usually in the home of the Heller family, where we conversed as well as we could in German, although we picked up bits of Hungarian also. I spent a great deal of time studying during the evening hours, but occasionally I helped Velma in her rug weaving. We had procured a rug pattern and the colored wool necessary to make an oriental prayer rug. Every knot was tied, and we became fascinated as the pattern emerged and the colors took on meaning. Each knot had to be done exactly according to pattern, as Arabic writing was in the pattern and the borders and designs had to be clearly defined. We have this rug to this day, and it is still quite beautiful. In Hungary, they usually hung their rugs on the wall.

When my prescribed time was finished in Szolnok, we informed the Hellers that I was to be sent next to Szeged, Hungary, for another surgical hospitantship. We had foreseen the general unrest in the country and the portent of misery and probability of war, and we tried again to convince and persuade the Heller family to leave the country and that we could help them to the United States. However, we could not stir this fine family to move. We were very concerned about them because of the noticeably increasing anti-Semitism becoming more apparent each day. They honestly could not believe their lives would be so tragically altered, and wanted to remain in their own home. Sadly, we bid adieu to our dear friends. We packed our few traveling bags and our friendly driver, Bela, drove us to the railway station. The faint, but shrill whistle beckoned and warned that we must hurry to board the train.

On our way out of Szolnok, we stopped and went through other villages. To know Hungary and the Magyars one must travel the backroads to the small eastern towns.

On such a route to Debrecen, near the village of Tiszafüred or Balmauyvaros (if one can pronounce the names), we encountered many horsemen along the way tending horses, cattle, and sheep. Farms with sheep and cattle were tended by the *scikos* or Magyar cowboys. It was a land of half-wild horses and the *csárda* [a tavern or restaurant]. The horses were ridden by the *scikos*, a swarthy muscular type of rough and tough individual. The cowboys, I believe, were as wild as the horses they rode, and every bit as rugged (or more so) than any rodeo rider I have ever seen. They rode wildly and danced the *csárdás* equally as wild; the ecstatic stamping dance with swinging, gesticulating arms and body portraying their every strong emotion. The music and songs of the Magyar are comparable to none throughout the European lands.

We obtained a special pass from the railroad to spend time in the small more Eastern towns of Hungary. We arrived in the afternoon in the village of Tiszafüred which is on the Tisza River. We enjoyed the town and spoke with many of the villagers and others who came in to sell their produce in the town market the following day.

We went to the inn which was quaint, artistic, and beautifully fit in with the country. It was obviously old as the roof was heavily thatched and covered with brilliant green moss, and sagging a trifle in the mid-section. We deposited our luggage and walked about the town. We saw a bewiskered farmer with a long black handle-bar moustache. We hailed him and he halted his horse and spoke to us. He had some melons in the back of his cart. We then bought one for a ridiculously cheap price and it looked so good we doubled the price. He gave us another type of melon also. We gave the melons to the innkeeper who insisted we sample it now. That *görög dinnye*—was indeed the most delightfully sweet and juiciest watermelon we had ever tasted.

After another tour of sauntering through the village we returned to the inn a bit past twilight. A traveling Segonya band was to play that evening at the inn. We requested the chef of the inn to prepare any type of Hungarian dinner he wished. The dinner was soon prepared. The savory odors from the kitchen were swirling about, tempting, tickling, and stimulating the olfactory and gastric nerves. We were told some of the tasty dishes such as fried *palacsinta* and *pörkölt*. Soon all tables were filled and the grape soon began to flow as swiftly and nearly as ceaselessly as the Tisza River winding its way around the village. Our watermelon snack again appeared and we suggested the chef to cut enough for all to enjoy. The band struck up a lively tune while the evening warmed. The band warmed with the liquid grape and the music tempo increased to the *csárdás*, the *czymbalum* [a dulcimer-like instrument] striking the beat. This rhythm would make a wooden legged man dance.

We sat and dined in this beautifully rustic and typical Magyar inn feeling the soft glow from a huge open hearth with burning logs. Occasional rockets of tiny sparks snapped from the fire—like tiny stars they would shoot, then lie and die on the flagstone hearth. We studied the other guests at the inn, and realized that we were also being studied as strangers. Our dress was different from most of the others, and they no doubt suspected we were German.

The lights reflected their black hair with auburn, coppery tones which seemed to sparkle with the flicker and glow from the hearth. Their skin appeared smooth, soft, and like the sheen of golden olive. Their cheek bones were wide, moderately prominent and accentuated a bit of facial triangularity and the straight Nordic type nose with delicate and sensitive nares. Their lips were full, beautifully curved, naturally sensuous, and with a cast of garnet. The most salient feature was the slightly tip tilted slant of the dark eyes. The young ladies may have been related and were seemingly unmindful of three men sitting at a table across the room. The men were probably *scikos*, with swarthy skin, muscular physique, auburn black hair, dark eyes with the slight slant: they were wearing rough leather jackets and trousers with the wide legs stuffed into black boot. We were looking and reflecting on the infusion of hundreds of years past with the invasions of the hordes of armies in conquest as they rolled across the steppes of Europe and over the Tisza and Danube Rivers.

Now we vividly see the cast of the Tartars; Attila the Hun and his hordes, who swept across Hungary leaving their bloody chapters in Hungarian history. There was also Genghis Khan with the mad Mongols: the Turks, known as the "Terrible Turks" in their Balkan conquest which ended at the gates of Vienna. The features and works of the Byzantium followed by Arpid the Conquerer with the bands and tribes of Magyars in1002. Down through the Carpathians into the fertile valley of the Danube are the remains of the arrogant Roman legionnaires under their leader Trajan (Marcus Ulpius Trajan) 53-117AD. The third table was occupied by a couple, both blond and with blue eyes and features of one from the Saxons, the Anglo, Prussians, Germanic armies, or possibly from the Crusaders from the north.

We found it difficult to leave our newly found friends. The villages and people of Hungary are ridden with history and we thoroughly enjoyed every minute of field, village, inn, city, or plain. We were now on our way and arriving in the Calvinistic-Protestant city of Debrecen. This is a city of intellectuals surely as there are so many world famous schools, colleges, and universities.

This city is often referred to as "The Calvinist Rome" and most of its people are Protestants. This area is one where many a bloody battle has been fought. The city has been bravely defended by the Magyar and has withstood and repelled the onslaught of the hordes of Tartars, Turks, and Austrians. The people here have been fanatically loyal to the true Hungarian ideals and their independence of thought and living. These people were strong anti-Nazi and proclaimed their faith and hope in democracy. The people here, like most Hungarians, are proud, self-willed, and singularly independent. It should be remembered that Debrecen is not only the largest town east of the Tisza River but is also Hungary's center of democracy and independence. It was here that the Dict dethroned the Habsburg Dynasty 14 April, 1849, and when Hungary was declared a free and independent state. It was here on 21 December, 1944, where the first Hungarian democratic government was formed. Debrecen is a beautiful city with wide streets lined with trees and beautiful homes. The historical background and the beauty of the city is well worth the travel to visit. We reached our objective in Debrecen and appreciated their mutual beliefs and world sentiments. These people will fight for their rights and continued peace and freedom. Now the journey to Szeged.

Szeged is located in the southeastern part of Hungary, where the Tisza River bends to the east into Rumania. The Rumanian and Jugoslavian borders meet approximately fifteen kilometers (ten miles) south from Szeged. Szeged has been until recently the second largest city in Hungary. I was sent to a larger hospital in Szeged Hungary. Here I was under the direction of Professor Doctor Hedry, Miklos, a deft, skilled technician whose surgical skill was precise and accurate. He was to a degree a showman, however, not ostensibly obvious. He knew the technique of teaching and the finesse of surgery. He was rapid when need be, yet meticulous where it was important. His skill came from a thorough knowledge of anatomy and pathology. His pre- and post-operative care was very good, however, not as intense and consistently accurate as in Vienna. His mortality ratio was the lowest and on par with the skilled professorial surgeons of Vienna.

Although my credentials were adequate, I was not allowed to perform surgery until I had been given another thorough examination in anatomy, physiology, pathology, diagnosis, and pre- and post operative care. These examinations were more encompassing than the ones I took in Budapest for placement. The Varozi Koskerhaus was an excellent, well managed, and very up-to-date hospital which at the time offered better and more practical surgical facilities than I had seen in several similar size hospitals in the U.S. at that time. My surgical time in Szeged was intensive, daily performing surgery with the professor as his assistant for the first month, then after the second month he observed and became my assistant; later the chief or second hospitant was assigned as my assistant. Here I also had war wounds to treat surgically from the aspect of secondary wound closures and definitive surgery. These were wounds which occurred in Spain during the revolution.

It is difficult to write extensively about this most unusual country. It was my pleasure to have been a visiting surgical resident. There have been many books written about this fabulously historic country with its unusual background. The people are different with their customs and we loved them all. The cities, towns, and villages were delightful, romantic, beautiful and extremely interesting. We hope someday to traverse this part of our world in a more leisurely manner to see and enjoy some of the worlds' most fascinating country.

The months passed swiftly in Szeged as in the other areas of study and application. My duty had been accomplished surgically. My Jugoslavian friends and acquaintances from the Serbian and Croatian areas could not be reconciled for a common cause. The Serbs gave full cooperation to the United States. Both were at odds with the other and for that reason more than any other would not coincide in a joint cooperative effort. Croatians chose to cater to the pleasure of Hitler much to their disaster, although both sects were countrymen and both very kindly to the United States of America, yet their ideals clashed one to the other. Here in the United States the Croats and Serbs seem to be the best of friends and all past issues of historic blemishes are apparently resolved as they should be.

Local and world shaking events were occurring while I was avidly pursuing surgical training and expertise. Data of these events and information was funneled in daily.

On one warm Sunday, Velma and I took a bicycle trip on our own out of Szeged. We chose to ride down an unpaved dirt road on the Hungarian border and followed the border between Rumania and Jugoslavia. We noted the flat farmlands, the many draw-wells, and the equally dispersed military posts and observation towers both in Rumania and Jugoslavia. After riding approximately twenty-five kilometers, we knew we were being watched even though unenthusiastically by the poorly equipped Rumanians in their tattered uniforms and straw clad feet. We were more avidly watched, however, by the uniformed Jugoslavian soldiers. One group called ahead apparently and alerted another small advanced group in another wooden observation tower, and as we rode over a small hill we were confronted on either side by two groups of military might manifested by bayonets on their guns.

We stopped and dismounted; conversation was limited due to the language barrier. First was the argument between the soldiers as to who should take us captive. It was decided that we were more on the Jugoslavian side of the road than the Rumanian. We had contemplated this action so had purposely moved to the right side of the mid line which we recognized as the Jugoslavian sector. We had cycled to the outskirts of the village of Mokrin. The Jugoslav soldiers were wearing all wool, high neck blouses and uniforms. It was an extremely hot day and the sun was beaming full force. We were taken, searched, then marched along a dusty road; they with their loaded guns and fixed bayonets. One soldier was to the rear of us, one on either side, and one in front. Obviously it would have been absurd to attempt any escape.

A devilish thought tickled our mental waves simultaneously when I said, "Let's gradually step up the pace. We may tire the soldiers."

We also concluded that we would arrive at our destination sooner and possibly conclude our problem. As the kilometers passed from our foot-pace of one hundred twenty to one hundred thirty per minute, the uniforms of the soldiers darkened with perspiration and our mouths were nearly parched. The day was hot and the pungent smell of their sweat irritated our nostrils. We kept the pace, however, and were marched to the village of Senta on the Tisza River, through the unpaved streets to the office of the commissar. We were looked upon as curiosities and I could glean from the conversation that we must be sent to Beograd (Belgrade) as we were thought to be spies. Our first examination and trial would be from the commissar of the village. We tried to converse to some extent in German and a few words of English. We produced our passports but they were sure we were German Spies. We were motioned to sit, and after a few minutes I was taken to a small room. In this room, which was approximately six feet by six feet, there were two chairs and a narrow ledge apparently for writing. I saw no light, and with the door closed, it was like a cocoon of darkness. After approximately five or ten minutes, the door was opened and I was told to come out and be seated with Velma. No explanation was ever given for the dark room. Should it be said I was "left in the dark?" The light of the sun through the window above was by contrast very bright. Our passports and visas were studied carefully and many questions asked in German and repeated. The questions were then like a cross-examination where I had to explain every detail and exactly what we were doing. The question was then debated as to whether we should be sent to Zagreb. I was questioned about the cities in the United States and manufacturing areas.

The last train had left for Zagreb and there was no suitable place for us to stay. Another young officer then appeared and went through more questions and finally asked about Detroit, Michigan. I knew very little about the city and the young officer then told us his uncle and brother were here working in the automobile industry. The chill and somber attitude then disappeared and we were offered tea which we happily accepted. The questions were then in a lighter vein and they were obviously more cordial and even a bit jovial. Many times the question arose regarding the possibility of the United States entering hostilities. We were also questioned about our regard of Miklailovich and Tito. We persuaded our interrogators that we were completely devoid of any political ties. We had not been involved in any problems or international affairs other than hearing and seeing the new headlines. Velma was a registered nurse and I, a budding surgeon.

The commissar carried himself well, and at first impression it was obvious that he was the Caesar who needed no laurel crown to denote that he wore the royal purple. His general attitude gradually softened, somewhat, he issued a few commands, gave us a pat on the shoulder, shook hands, and wished us well. The young officer then took us back to the Hungarian border from where we cycled back to Szeged.

CHAPTER EIGHT
HOLLAND TO SCOTLAND,
ROYAL COLLEGE OF SURGEONS, & RETURN TO U.S.

Any alert individual knew, if he were attuned to world events, that the early germination of the seeds of war began to be evident in 1931, when Japan began bursting at the seams of land boundary lines. The Japanese nation was being propagandized by their military leaders. Japan forced a so-called "incident" in an endeavor to conquer a great and wealthy section of North China. A subservient state called Manchukuo was formed, which later declared war on China, as well as opening hostilities against Russia. Many of us in the United States read of the brutal war on the Russian-Manchukuo border and knew this could be the spark to ignite the world.

Mussolini, the pompous little maniac, swelled his stature like a singing toad, extolling his fascist doctrine. He then found a weak, underdeveloped, poor, starving, and primitive nation he thought he could conquer. In October of 1935, Mussolini, and his hordes of 'brave Italian' soldiers opened war on Ethiopia. The poor, naked natives of Ethiopia fought heroically, using spears and antiquated planes, tanks, and heavy artillery, but the cowardly war machine from Italy slaughtered the Ethiopians. Haile Sellassie pleaded and begged with the weak and crumbling League of Nations for help, but the League was less effective than a paper tiger, and the antithesis of the might of both Germany and Italy. The plea of the Ethiopian Emperor fell upon deaf ears. The same words were voiced by the Lord in the Old Testament, Jeremiah Chapter 6, Verse 21 when he said, "Hear now this, O foolish people, and without understanding which have eyes and see not; which have ears and hear not." The slaughter, misery, and suffering of the Ethiopians continued until the poor nation was to its knees and the Italians were in control.

Bloody and heart-rending conflicts were also being carried out in Spain with the Civil War there. Germany and Russia used this arena to test their weaponry, while aiding and abetting Generalissimo Franco and his government. I treated many wounded soldiers from the Spanish war who were sent to our hospital in Szeged in 1937-38 and they were actually unaware of why they had been sent to Spain to fight. However, this is not uncommon in any war. I recall talking to a wounded eighteen-year-old Italian soldier whose story was that he had been on a ship coming from the war in Ethiopia. At least he had been told he was coming home. However, instead of debarking in Italy, he was mustered out, with other Italian soldiers, not in the Bay of Napoli, but into the Bay of Barcelona. There they were led into battle, being told it was for the glory of Italy and the preservation of the Church. Many of these same men died, screaming, *"Mama Mia."* The Germans echoed this same type of cry, and died, murmuring, *"Warum?"* (why). The Russians seemed to be the most stoic, yet they also cried, *"Pochemou?"* (why). I asked everyone I was in contact with about their purpose in the war. Most did not really know.

The soldier of World War II "knew" the reason war was necessary; he knew the issues, where they led, and understood the ultimate stakes. It is our inheritance to have strong devotion to liberty and stand for that right. We feel we know the meaning of justice and have a sensitiveness to mercy. Most of us know and understand that civilization is not to be found in the power to convert millions of men into abject machines or slaves shorn of human emotions, or to be iconoclastically obedient to the unjust and evil will of a despot. It is difficult for the average American to conceive, much less commit the atrocities, horrors, and bestialities which were devised in cold blood by the Hitlerian hordes. I have confronted many of the S.S. Troops, members of the Brown Shirts, and Hitler's personal staff with questions of why. Their answers were, "War is war; it is total, it must be, for the extermination of the inferiors and subjugation of the defeated." The misery and atrocities of the Nazi regime were all premeditated and so obvious it was impossible to deny. The murder of masses of innocent civilians, the burning of towns, and the starving, torturing, and enslaving of entire populations were not simply an on-the-spot burst of bloody passion but were precisely plotted, deliberately ordered, and performed by those obedient to Hitler.

One major belief of the Prussian General Military staff which carried over to influence Hitler was that all men have an element of bestiality—it needs only nurturing by propaganda and insidious teaching to unleash this geni and put it into action at the proper time. One only needs to read the background of civilizations to understand trends and actions of today. The

Teutons, Huns, Goths, and Vandals were the ancestors of the Germans who retained certain hereditary characteristics from them and which may be latent. However, they are manifest, and have been since the beginning of history. Cruelty was fostered by these tribes for fifteen hundred years. With clever early training, and with war as a goal, the inner nature of violence and hatred is enlarged, and the beast is unleashed in time of war. Germany, including both East and West are great nations, and will continue to be so, however, it is imperative that they be controlled. They will rise again unless their traits are softened and blended with the basic foundations of humane understanding. It is true that Germany is a so-called Christian nation, yet they allowed the few who had lost their precepts to influence those not so diabolically inclined. Many people, however, will not agree regarding the basic nature and characteristics of a group or nation of peoples as having hereditary factors of violence rather than an inculcated or environmental factor. The average German knows and firmly believes he is of the greatest and most superior of all races. His belief is that Germany will rise again as one nation. In World War II one of the repeated maxims of the Germans, other than "*Sieg Heil*" was "*Deutschland Uber Alles*," and "*Heute Deutschland, im morgen die Ganze Weld*."

A factor in many of our post-combat or post-war battle fatigue and depressive reactions is secondary to psychogenic maladjustments in trying to logically analyze our own thoughts and actions. We have, in war, negated our basic teachings and the rules of the old Bible, as well as the precepts of Christianity. Then we are thrust into a position where we are told it is to save the ideal of freedom. To save this ideal we learn to hate our adversary—kill, maim—call it by any name, it still is murder. After the war is ended, then there is a period of re-adjustment back into a society where we are told to "love thy neighbor as thyself." I know of none who have not had some phase of depression with which to contend after having been in battle. It is understandable.

In *The War and America* by Hugo Munsterberg, he stated, "Ye shall love peace as a means to new wars—and the short peace more than the long, and war and courage have done more great things than charity." However, in contrast to this idea the German philosopher, Friedrich Nietzsche, 1844-1900 (born in Saxony and later a Swiss citizen) has written, "I even feel it my duty to tell the Germans, for once in a way, all that they have on their conscience. Every great crime against culture for the last four centuries lies on their conscience—and always for the same reason, always owing to their bottomless cowardice in the face of reality, which is also cowardice in the face of truth; always owing to the love of falsehood which has become almost instinctive in them." Goethe, one of the world's greatest immortal scholars and a German writer and poet, stated empirically, "The Prussians are cruel by nature; civilization will make them ferocious."

My parents recalled the days when both Russia and France were vying for Supremacy, however England held the reins. England, at that time, controlled a vast Empire which encircled the world and held control with the greatest Navy in the world. Germany, at that same time, was striving for a greater control of the seas by building a great navy. In all German officers' clubs and elsewhere the toast of the times was "*Auf den Tag*" meaning "To the day" when we will be powerful enough to master the hated English. Superiority and the idea of a super race has been taught and inculcated in the German schools and institutions since long before the France-Prussian war. This has been a boon as well as a disaster to the nation as a whole; it fostered pride in their work, their thrift, and their industriousness. No one can deny that they are an aggressive nation of achievement.

We found Rotterdam a very interesting and beautifully different city laced with canals and bedecked with flowers. A most disturbing occurrence flared suddenly, soon after our arrival in Rotterdam, Holland. My meal of the preceding evening had not settled well. My gastrointestinal tract was attacked by sudden cramping pain, as the gas rolled around in a barrage and acute nausea struck. I saw a mid-block shelter with the sign "*Damen*" and "*Herren*." My pace quickened to a trot, then a dash to find the comfort of the throne in time. I was soon confronted and profoundly embarrassed by a little Dutch woman who suddenly entered my privacy and tried to pull me off my recently acquired seat. She was screaming something but I was in dire pain. I finally managed to dislodge her from the tiny compartment and told her to find her own place, thinking she may have the same urgency, I shouted at her as she sat just outside the swinging door and told her in German to please leave me in my moment of stress and misery and find her own throne in the place for "*Damen*." On opening the door, I practically fell on an immovable object—the woman! She finally told me in Dutch that I owed her ten gilder or similar amount. She turned out to be the gate keeper of the Glory Hole and had to be paid. I had no Netherlands exchange money, however, gave her all the change in my pocket comprised of a few French francs and some shillings from Austria. These she accepted and gave me a few necessities in return. I washed and shined a bit, felt limp as a bedraggled cat, and went about to replace my electrolyte loss. In spite of the painful inconvenience upon our arrival, Velma and I enjoyed the city and their open hospitality.

I made the appropriate contacts and were told we had passage over the channel on a lettuce boat up the North Sea to Newcastle upon Tyne: to leave at a certain time from a specified dock. Early the following morning, we were awakened, given a short fast snack of fish and gruel of some type, then hurried onto the boat ready to leave. The captain said he expected us and hoped we were seaworthy sailors as the crossing was expected to be a bit rough. This proved to be the greatest understatement of all time. We thought a bit however, we did not wish to waste time and knowing quite well that between us here in Rotterdam and England lay the most deadly body of water in the world, the English channel and the North Sea, over which one hundred fifty miles were necessary travel. This body of water which has wrecked famous armadas of the past and dozens of ships every year in the mountainous gale and hurricane waters which roar unpredictably through and down the funnel from the Arctic, Antarctic, and Atlantic Oceans. The only nearly comparable place is around the tip of Africa.

The fog lay on the glassy waters like pearl filled cotton. We were a bit querulous when leaving the dock as a huge fog was rolling in. We could hear moans of the mournful fog horns. The captain told us the weather was sour, and that we were going along the coast and would be through the fog within the hour after departure. The shadowed sun turned gray and as we moved out from the coast other ships echoed the mournful and more frightening, irritating fog horn hoots. We had cast off and were quickly engulfed in a shroud of white, drifting mist. The fog horns continued to screech and bawl from every direction.

After about three hours into the stormy sea, we were slipping and sliding along the deck as we heard the captain shouting commands, ordering all below, and to batten down the hatches and secure the ports. The land was suddenly clothed in darkness the complete shut out by night. We were beginning to plunge into the wall and depth of a monstrous hurricane. The point of no return had been reached, the sea was now treacherously confusing. The gleaming crest of the waves were becoming mountainous in their all-out rage to engulf and swallow our small ship. A not too silent prayer came spontaneously through tense lips—a prayer of hope for all, and to be guided away from the rock bound areas of the Danish coast.

For some reason or other, my feelings were not of fear as I tried to analyze my intermittent waves of tension corresponding to the dipping and heaving of our ship. Surely my heart felt as if it had skipped a beat, but in feeling my pulse—all seemed regular, normal and steady. I wanted to go below because of the possible danger of being struck by a monstrous wave and being washed overboard. My thoughts were then directed to one of my direct paternal ancestors who was washed overboard in a storm as his ship was rounding Cape Horn. I had no intention of making a second historical family wash out. The sea did not appear to be uniform in its extremity—surely if the gale or hurricane was directed by wind currents the waves would be uniform in their geometry. Here there was no one directional phase, there was no uniformity of scenery except disorder. The horizon was no longer horizontal, the ship and the sea were bounding over the vertical, oblique, sending all plane geometry a twisting, losing all perspective. Now again looking through the port hole, I found directional bearings were impossible at this point. My thoughts were on the ship's captain, however, knowing he was a seasoned tar was consoling as he was surely aware the prow was dipping into the dark waves sending walls of sea water and the foam skidding and rolling over the deck, washing and smashing everything not locked down.

Our small ship delved into the cave-like darkness of the water and echoed with the grind of the motors, with an occasional unsynchronized beat. Surely the sea would engulf us, we thought. Would the black walls keep a wide enough trough for our comparatively infinitesimal hull to gain travel? Before we could answer ourselves we were thrown like the emesing of a giant, up to the top. Up we shot. The beat of the motors with this maneuver sounded like a thrashing of turbines. The waves hissed and rolled as the hurricane-wind blew out of the black night. We tossed about like a cork in every direction including up and down, but not quite turning over. We would rise for seemingly an interminable height, and looking through the port hole we could see mountains of white glaciers of water then down we would fall seeing the various shades of water, from light green to light blue, then to dark blue and finally dark black. Surely we had struck the bottom of the ocean and the sea would close over the tip, totally engulfing us. Then up we would jet at any and all angles back to the crest. Wrapping our arms around the bunk head posts and trying to peer through the portholes, the ghastly picture was absolutely frightening as the ship's lights were cast out upon the tumultuous upheaval. The immense waves crashed against the ship's side, like a huge flat side of an ax crashing against a hollow log. Everything breakable was broken, the ship's turret was rocking and the lamps continued to swing. We rocked, rolled, pitched, tossed, turned, peaked, dived, and dropped like a blind ship roaring into eternity.

Suddenly a tremendous blast from a near fog horn rent the oceanic sounds. Our fog horn bellowed and moaned; the tremendous blast seemingly emanated from immediately above our deck. We peered out the porthole as best we could, bouncing against an upturned wooden bucket. A huge black shadowy mass rolled by as all our engines were ordered to a complete stop. We were told later a large tanker nearly struck our ship and it later foundered on the Danish coast, along with sixty other channel-going ships. We heard many distress calls and learned later that several ships had been smashed along the coast of Denmark in the storm and the six hour trip extended to twelve hours then to twenty-four hours. I was trying to convince Velma and myself that the sea-sickness she was experiencing was psychological and mind over matter. It simply would not work, however, and that was the first and only time I have suffered with *mal-de-mere*. Velma had plenty of company as we practically turned ourselves wrong side out. Our legs were like wet spaghetti. Our faces were white and wet and our eyes felt like exopthalmic balls popping from their sockets. Our jaws sagged as we uttered a prayer for our ship and all hands aboard; hoping to be included in the over all request. The fog horn blasts became more distant and after twelve hours of foundering we finally either blanked out or fell to sleep from complete exhaustion, both resting in the lower bunk, so it would not be so far to fall.

We awoke after a short rest from total emotional exhaustion of two hours. We were continuing to roll, but were not following a contorted course. We were moving relatively slow along smooth waters into the Tyne River harbor, then finally ending our forty-eight hour harrowing experience which was to have been a six hour voyage. In darkness, we limped into the port of New Castle Upon Tyne, England. The sailors were extremely helpful, however, we managed to make connections with the train, *The Flying Scotsman*, leaving at that time for Edinburgh, Scotland, which was our destination. The world and everything in it continued to whirl. We arrived in Edinburgh about four in the morning.

The station was empty, cold, bleak, and reeking from leftover food on the tables with dirty tea cups. I had Velma lie on a bench while I went out to attempt to find lodging. One would think I was trying to bomb the hotels. No taxi cabs were available so I walked and knocked on barred hotel doors.

At seven I managed to find one. The proprietor opened a second story window and called down, "Wot you knockin' on door at this hour fer?" I replied that I wanted to gain entrance and get a room. He said he would open only at eight-thirty.

I then returned to the railway station. Here I found a policeman ("Bobbie") giving Velma considerable trouble in not allowing her to stay in the station. After a few choice words broaching a bit on the old Anglo-Saxon verbiage, it was either she stay and lie on a bench until I could get a taxi at eight, or we were going to really have one whale of a donnybrook. We stayed and rested then until I was able to get a taxi.

Traveling has taught us a bit now and then, particularly to inquire the price of any item or purchase before finalizing the bargain. On inquiry regarding the taxi fare to the hotel the reply was, "Oh Mon, aboot a bob r-r-r-two." I again asked the price. The driver looked us over and asked "Ar-r-e ye from Americky?" I gave nothing but a dour look and he then said, "Likely a bob." After paying the grumbling taxi driver the equivalent of a bob in Dutch coins I had exchanged following the Dutch controversy, the driver looked at the coins and said, "I canna take this lot." I replied, "Bite it or eat it, as it may be gold." Off he went muttering, "Crazy people in early marning."

Our fatigue, instability of equilibrium, along with the pale washed out appearance was one with the drab grey stone buildings. The Temperance Hotel was a drab looking place. I am sure our reddened eyes appeared like two holes in a blanket, as exhausted as we felt. After gaining entrance and entering the small lobby to be greeted by a slovenly, dumpy, balding little man whose accent placed him truly in mid-Scotland with the heavy burr in the brogue. Whoever chose the tired carpeting must have been blind or attending a burn-out sale. The heavy lace curtains did to some extent partially obscure the dirty grey windows. The bed was of the old brass and knobby type, quite tarnished with age. There was a wardrobe of antiquity with a loosely hinged double door, one side faced with a mirror. Velma took one look and said, "no, that can't be me," the shock was salutary and quite a jolt—"who is the hollow eyed old hag in the mirror?" She flopped on the bed as I stole a look at myself. My only comment was, "By all appearances we were made for each other, but who is the man in the mirror?" The effect of dehydration sneered at ourselves from the depth of our eye sockets—we looked and laughed. I am sure Velma laughed to keep from shedding a tear, which she was never wont to do.

The room reeked with the smell of damp peat emanating from a blackened fireplace which may have been partially cleaned the past year. "We can't manage breakfast nor do we allow food to be brought in, mind you," the churlish innkeeper said as he prattled on.

I immediately had Velma go to bed for much needed rest while I went down to see if I could get a bottle of milk as she was quite feverish with dehydration.

I found it impossible to get pasteurized milk anywhere in Edinburgh. All meat, fowl, cheese or fish were placed in a large ice box along with mutton, and all items kept in the box then reeked with the smell of mutton.

On returning with the few parcels and milk, the hotel manager stopped me stating, "You canna bring food in this hotel and are you married? You dinna tell me wuther or nay ye were a German or an American?" On telling him we were American, he then said, "Well mon, ye mus be from Chicago?

Be ye a gangster?" I walked him over to the window, told him I was from Missouri and asked, "Just how far must we go to get away from the slums in this city?"

With this he flew into a Gaelic rage while I continued up to our room. 'Twasn't exactly seventh heaven, however adequate. We convalesced and recuperated the remainder of the day and night.

The city of Edinburgh is beautiful and steeped in antiquity. We were located directly across the street from Holyrood Castle, the former abode of Mary, Queen of Scots. A call was made to the name previously given to me regarding assisting in surgery, and he already knew we were in the city. It was hoped my bit of adversity had not preceded my call. He told me to go to Argyle Place across the meadows from the Royal infirmary and the Royal College of Surgeons at the University. The next morning we investigated the quarters in Argyle Place and found them to our liking. We moved in and Velma made the nest while I went to the Royal College, talked with an acquaintance, a doctor who was now teaching on the faculty of surgeons, Dr. Ian Aird. Dr. Aird had taken post graduate surgical training with one of my relatives in the Washington University, Barnes Hospital of Saint Louis, Missouri. A residency was arranged here and I was to be under Sir John Frazier for one section, Sir D.P.D. Wilkie, another section in surgery, and Mr. Smith for an anatomical review.

In the hierarchy of British medical men, one becomes a doctor with the M.D. or commensurate degree upon graduation from Medical School. After a period of internship, specialty residence training and more time and study, one may then sit for the fellowship in the Royal College of Surgeons, which is given by long periods of examination in specific centers in the kingdom such as London or Edinburgh. If the examinations and all qualifications are successfully met the doctor then may become a Fellow and thereafter be addressed as "Mr." Knighthood may be bestowed by the king or queen upon one of great selection if, after many years of outstanding distinguished service to the country, and thereupon he may be addressed as "Sir."

My daily duties were outlined. Although our primary introduction was a bit adverse, we found the city and the Scots generally very hospitable. Many of my family on the paternal side lived in this area. This country of Scots seems to be in a different world entirely and such a contradistinction from the Europe we had just left. From our window, we could see the colorful hills and crags along the sea coast. There was the cleft called King Arthur's Seat along the crest; the expanse of continuous hills was covered with white and purple heather. Velma was still feeling a bit uncertain and we continued to have the slight vertiginous instability of the rolling ship on the mountainous sea. We were able to retain a small amount of broth and gruel brought by our very kind neighbors, Mrs. Lauder and Mrs. Duncan. The fireplace was glowing with coals of peat and casting the scent of smoldering warm peat from the fire hearth edge.

That evening we munched some of Mrs. Lauder's crumpets, drank two cups of tea and retired to stop the room from the slowing spinning movement. Velma said she tried to stop the room from whirling and failed.

The next day we were awakened by someone shouting, "Coal, Coke, Peat." It did seem to be a bit early for the huckster to be hawking his wares before six o'clock, so back into the warm fluffy covers we dived. No sooner were we asleep that a most unusual clamor or sound awakened us that was recognized as a bagpipe group of Argyle, kilt-clad Highlanders, parading and blowing their loudest at six in the morning. Time to arise! The bagpipers were playing "Annie Laurie," among the other melodies, which I did not know by name, but they were tunes my paternal grandparents used to sing when I was a small boy. The house was stirring as the pipers paraded around the meadows. The pipers soon left and we were told the Highlanders paraded and played on Wednesday and the Black Watch paraded and played on Saturday mornings same hour, same place, as a tradition.

For breakfast we had the old stand-by, rolled oats and kippers as there were no eggs. This was one of our firsts, having dried fish for breakfast. We were told that one soon develops a taste for kippers or herring. There were things to be done and the time was here, so I finished breakfast and was off across the meadows to the university classroom.

The great stone nineteenth century building stood as sturdy as the Scots who had placed rock on rock, stone on stone, and bound them together with tough, hard mortar. My introduction to the professor was short and firm as the lecture and diagram began. The professor then began a barrage of questions which, at this phase of my training, were didactic and simple. The first hour was then followed by an hour of questioning on complete muscle action and innervations. I had a ten minute break at ten, followed by more questions, this time on anatomical action following various types of injuries and physiological changes wrought by injury.

Eleven-thirty was snack time followed by twelve-thirty hospital introductions and grand rounds at one-fifteen. I was startled to find so many patients of all ages afflicted with the changes and surgical effects from Bovine tuberculosis, including scrofula, which is glandular involvement around the neck secondary to the inroads of tuberculosis. There were people afflicted with diseases I had studied, but had never seen, such as Pott's disease (tuberculosis of the vertebrae with degeneration). Tuberculosis of the female breast was not rare there, also Addison's disease, otherwise known as bronze diabetes which is tuberculosis of the adrenal gland. Following grand rounds by the eminent and brilliant Sir John Frazier, he then questioned me. I made the comment that it seemed odd that so many were suffering with Bovine tuberculosis when it was entirely preventable by proper methods.

Sir John replied with a heavy Scot burr, "Dr. Graham, you will learn that your forefathers and the Scots are yet a bit slow and reluctant to accept innovation." He stated further that they were making strides, however, and he said that he felt sure that before the century turned again, the frugality of these dear people will have been released enough to yield their cause to the inevitable process of vaccination. He said that many were becoming convinced that it was the wish of the Lord and His will be done. They figured that since the prophets allowed man to learn of the discovery of new treatments and preventatives it should be considered as a heavenly gift so they slowly began to change and that pasteurization would also come about.

He stated that, "In the meanwhile, we shall pursue our duties as they are presented before us. Mr. Graham, you have a guid nom, do you have your tartan and kilts for festive occasions?"

I replied, "No, Sir John, I too have been a wee bit slow as a newcomer, however, I pray this too shall come before the turn of the century." There was an immediate inner glow of friendship that was felt right off.

The days and nights passed and the weeks flew by. Most weekends were free when we enjoyed the rides and walks through the land of the Scots. It was easily understood why the Romans built a great wall across the land of the Scots. Since the Scots could not or would not be conquered, they were walled off to keep them from constantly irritating them and also to stop them from stealing from the Englanders. Time was never found idle; every minute of all waking hours was utilized whether in study or leisure. For our pleasure, not knowing if we would ever return, we traveled to new and interesting places. The country has beauty where one sees it and Scotland is filled with natural beauty. We may be in Coventry or perhaps the Firth of Forth in the moors, the castles reeking with antiquity, history, love, and war.

We spent the off times away from clinic and study or on occasion to walk through the interesting but ragged parts around the lakes (called lochs). I have never seen lochs so dark blue-black as in Scotland. We were told this was because of the extreme depth of the water. Although we have searched several lochs for evidence of a Loch Ness monster it was never seen by us, although we did feel a foreboding excitement scanning the water for this elusive and fabled monster.

One weekend we decided to get away from obvious civilization and buildings to see the Scottish lochs and moors. As we headed up the craggy glen stumbling for footage and grabbing at the gnarled pines, we stood just long enough to catch our breath. Surveying the moors from that vantage point, I felt a surge of euphoria, that joy-of-life feeling which is often communicated to me by visualizing the beauty of nature surrounding me.

Grasping the pine which the harsh weather and uncaring winds had ironically bent and twisted into artistically shaped forms gave me a renewed feeling of respect. This pine had weathered the heavy storms for years bending and twisting with the force of wind, sea, snow, and rain.

Our next destination was to climb down the other side of the precipice onto the moors. It was exhilarating and I must say a good deal less exhausting. This country, so fresh and lush, took me back to an imaginary time and made me feel that we were the first and only two people ever to place our feet in the damp, cool, mossy glen. It was a sacred and awesome feeling.

It was understandable to see why the Scots had such ruddy complexions with rosy cheeks. The winds were cold, sharp, and cutting as they whip over the crags and moors at certain times of the day, and our own cheeks were rosy, being whipped by the gusting wind over the grass. The rushing streams seemed colder than ice. Trees were grotesquely bent and gnarled, due to the constant strong winds dotted along and near the crest of the hills. Scotch pines, rhododendrons and heather were growing through the moss and grassy areas lining the lush glens. The oaks were also heavy and gnarled, often covered with moss. The glens were always beautiful, green, damp, and cool.

There were many other interesting things to do, and one of these was to watch the Scots play ten pins and curling.

We found the most practical clothing to wear were tweeds, as there was a time almost every day when it was damp. The woolen tweeds seemed to absorb the limited moisture without becoming unbearable or causing one to be wet and cold. A bit more than a light mist would fall daily, not enough to call rain, yet too heavy for fog. For many months throughout the year there was no darkness, consequently no actual night.

We have walked down Princess Street past the Sir Walter Scott Memorial at three in the wee hours of the morning in broad daylight. In a manner, we seemed rather detached from the world while in Scotland. The troop movements and saber rattling were only like yesterday's bad dream except for the daily reports. These would point up troop movements. France and Poland were now gone. The question now was regarding the next major move by the Hitlerian forces. The Scots and English were seemingly shaking themselves into the realization they might find themselves defending their shores and their homeland. The talk of the probability of war was becoming more apparent in daily conversations.

My work in surgery continued and it must be stated that my share was more than adequate. My weeks were spent under the aegis of Sir D. P. D. Wilkie, a master of surgery as well as being a superb professor. Didactic lectures were given by Mr. John Bruce and Mr. Ian Aird while Mr. Smith continued to hold the surgical anatomy section.

The weekends were spent enjoyably traveling and in the out of doors. Velma's remonstration was that we should have more freedom during the off hours. She has often said that I must always have an objective or a goal to have real enjoyment. This thought had never occurred to me, however, it must be one of those inner demands.

A trip to the Graham, eighteenth century castle in the mid-Highlands was coldly interesting; multiple towered, turreted, and bleak as a tomb. A remark was made regarding the somber tranquility. Yes, it was agreed, so tranquil it was dead a few centuries past. It would be no surprise to see a ghostly knight in armor riding out on a galloping horse any moment.

Velma was appearing her pretty, sweet self; her cheeks were rosy from the sun and wind, and we soon were aware that she was becoming a bit rotund. She was known by all as a marvelous cook and we never lacked for guests. She repeated that the only reason the food was different was that she spiced it up a bit here and there with a bit of peppers, spices, lean and fat in the right places. This was a change from the overly boiled, seasonless foods for which my forebearers and grandmothers, Scot, Graham, and Wallace were famous.

My conferees called me for a meeting and they wished to know my plans. My informant notified me that there was question regarding my joining the British Army as a ranking officer. The reason being was that they were somewhat suspicious regarding my activities and associations in Germany. They knew my commissioned rank in the army of the United States. On inquiry as to my joining the British Army, the matter was studied and I was rejected. After much questioning, I was told by a friend, whether true or false, that I was considered a counter espionage agent. On further questioning, it was found that I had been a member of a dueling society while in Germany and Austria. The irony of this is, that I had proceeded on to Edinburgh and studied in the Royal College of Surgeons, then in the war I was assigned to the British Second Army under General Montgomery, and with the 6th Canadian unit in Holland while attached to the 101st American Airborne Division. No further action was taken for my enlistment into the British Army at this time.

After migrating from the fogs of Edinburgh and the great centers of learning and surgical knowledge, we set sail for our homeland on the USS *United States*. The sea filled with plankton: gray, red, brown, and green in the light of day and sparkling like millions of dazzling colored jewels at night tossing, leaping and lighting the ship's wake thrown by the monstrous turbines. The brilliance of these phosphorescent gems is likened to the pirates' treasure chests open in the sun. My respect for the sea by this time was great, knowing now by experience that the quiet serenity of its blue bland depths withholds the horrors and potency of its mighty potential.

The days were quiet with this ocean crossing and I had time to contemplate my future. Basically, it was my wish to continue study in residency until the call came for active duty with the army which I knew would be imminent, and even give me a sense of relief to become actively involved, happen what may, as I felt I should fulfill my duties as a citizen soldier and surgeon. Many thoughts and contemplated plans crossed my mind. Foremost was how well did I know my parents' wishes, and what could I do for our mutual benefit? Neither Father or Mother had ever mentioned any specifics. I had learned much, yet realized full well it was infinitesimal to the necessary knowledge yet to be gained.

I dreamed about how good it would be to arrive on home ground again, and the necessity of having permanent quarters was becoming more eminently obvious by the day. Velma was becoming enormously rotund, so the first addition to the family would soon arrive. We felt sure it would be a boy because it was so very vigorous. Now at this late date we both began to think it would be a mule as the explosive kicking nearly jarred the door loose.

Many hours were spent with the ship's passengers, standing around the rail and pointing out phantom enemy battleship. Rumors were flying from lip to ear, and I must say, it did make the passage more exciting. After our five days' voyage, we returned to the arms of our Great Lady who stands on Staten Island, New York, our Statue of Liberty. Pre-docking in New York was a great thrill after having been living in a foreign country for over a year. The Statue of Liberty and the New York sky line were welcome sights and we felt a warm glow of kinship with our nation. We looked at the great Statue of Liberty and reflected on the generosity of France in this great and meaningful gift and realized that France had long been our staunch ally from our early days of the revolution.

We were met at the pier by my mother and father, with whom we had a very joyous reunion. Then we went through customs and routine inspection before getting to the car and driving off for the home of my Aunt Ella and Uncle William Henry in Earlville, New York. We had a good time exchanging stories of the past year's experiences with them. After this visit we drove on to Missouri and Kansas City, where we were delighted to see Velma's parents, Mom and Dad Hill. We had not told them of their impending grandparent status, and they were very happy. I was quite aware that, from my army reports, I would possibly be requested to report for active service with the army in a very few weeks.

Returning to the United States of America was a great thrill. In a manner, our return was as though we had left a social and political world of chaos, misery upon misery, and horror upon horror, with the ominous portent of world involvement. We left behind also a wealth of friends, while bringing the gained knowledge of pathology and surgical skill learned from the masters of the time. We had passed from the shadows and darkness of war and conquest into a world of disbelief, or refusal of acceptance. Our War Department knew full well of the potential involvement, however, generally speaking we continued to exist here in the fairyland of make believe, dancing on the inexorable route to possible destruction.

Inquiry was made regarding active duty, and I was informed that I could continue in surgery with my father until notified to report for continued army duty. It was also requested that I should take a series of extension courses related to changes in army structure and activities to keep me better informed and up-to date. It was a pleasure to be associated with my father in his practice and become acquainted with various surgical techniques varying, to a degree, from the European masters. My duties were numerous in keeping pace with my father, who was precise and exacting regarding time, place, and complete knowledge of every possibility which might be encountered in the various surgical procedures. Days were full, and many nights were taken with urgent cases. I certainly was much too busy to take an active part in the life of the city. Also, Dr. James G. Montgomery asked me to assist him in surgical procedures; this I considered an honor, as he had been one of my chief mentors during my previous time in the Kansas City General Hospital. Added to my other duties once a week it was my pleasure to teach a class of nurses of Saint Joseph Hospital a course in Surgical Nursing Care and Anatomy. When the opportunity presented, I found it enjoyable to write about some of the very interesting and unusual case studies we had. The experience gained in Germany and Vienna was now found to be most valuable.

PHOTO GALLERY ONE

Wallace Harry Graham,
age four sitting on a trunk
holding a black cat.
1914, Highland, Kansas

Neighborhood "gang" from Troost and
Forest Streets; Kansas City, Missouri
Back Row: Wallace Graham, Ranny
Wenzel and George Blender
Front row: Murray and Lew Wenzel

Transcript of note handwritten by Wallace
Graham at age twelve on the fabric debris
of a crashed plane :

Aug 17-1922
About 10-30
While visiting Grandpa Veneman at
Almena, Kan's, [Kansas] we got into the car
and went to John Warner's farm 1/2 mile
east of Grandpa's and found this piece of an
areoplane which belonged to Dr. Brewster
of Neb. His boy was lying unconcious at Dr.
Bennies. The pilot was knocked unconcious
for 40 min. I met the Dr's other boy and we
are both about the same age, he fat and I
lean. We both agreed to be Dr's.
        Wallace Graham
The Areoplane was wrecked at Almena,
Kansas Aug 16-22

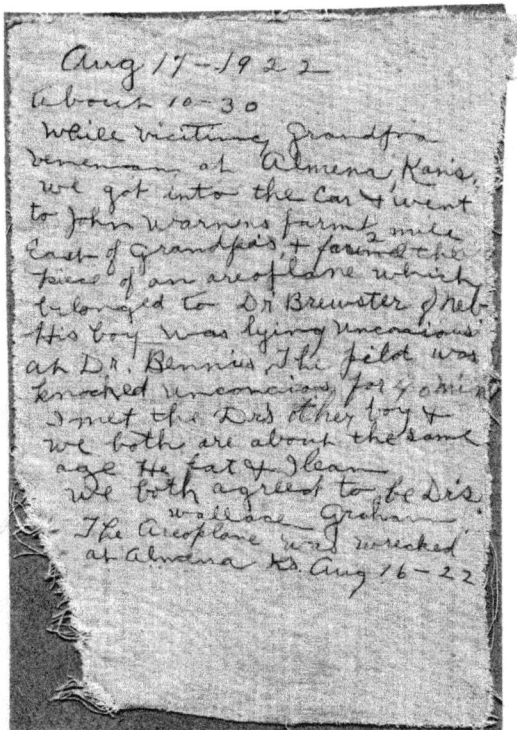

Wallace H. Graham, Eagle Scout 1924

Where the Streetcar Stops, Page 64, Chris Wilborn, author 1991
Photo reprinted with permission. Wilborn and Associates, photographers

Wallace Graham Track team at
Central Missouri State College;
Warrensburg, Missouri – 1931

Unsuspected by his father, Wallace "Wally" Graham boxed his way to the Welterweight Golden Glove championship and beyond. He even tried out for the Olympic team.

KANSAS CITY FIGHTER WINS IN ST. LOUIS

Wally Graham, Kansas City middleweight, fighting in St. Louis, scored a technical knockout over Bill Fagan, New York, in the third round of an Olympic tryout bout there Friday night. Jack Runyon, another K. C. fighter, lost on a knockout to Don Bayliss, St. Louis, in a heavyweight bout.

"WALLY" GRAHAM SCORES KNOCKOUT IN ST. JOE BOUT

"Wally" Graham, College student, knocked out Joe Bazanno, St. Joseph professional heavyweight boxer, there Thursday night. Graham scored his knockout in the fifth round.

The bout was a ten-round affair and was staged in the Rubideaux Club as the main event on the card. Graham sustained a small cut over the left eye and a portion of one of his teeth was missing Friday. These were his only injuries.

January 30, 1932

"Wally" Graham Wins Middlewest Title

Decision in St. Louis Gives Student Right to Take Part in Olympic Tryouts

Wallace Graham, College student and Kansas City middleweight, scored a technical knockout over Bill Fagan of New York, in the third round of an Olympic tryout in St. Louis Friday night. The fight was staged in the Central Athletic Club building.

Graham knocked out "Kid" Champlain of Chicago in the second round of their bout the Friday before. The judge's decision over Fagan gave Graham the middleweight amateur championship of the middlewest. He was awarded a medal and is eligible for national Olympic tryouts in New York in June.

He is a senior and was recently chosen the College's most popular student.

WALLACE GRAHAM TO TRY FOR U. S. OLYMPIC BOXING TEAM

Wallace Graham, Kansas City youth and a student in the College, will try-out for the Olympic team in the spring in boxing events. He won a letter in track at the College last spring.

Graham started intensive training this week which includes a four-round bout and light run daily, and on Saturdays hard workouts with Joe Milhelm, a member of the American Olympic boxing team, in Kansas City.

Preliminaries for the Mid West elimination for the team will be held in Kansas City sometime in March.

High School sweethearts, Velma Hill and Wallace Graham; Kansas City, Missouri

Marriage of Wallace H. Graham to Velma R. Hill, R.N.
September 15, 1935
Kansas City, Missouri

Left: Wallace H. Graham, M.D. and 1st Lieutenant U.S. Army, with
his mother, Elizabeth and father, James W. Graham, M.D., upon
graduation from Creighton Medical School
June 4, 1936—Omaha, Nebraska

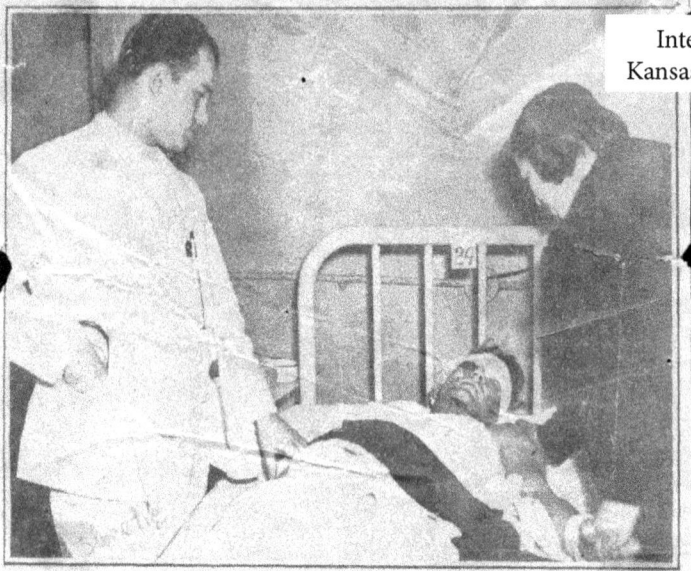

'Ride' Victim Near Death in General Hospital

Intern and Residency at
Kansas City General Hospital

June 30, 1936
Kansas City Hospital Intern

THROAT INCISION BELIEVED TO HAVE SAVED MAN'S LIFE

General Hospital Physicians Operate to Enable Patient to Breathe.

An emergency operation, performed in the receiving ward of the general hospital, after application of a stethoscope had failed to give any evidence that the patient still was breathing, probably saved the life Saturday of George Mason, 32 years old, 1000 the Paseo.

Mason walked into the receiving ward and told the clerk on duty that he was experiencing difficulty in breathing and desired treatment. There was no physician immediately available and the clerk asked Mason to take a seat.

He sat down on a long bench on which were several other persons. Just as Dr. Frederick Hall and Dr. Wallace Graham stepped into the room, Mason collapsed.

Emergency Effort.

The two physicians ran to his side. His face had become purple and it appeared that he had choked to death. Dr. Graham applied a stethoscope but there was no indication of life.

The physicians injected adrenalin into the man's heart and then started artificial respiration. When it seemed that Mason again was breathing, Dr. Graham decided to perform a tracheotomy.

There on the bench in the receiving ward, he made an incision in Mason's throat. Then he took a piece of tourniquet hose 6 inches long and inserted it in the incision.

Recovery Expected.

Mason's breathing became more nearly normal. After the two physicians had worked with him for approximately an hour, he was taken to a bed. Saturday night he had not regained consciousness, but it was believed he would recover.

The physicians learned later that Mason had complained for some time that there was an obstruction in his throat that prevented his breathing freely. He had been advised by other physicians to enter a hospital for an operation, but had neglected doing so.

Mrs. Mason, it was said, was visiting in Jefferson City.

134

1937-1938

Velma and Wallace Graham
as Austrians

Velma and Wallace Graham
Passport photo 1937

Wallace in *lederhosen*

Velma in Tyrolean Sweater

Velma and Wallace Graham in Hungary

Wallace and Velma in Hungarian folk clothing

Vienna on return trip
"The Nazification of Wien" 1938

Returning Austrians (former Nazis who fled from Austria under the
Nationalist regime) singing the "Horst Wessel." April 5, 1938

Left: Goose stepping along the streets of Wien 1938

Vienna, Austria 1938
Hitler with Goering, Hess, and Goebels, et al., at the Opera

Left:
Adolph Hitler (light uniform) standing in balcony of Rathaus in Wien

Right:
The pigeons being liberated at the same time Hitler announced to the world that Austria was now all one with the fatherland (the Vaterland).

Nazi Tanks

Officers looking on

"Heil!"

Medicine Bluffs, Fort Sill,
Oklahoma, 1941

Piano provided for down-time
in tent on maneuvers

Wallace on training maneuvers

Above and below: Louisiana maneuvers with
6th Division 80th Field Artillery Battalion 1942

80th Field Artillery Battalion

Heather and Wally with their mother,
Velma Graham on maneuvers
1942

Wallace H. Graham with his children,
Heather and Wally on maneuvers
1942

1942-1943

Being true to the Boy Scout
motto, "Be Prepared," Dr. Graham
learned how to operate different
vehicles in an emergency.

Wallace in the middle with his visiting parents, Dr. and Mrs. James W. Graham at rental house in Indiana. Graham was stationed there for a couple of months at Camp Atterbury. March 28, 1943

Wallace target shooting with his father, past pistol team member, Col. James Walter Graham, M.D., who served in WW I as 1st Lieutenant, and as Colonel in the first part of WW II.

HOSPITAL UNIT IS FIRST OF SECOND ARMY TO ARRIVE

By Cpl Charles S. Gwynne

What is believed to be the first unit of the Second Army to arrive in Camp Tyson, the 24th Evacuation Hospital (Semimobile) with Col Carl M. Rylander in command, arrived recently after a 3-month maneuver stretch spent in the lovely, cool hills of Tennessee.

The majority of the men are from New York, New Jersey, Ohio, West Virginia and Kentucky. Approximately 3,000 patients were treated by the hospital during the summer, including everything from a chigger-bite to a tank crack-up. With a capable and competant staff of doctors and nurses, excellent care and treatment was given to the men who became ill or injured on maneuvers.

Together with the moving every two weeks on trucks, over dusty rough roads, often through a downpour, and with 24-hour ward service, the entire staff was really kept on the "never-a-dull-moment" stage ever since we opened for "business" on June 14.

Men in the service today should hold no qualms as to what their treatment and care would be if they were to become ill or injured on the field of action. The best of medical attention, service and equipment is at their constant and instant disposal. Completely furnished and supplied x-ray rooms, operating tents—all well staffed with capable surgeons in every medical and surgical line as well as atractive nurses and trained technicians—is at the disposal of the enlisted man at any time, entirely free of charge.

Diagnosis, operations, plaster casts, x-rays were all carried out in the field as efficient as any modern city hospital could have done. Red cross field workers and the USO brought in stationery, toliet articles, movies, games and magazines to the patients. Our field PX was open from 10 o'clock in the morning, until 10 o'clock at night. As one patient expressed it, "I hate to leave; I've gained a pound in my one day stay, and had the best night's sleep in three months".

The 24th men are proud of their organization's accomplishments and they say, "if you think we did a good job while on maneuvers, just wait until we get into the field of action". They are all set and straining at the leach to get into active service.

The 24th's staff and its men like Camp Tyson very much. We appreciate the cordial and warm welcome we have received since arriving. We wish to thank all of you for your patience and helpfulness in answering our many questions and directing us about. Questions like, "What time do the movies begin? What time do they stop selling beer? What is Paris like? What time do the balloons go up? . . etc." We are confident that our stay here will be a pleasant one.

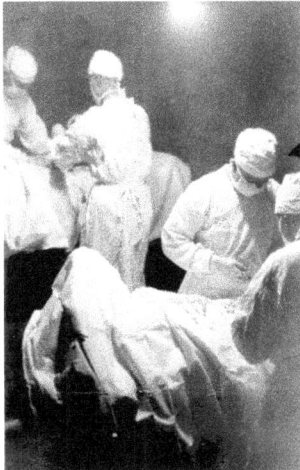

Field Hospital La Cambre, France June 1944 Arrow at right points to Dr. Graham.

Saint Lo, France bombed out.

Saint Lo, France June 1944

143

June 1944
Bombed out town,
Signy, France

Death camp furnaces

CHAPTER NINE
PREPARATION FOR WAR

The letter finally arrived from the War Department with their greetings and notification for the call to active duty. I was then sent to the nearest army instillation for examination and induction. I went to Fort Leavenworth, Kansas for mobilization and re-examination. Dreams of yesteryear flashed through my mind—of my grandfather, John William Graham, fresh from the East to the Kansas prairies looking for adventure, and imbued with national pride. He believed in a strong, undivided nation, had a beleaguered feeling of sympathy for both North and South, but opposed slavery. It was here in Leavenworth that my grandfather stood for examination, indoctrination, and induction into the Army of the Union in October, 1861, and was assigned to Company D, 8th Regiment, Kansas Volunteer Infantry, under command of Colonel Robert H. Graham. He was involved in many battles and seriously wounded in the Battle of Murfreesboro in March, 1863.

His many stories were vivid but revealed the misery as well as heroism of his fellow soldiers. Granddad lost his left eye and he sustained a bayonet wound, revealed by a scar on the left, anterior upper chest, and left shoulder. He carried a minieball in the anterior right thigh for many years.

I also thought of my father in 1917, having his examination for active duty in World War I. Dad was a reservist who went on active duty as a captain in the Medical Corps. I was stirred from reflection by the examining officer's booming voice, "Lieutenant Wallace H. Graham." He further announced, "Any medical doctor able to hear my voice and able to see and walk over here is in good physical condition. Lieutenant, you have a good record and you are physically fit." My assignment was to the station hospital at Fort Leonard Wood in Missouri as a surgeon. The adjoining examining room where a great number of inductees were being examined, was like a bare-bottom menagerie. There were occasional guttural sounds and a bit of the old Anglo-Saxon, earthy verbalization:

"My gawd, Sarge, you didn't have to jam the damn needle clear through my rear end."

"What's all these shots for—where you sending me to?"

"Man I'd rather have the yaller fever than these darn shots. "Suddenly a loud thud was heard, and the floor shook: "OK, pick the big guy off the floor or step over him."

"I don't believe in shots, Sergeant, do I got to have 'em?"

"You are damned right, soldier, and you're gonna have so many shots that if they were stickin' out of your hide you'd look like a porkypine."

"Man, I can't raise either arm and I can't sit down, I had so many shots."

"Okay, next for eye exam. Read the top line of letters on the sign over there on the wall."

"What wall, Sarge? I can't see no sign or no wall."

"Okay, you pass. You saw well enough to walk through the door."

"Hell, Sarge, I felt my way in here follerin' the butt-end ahead of me."

Bits of conversation in the officers examination section were more serious but without enthusiasm. Many comments were made regarding the pact between Stalin of Russia and Hitler of Germany, and the nonaggression pact signed by Joachim von Ribbentrop. We were aware that Prime Minister Neville Chamberlain had explained, in tones of fatigue and defeat, that Hitler and the German military staff were giving no assurance of peace and that Britain was committed to war. Comments such as, "It does seem odd that some person can't or will not shoot that crazy, wild man, Hitler."

"We can count the Allies on one hand of those who would help England." "Let's hope they can hold out for a few months. They are having a miserable time." "No one can depend on France, and they will not fight."

Some were saying the French preferred Hitler to Blum, and that France was rotten to the core with communism, and French industry was generally ruled by communism. Further comments of: "The British have the guts to hold out if they have the material." "God knows we should give them everything they need to hold the line until we can fortify ourselves."

It seemed to be an accepted fact that we would be involved in the war. The spirit was good and the attitude not that of heroic venture, but more of duty. The average answer pertained to national pride and protection of what we had and that we would do whatever was necessary to protect the democratic way. The officers' attitude was altruistic; few recruits however, had visions of glory.

Fort Wood was named after General Leonard Wood who had been a medical doctor imbued with the ideals of nationalism, and he believed he could accomplish his objective and be of greater service to his country as an officer in command of troops rather than in the Medical Corps. After graduation from Harvard Medical School and serving in the Medical Corps, he gained recognition as a leader of the Rough Riders in the Spanish-American War. He later commanded U.S. forces in the Philippines. He became Chief of Staff and in 1920 almost received the Republican nomination for President of the United States. He served as Governor of the Philippines, and died in 1927.

On 4 April 1941, I reported to Colonel Vanderboget of the station hospital. He was obviously a consumer of abundant food, and a pleasant officer. My salute was returned as I proceeded in the strict military manner of self-presentation. The colonel ordered me to stand at ease. He then stated that he had my 201 file; my assignment would be in the surgical section, temporarily in charge of a ward. He remarked that it was questionable whether there were enough patients to keep me busy. "I see according to your file," he said, "that you have had considerable experience in the military and were a very efficient noncommissioned officer in the infantry and in a splendid outfit, Company D2, and machine gunner under Lieutenant Cassidy from the Point. Well, you will be very useful in training our medical personnel in proper military tactics, ethics, and drill. You will be in charge of teaching them how to maintain themselves as officers and gentlemen and teach them how to be soldiers. You will find some of the doctors difficult, I am sure, as most of you are like a bunch of primadonnas and individualistic. Most will probably abhor any duty that does not involve their particular specialty in the field of medicine and surgery. I see you were a drillmaster and were proficient in advanced military tactics."

My reply was, "Sir, it may prove to be difficult if I have superior ranking commissioned officers to command."

He growled, "Lieutenant Graham, at this stage they don't know a private from a colonel, nor do they know where or how to wear their rank on the shoulders, cap, or seat of their trousers, and the most of them don't give a damn. I have read the files of all those assigned. You, Lieutenant Graham, will have your regular hospital duties, and in addition, we shall name it a training command. At this time you and the command will arrange your rooms in the hospital complement."

My room was assigned, and after drawing bedding and other essentials from the supply sergeant, I found a need for a shelf or two for books. I recalled having seen a large pile of scrap lumber in the middle of a field, stacked in readiness to be burned. A bit past twilight in the dusk of the evening after-duty hours, a fellow officer, Lieutenant Jack Moriarity, and I walked to the outer limits of the camp where the lumber scraps were piled.

We were amazed to see a fully armed guard marching around the field with a gun over his shoulder. Not knowing exactly why an armed guard should be on duty for scrap wood, we were both skeptical and cautious. We devised a plan to crawl into the scrap pile as the guard was past the midsection, away from us and across the field, then to choose our pieces and bits of board and wait until he made the next trip around. The plan worked perfectly; we picked up our boards and made a successful retreat. We were carrying the boards into the quarters when suddenly Captain Albert I. Lieberman, Jr. stepped out of his room. He wanted to know where we got the lumber. We told him it was a military secret, known only to much higher authority. We hammered and sawed until our bookshelves were in place. Captain Lieberman again appeared on the scene, stating that he was going to report us for stealing government property. Lieberman had gone to the lumber pile to get a scrap of board and confronted the guard. The lumber was to be burned the following morning but no one could use it. The captain reported Lieutenant Moriarity and me, but there were no witnesses, and the guard knew nothing about our evening requisition, and had seen nothing. Jack and I had difficulty remembering where we got the boards, and the case was dropped.

My duties were numerous, and I was happy not to have duty as latrine inspector. To the best of my knowledge, I think Captain Rolly Elkins had that duty. Probably the commander considered it a compliment, as the captain was the station proctologist and the best of good fellows, otherwise known as the "Rear Admiral."

It was a bit difficult to explain to a group of recently inducted medical officers why they should stand in line and learn to march and drill like West Pointers. I got the point across, and they took it well. We were all in this together and there were command performances. After many days and drills we became proficient, and our station complement won first honors in review at dress parade.

My mother notified me that my father was called to active duty in the army. He was delighted to have part in our war preparation. His duty was to establish the station hospital in Camp McCoy, Wisconsin, and fulfill his duties in the rank of colonel. Nothing could have made me more happy, as he said it made him feel useful for his country and twenty years younger.

After my third month in the station hospital, my wife with our children, Wallace Scott and Heather Ellen, decided to move near Fort Leonard Wood. The closest place was in Rolla where they rented a small house. Rolla was thirty circuitous miles from the fort. Time off the station was limited, and only by permission or pass. I commuted as often as I could, although the crooked route was a challenge.

While in service at Leonard Wood I spent my spare time in special studies. Among my extra-curricular activities was learning to fly every type of plane. The thought was self-preservation in event of necessity. I considered capture by the enemy, and having added knowledge for escape might be a valuable necessity. I learned to drive basic vehicles including tanks, large and small trucks, jeeps, command cars, and later handled every type of weaponry. I had a good part of this in earlier years when trained as a soldier.

On weekends and after duty I drove to Rolla where there was a large pasture, or field, used as an airport and for teaching aeronautics. The instructor was James Rutherford who taught basic elements of flight in a Piper Cub and a Waco biplane. Neither aircraft was equipped with brakes. I learned the basics of wind currents, navigation, and then flight instruction progressed well until the day of my solo flight. Velma and our children were watching as I made my debut. My first surprise came when I saw that the plane was different than the one in which I was taught, although it was a Piper. I stepped into the plane, buckled down, checked the instrument panel, tested the ailerons, compass, altimeter, gas and oil pressure, then looked around for a parachute, but was told none was available. On search I found no radio; there was probably no one to talk to anyway. I turned on the switch, the instructor spun the propeller, and after a few turns it clicked and spun. Blocks were removed from the wheel and flaps checked out okay. I revved the engine and had a successful take-off. The field seemed extremely short and there were high-tension wires at either end of the field. There was an army encampment on the north side of the field separated by a barbed wire fence. The last admonition was to, be sure to miss the tension wires. I had no idea of striking them and being fried by electricity. I waved and took off; the plane lifted gently, I skimmed over the wires, climbed to eight hundred feet, took a long sigh of relief, and flew around for an hour before deciding to land. Correct turns were made to enter the flight pattern—the only thing wrong was that I forgot how many section lines it was when the engine was to be cut down to glide in—I recalled it being an even number, two or four, so I chose two and literally dropped down. I dropped past the center of the field going eighty miles an hour. I looked for brakes and could find none. To turn would put me into a ground loop and a wreck; to continue ahead would be disastrous, a crash into a tall wooden fence. To take off again would mean that I would strike the power lines. I pushed the throttle all the way forward, lifted the plane, and turned to the left toward the army tents. I cleared the barbed wire fence by inches. A soldier walking guard threw himself to the ground and I can still hear what he shouted, and it was not printable. Clearing the fence I banked sharply and put all the climb I dared without mushing into a stall, then headed for the power lines hoping to clear them as I tried to gain height. Surely the good Lord did not want me then, as I skimmed over them without mushing or dragging my tail. Wires were now under me. I took a gentle climb to a thousand feet, said a sincere prayer of thankfulness, and took deep breaths.

My next thought was how I was going to get down. Again searched for a parachute and there was none—1 would have been happy to jump out with a chute; no such good fortune. I could not send a message without a radio. The thought struck me that I could write a note, drop it, someone could number the section line—how absurd! This was impractical and impossible.

I saw a plane approaching and prayed for it to land and would follow. It was a bit larger and much faster, and by the time I had turned to follow at the proper level the other plane had landed. By this time I was flying around with the fast-setting sun, which meant it would soon be dark. I saw Velma and the children, Wally was three and Heather two, down below trying to wave me down. I then saw a large transport plane—perhaps it would land and I would follow. My move to get behind was successful, but suddenly my plane began to rock and toss out of control. It was then that I learned what cavitation meant in the extreme turbulence caused by the wind in back of the large plane. The large plane flew on, and my plane was finally sighted. Lights were being turned on and I had none, so I thought, "Now I shall cut the engine down at the fourth section line and hope to glide adequately to miss the tension lines at the near or west end of the field." My gas was getting low and there was no other appropriate field as everything else had been plowed. I made my descent, missed the lines, nosed down, leveled off, and made a perfect landing, rolling to a stop. My legs were weak on the dismount, but my joy unbounded. The instructor asked if I had been "shooting landings." It was forbidden to fly over the army encampment, he told me. My only reply was that I was happy to walk away and he complimented me on a perfect landing. My family did not learn of my escapade and fears.

On other days flights seemed easier and I enjoyed the open cockpit of the Waco, although it too had no brakes. I was happy to understand a few basics in flying but knew I would never be a pilot by choice.

Daily duties rolled along in routine back at the Fort. Men and officers were sent to us until our table of organization filled. Everyone was trained. Noncommissioned officers were appointed as efficiency developed. When our units were trained to top function, we would lose the most efficient to other units. They went off as a cadre to train others in the same manner.

This procedure was disheartening but we understood its necessity for an efficient army. Recruits continued to be sent and we were never told when our unit would be judged full strength with capability of maintaining efficiency under fire in combat. Drills, obstacle courses, hikes, care of equipment, and hospital function with patients was a daily duty. We would have competitive inspections between sections, and as an occasional reward an extra pass or a weekend. We had pride and esprit. Hours and days passed and with multiple inspections. There was spick and span, spit and polish. The station pathologist was transferred to another hospital and we could not get a replacement for two to three months. I had credentials, having been in post-graduate pathology longer than anyone and the duty of station pathologist fell on my shoulders, an unwelcome ton of bricks. My duties were now above routine, and I was on call twenty-four hours a day, as there was no replacement.

We were exceedingly busy, not so much with appendices, hernias, and surgery routine, as with maimed bodies from automobile accidents. The toll of maimed and dead was almost like that of a weekend of warfare in combat. Many weekends were traumatic as each ensuing day of liberty saw men leave the Fort on pass, take on a load of ethanol, get in their cars, and roar down the curvaceous highway between Fort Leonard Wood, Lebanon, and Rolla. The highway had been an old Indian trail around the base of the Ozark Mountains. In our time many a modern young brave's life was snuffed out before it had a fair start. It was my task to determine the exact cause of demise and other details. After three months a suitable pathologist was found, Lieutenant John Foster from Fort Smith, Arkansas, whom I warmly welcomed.

There is something in my makeup that enjoys discipline and regimentation. Even though confronted with many duties not to my preference, I performed them for the welfare of the organization, to see that machinery was oiled to move. It affords me satisfaction in observing a functioning hospital. It was helpful to have been trained in military science and tactics as I could explain military moves, objectives, and casualties.

I enjoyed the meals and never purposely missed any of them. We learned never to grumble about army food, at times appropriately called the mess. The first officer who complained was assigned as mess officer, and regardless of base assignment he was sent to a briefing in the Cooks and Bakers' School, for later assignment to food preparation.

During this time the United States entered the war. I remember the startling announcement of the attack on Pearl Harbor which came over our car radio when my family and I were returning from a few days in Kansas City. I do not think either of us was shocked. We knew it would be soon, but expected it to be Germany. German submarines had been sighted off the Atlantic coast, and the most likely provocation would be for the Germans to attack our shipping. Pearl Harbor struck like a bolt. We were silent and sorry; our first words were almost identical, "What a miserable shame!" Having lived in Germany throughout the years of preparation, we knew our nation had to face the challenge. The following day, 8 December the United States declared war on Japan. On 11 December 1941, the United States declared war on Germany and Italy.

After a few months of training, we of the station hospital complement received official letters, to be answered immediately. We were given a choice which was unlike the army, as to where would we prefer duty: Alaska or the Philippines. I chose the Philippines as a nice warm and comfortable place to carry out my duties.

Soon personnel changes occurred and vacancies were filled. Three of us officers were transferred to line divisions or battalions, but the main hospital unit was readied, placed on alert basis and confined to camp until all were shipped out to the South Pacific. On 2 August, 1941, I had been transferred to the 80th Field Artillery-155mm Howitzer section of the 6th Division as battalion surgeon, under command of Major Walker Henderson, Division artillery surgeon. The Division medical commanding officer was Colonel Jerry Huddleston. My duties were to care for the medical and surgical problems of the 80th Field Artillery. This was a welcome, enjoyable change. Here my duties were with the finest officers, commissioned, noncommissioned and enlisted men, all of whom were proud to be in this unit of the 6th Division. There was never a dull moment in this organization.

My other assignment was with Lieutenant Jacob Mynderse and we were assigned coaching duties of the boxing team. An interesting note here is that Lieutenant Jake Mynderse, later following duty in the Southwest Pacific, became colonel and military attaché to Moscow under Lieutenant General Bedell Smith when he later became ambassador. Jake was later military attaché in Afghanistan. I had completed the extension courses of study for a captaincy in June, 1940. My promotion to captain came on 24 December 1941.

After several weeks of training, field problems, and general conditioning our artillery battalions were sent to Gunnery-Artillery school for firing at Fort Sill, Oklahoma. Here our 80th Field Artillery excelled. Here also I saw where the great Indian leader, Geronimo, had been incarcerated. He was deceived, lied to, captured, and kept in a dungeon not fit for a dog. I studied the history of this shameful event by our army stalwarts. At one point, we of the 6th Division were chosen to parade in Chicago. The Chicago trip was a thrill, traveling along with the convoy of heavy artillery. On the day of the parade we were spic and span and imbued with the thought that our division was the best in the army. The rolling rifles were so long there was difficulty getting them around turns. Every individual was properly positioned, sitting like statues in their appropriate places, either on the big guns, rolling rifles, 155mm howitzers or 105mm batteries. Crowds were lining the streets and packed the parade route.

The parade accomplished, with all fanfare and excitement, we went back to our fort in the Ozarks'. On arriving we brought all sections to top efficiency. Orders were received to assemble and move out for maneuvers, simulating combat throughout south Missouri, Tennessee, Arkansas, and Louisiana. My friend Jake Mynderse received his promotion to captain at this time. My present duty was as medical officer now on maneuvers with the 6th Division, 80th Field Artillery, as battalion surgeon. Army maneuvers were interesting as life-saving tactics in war games and sham battles, with the ploy of deception by thrusts, feints, retreats, pincers, and encirclement to force exposure, destruction and annihilation of the enemy. We were now under Lieutenant General Walter Krueger, to learn about the forces of destruction and annihilation or neutralization of the enemy. On 1 June 1942, I was promoted to 6th Division artillery surgeon.

Many people believe war is a matter of the constant clash of opposing armies, slashing ranger and commando raids, or firing of high explosive shell and rockets, of massive airborne activity, parachuting infantry and artillery drops in the midst of the enemy, fighting out of predicaments. This is largely true, but the greatest effort is planning, and learning the psychology of the enemy. We took time to learn the proper use of material, weaponry, fire power, resources, supply, food, clothing, and reserve replacements. We acted out the lessons we learned in basic training and in encampments. Army maneuvers are the toughening process preparing for the real business of war. Aid stations, litter bearers for wounded, field hospital units, evacuation and general hospitals, all must function to save lives, repair torn bodies, relieve pain and suffering. We must instill in our fighting men belief that if wounded and in the hands of medics, they would have the best care and would live. For some the war would be over, others would return to duty. War games, like war, were hard work, on alert, with rough, tough, rugged days and nights. There were sleepless cold nights spent digging, crawling, and shivering in foxholes or slit trenches, inching our way over rocks, mountains, mud, rivers. Believe me, the foot-slogging soldier has one rugged time crawling, running, walking, and sweating through mile after mile. Our fighting men and heroes deserve praise and accolades. This may continue day after day without compensation. You are with men you trust, and you know there is no way to get through except by battling hardships together.

We marched, camouflaged as we would do in combat. We had forced marches of twenty-five and fifty miles and more, waded through rivers with water up to our necks, sometimes using pontoon bridges. We learned to remove wet clothing at the appropriate time and care for feet and bodies. We learned how to bathe and shave out of a helmet. When the nights were unbearably cold, the ambulance occasionally proved great shelter. We would trudge through mud and swamps at any hour, day, or night, to attain objectives. Our guiding light through forests and hills would be a dim red light held by the forward scout. It could be the phosphorescent glow of a piece of rotted tree stump.

I recall one black night in a pouring cold rain when we were tired and hungry as a pack of starved wolves. The mess truck or chow wagon, as it was called, came wheeling through mud and water up to the hub caps. We lined up and the chow was forked out by the K.P.s (kitchen police). We could see nothing as we had to keep strict blackout. I pushed my mess kit up to the beef line and got what felt like a nice piece of beef. The icy rain hit my helmet like a hail of nails and drenched my food, which floated in ice water. If we bent our heads forward, the rain would pour off our helmet and down the back of the neck. I tasted my beef and found it was huge glob of fat-cold fat. I devoured every bit, though, but did not know what the next bite would be. It filled my stomach. All this rugged training never bothered me as I knew it was all for the hardening process, for possible survival, and knowing it could be worse.

We waded through the Red River in Arkansas, and again in Louisiana. It was amazing how many lessons learned in Boy Scouts, nature study, and Indian lore helped in survival. We had an extensive mock battle near Cookeville, Tennessee in which the 80th Field Artillery was victorious. We were elated over our performance. Louisiana maneuvers now completed, the division moved back to Leonard Wood.

On return I was surprised to be questioned by a group of 2nd Army inspection officers. Among them were Colonel John Cullen and a Colonel Stryker from the 2nd Army headquarters medical department under Lieutenant General Ben Lear. I was questioned regarding many tactical details, all of which were not strictly medical matters. On 29 August 1942, my appointment appeared as executive officer of the 9th Evacuation Hospital. I later received orders to report to 2nd Army headquarters in Memphis. My duties as executive officer of the 9th Evacuation ended on 15 January 1943. Orders came assigning me as 2nd Army headquarters staff inspecting officer for evacuation hospitals, advising units on combat readiness. I was proud of this promotion and believed in my duties; I tried to fulfill my duties in this great war. I enjoyed assignments at many hospitals where personnel and officers were of top quality and generally performed duties in the most skilled manner. Among my assignments were those of acting executive officer of the 95th Evacuation Hospital in Fort Francis E. Warren; Cheyenne, Wyoming, as well as that of army inspector. Weather was a bit wild and unpredictable. The fourth of July in Cheyenne is the big rodeo day. On that Fourth the day began hot and windy, but by noon was snowing like a blizzard. Up to this time Fort Warren was the only place I had been where the wind seemed to blow in every direction, including up and down. The soil was so sandy that forced marches were difficult, and many men complained that for each two steps forward we slid back one.

It was a pleasure to work with the 95th Evacuation Hospital. Organization was well-knit and commanded by superior commissioned and noncommissioned officers. The hospital was under the command of Major Hubert L. Binkley, later lieutenant colonel, an excellent officer who took pride in the efficiency of his command. Captain Thomas Matthews, later colonel, was a splendid training officer who contributed to our efficiency. This hospital unit had an unusually high esprit engendered by First Sergeant Richard C. Seymour, later awarded a battlefield commission of lieutenant. One of our exercises was to break camp and move with haste and without confusion. We could set up the entire two-hundred -bed hospital in less than two hours, including supply, with all ward tents complete. We could break and be set to move out, fully packed, within the same time, and with efficiency.

Once in late fall or early winter on my assignment to Fort Warren as 2nd Army inspecting officer to the 97th Evacuation Hospital,we were bivouacked in nearby Pole Mountain out of Cheyenne. Having learned, I decided to fly over the encampment and test our camouflage with the tents all in place. I took a jeep and drove to Breeze Airport in Laramie. My credentials and flight card shown, I took off in a Piper Cub. The take-off was uneventful, and over the mountains I flew. The unit encampment was difficult to find. The unit had perfect camouflage.

Winds were a bit stout, and I decided to fly down the valley at increased altitude, get out the opposite end of the mountain chain, then back to the airport. The down draft was so heavy it was necessary to push on full power and climb to a higher altitude without mushing into a stall. I climbed two thousand feet, to a total five thousand feet up from the valley, when suddenly a down draft caught me and the plane dramatically dropped fifteen-hundred feet with full power. This jolt gave me a frightful thrill. I crippled up the valley, with the right wing flopping down; then the left wing elevated and vice versa, regardless of full power. I was as helpless in the plane as if I were riding a flipping leaf. My command and control of the plane was almost ineffectual. Between prayers, dives, and climbs, I crawled into the Breeze Airport. The attendant thought I had lost my mind, as the moment my feet hit the ground, I tore my flight card into many pieces and handed these to the young man. It did not ease my mind in relating the flight when he replied, "No one would dare fly down the death valley, especially on a windy day like this."

It was obvious that I was not in command of the small plane nor would I ever care to be in the same situation again. My problems were not over for this exercise, as in arriving back to the encampment it was a bit late, with only time to report and have evening mess, clean the mess kit, and prepare my tent and sleeping bag. The bag was double and filled with eiderdown, and always warm. I slid into the bag, snuggled down, fastened the neck-piece, and thought I felt something move, but knew better, and gave the end of the bag a kick to straighten it out evenly. A sudden severe pain hit my foot. I thought surely a snake had bitten me, and flailing around in trying to extricate myself from the bag I knocked over table and chairs and other paraphernalia and finally wriggled out. Looking down at my lower extremities, I saw a handful of black and white barbs protruding from my bloody foot. Another officer came to my rescue and removed the barbs not without an ouch. We carefully turned the sleeping bag inside out and there sat a docile, unperturbed, fat porcupine looking up at us. The throbbing pain roared up my foot and leg to my rear end. We pushed old Porky out with a shovel and spent an hour pulling other barbs out of the bag. We treated the puncture wounds and I finally got back to bed with cold chills and a sore extremity.

Next morning I was beginning to wish I had not been so insistent on all men being clean-shaven at reveille. The stream nearby was frozen over and we had to break the ice, wash, spot bathe, and shave with ice water. My de-barbed foot remained one sore reminder for several days. Nevertheless the bivouac was a real success as a smooth, functioning organization. The hospital unit was later placed on alert and my replacement arrived. He was briefed first regarding duties and personnel, then readied and sent to the combat zone within the month with the unit.

The organization progressed well and was then ordered to Camp Breckenridge, Kentucky, where I was ordered for more training. This move was more for intense training while filling the unit with its complement. From this camp the hospital unit was sent to a staging area to leave for the war zone in North Africa. I was retained for the training command of newly formed hospital units building from cadres from more seasoned organizations.

Upon completion of my duties in Breckenridge orders sent me to Camp Campbell near Sturgis, Kentucky. The family moved to Sturgis. Camp Campbell was interesting and in different terrain. As we drove along country roads in that area one evening looking for a bivouac area, we became lost. We followed the rutted dirt road through the woods where we became confused. We came upon a working still, where rough-looking men appeared and told us menacingly that we had no business there and to get out fast. The brewmaster, if that is the proper eponym, was armed with an ancient musket. He was direct and earthy in his warning that he "ain't wantin' no sogers trampin' around my gol durned place of bizness. Now get out afore I fill yore tail ends full o' lead." We understood and took off fast, over the many miserable partly hidden and narrow roads through the woods, until we found our way back into Sturgis.

My next interesting station assignment was in Camp Atterbury, Indiana. While stationed in Atterbury, my family lived a short time in nearby Martinsville, and later moved to Columbus, closer to the camp. I was inspecting officer for an evacuation hospital going through the paces of training and placement of officers and other personnel. Trained surgeons who were Fellows of the American College of Surgeons or certified by the American Board of Surgery, were placed with or sent to units where their skills were applied in their specialty. In Atterbury we had fine friends, whom we have retained through the many years: Captain Irving Brown, Jr., Army Medical Corps, and his wife Ruth. They now live where Dr. Brown practiced medicine, as an anesthesiologist, in New Market, New Hamphsire. In Atterbury were other fine hospital units to be trained for combat readiness. We shared camp with the 83rd Division. Captain Irving Brown was an outstanding medical officer assigned to the 83rd Division. Following preparation of the Evacuation Hospital to efficiency, and notifying army headquarters of its readiness, the unit went overseas. At the end of this tour, I was ordered back to 2nd Army headquarters in Memphis. Here with my peers and commanding officers we analyzed remaining evacuation hospitals. Vacancies were noted and evaluated.

After many assignments an unusual opportunity came to choose what I considered an efficient functioning medical unit, and I chose the 24th Evacuation Hospital under command of Colonel Carl M. Rylander, a proficient and decisive commanding officer. He always maintained accord and discipline, not by vociferous demands or bombastic maneuvers, but in a quiet, reserved, firm manner. One never misunderstood what he meant. In straightforward manner he was a good military officer, as well as having principles. His organization ran smoothly, and it was later considered one of the outstanding Evacuation Hospitals in the army. By vote of many it was adjudged one of the most distinguished and efficient in the European Theater. Our Evacuation Hospital would take three hundred casualties and was easily reduced or expandable. While on maneuvers we would set up in every imaginable manner. We would try many ways to determine the most expeditious setup of tents using diverse locations, as well as adjusting to buildings. We were mobile, fast, efficient. To effect more realism, we would perform surgical procedures in the field, the same as handling the wounded when we were committed to battle lines.

One way to obtain casualties was by having inspection of the men. We convinced all uncircumcised men that they should be circumcised, also any moles, warts, or questionable body lesions should be surgically removed. One soldier had a large blue-black mole which he thought had been growing the past six weeks. The mole was on an appendage, where he should also be circumcised. Following thorough triage, skin prep, proper gowning and care, he was brought to the surgical area by litter and properly placed. Following induction of anesthesia and proper draping, the surgical technician thought he saw the mole move. It was passed off as a joke. The mole and circumcision were both accomplished. Tissues were sent to pathology and the mole was found to be a huge blood-filled tick.

In one phase during a bivouac there was inspection of vehicles. We were not supposed to use gasoline to clean the motors, but it was done in a few instances. We were bivouacked in an abandoned farm where there was an outhouse, commonly known as a Chic Sales or three-hole privy, also called the latrine. Dirty oil and gasoline was thrown into the privy. The following morning we heard a resounding explosion, and the privy rocked. One of the men was lying flat, having been blown out the door. He had been smoking while evacuating, and dropped the cigarette in the next hole and combustion followed. This resulted in a severe burn in a vital area, which we took care of immediately. He later needed some split skin grafting. No one admitted any knowledge of how the gasoline accumulated in that area. One opinion was that the one who dug the hole years ago overlooked a gas or oil well. Others put the entire blame on Sergeant Farkas, the head of the mess, for feeding such food the evening before.

Our unit gradually received enlisted men, noncommissioned and commissioned officers, to fill the table of organization. We knew our stateside days were numbered and anxiously awaited the big move. The unit was stationed in Barrage Balloon Camp in Tyson, Tennessee, near the town of Paris. I reported for duty on 19 July 1943. The camp was practically covered by large, silver, fat, cigar-shaped balloons. Townspeople were generous and pleasant and we enjoyed their hospitality for which the people of the South are renowned. Our unit, the 24th Evacuation Hospital, was so expert in every phase of military medical and surgical expediency that units from distant areas came to see how we functioned. Families were permitted to stay, prior to the day of departure to the point of embarkation.

Velma and our two children stayed in a single-level house supported on a few concrete blocks. We shared this small four-room dwelling with Chaplain Captain Backenstose and his wife Mary, from Lebanon, Pennsylvania, the most congenial, delightful, wholesome, intelligent people it has been our pleasure to have known. They were Pennsylvania Dutch, with the associated brogue. When we were not on bivouac or night duty we enjoyed ourselves throwing balls at the huge rat trying to chew a hole in the floor next to the drainpipe from the sink. We would throw the ball and the rat would dodge and duck, then resume the gnawing, never dismayed nor fearful. If we plugged the hole with putty, paper, wood, or a bottle, the rat would deftly move the obstruction, keep an eye on us and continue to gnaw at the hole. Our one stove was a hand-carried kerosene two-burner, which we used for cooking or heating. On several occasions it would burst into flames, to be smothered by a blanket or carried outside and the flames smothered while getting scorched ourselves. This is the first place we had ever seen armies of huge white-gray, long-legged crickets.

In camp we had daily inspections, general and showdown for all equipment, multiple "shots" for immunization. We had forced marches of twenty-five and fifty miles.

Final leaves and furloughs were canceled and all phones silenced. We had received orders. The last days in camp, in November and December, marked a time of year when daylight was becoming shorter, and we went on duty and off duty in the dark. Weather was cool and the wind sharp and biting. Humidity was wet, the earth muddy. The heavens rolled and opened to allow a bit of sunshine. Living an unnatural existence, making the best of it, we were happy to be with our loved ones, yet anxious to expand ourselves, anxious to get to our destination and perform duties for which we had been training the past three or four years.

The time came to entrain, 10 January 1944, beautiful and sunny. A song at the time was "Oh What a Beautiful Day," and my wife tells me I sang it too enthusiastically. The band played as we loaded our duffel bags and boarded single-file onto the train. There were kisses and waving as the whistle blew. The sliding doors were secured, the coupling of the cars grumbled with a slight jolt. As evening shadows lengthened we peered over the rolling hills and valleys of Tennessee. The music of the band diminished as twinkling lights shown from the small houses between the leafless maples.

Now as I sat peering out the window, the world seemed a bit more taut, the vagary of time and future was about to unfold. The horizon to the East held our answer. We were closer to functioning as a cog in the machinery of war, for a purpose of liberation, to smash the destroyers of freedom. Reality was war and we were a proud if small part. The little village was left in the dusk, and windows darkened as we peered into the void, catching a flicker of light from a far-off farmhouse. Some of our men were chattering, others playing cards, while a few prepared for bed. I listened to the clickety-clack of the train rolling over the rails, heading eastward—destination unknown. Our day had been hectic. We were all tired. We made up our own sleeping quarters rather than wait for the porter. Darkness was falling like a cloak enveloping little towns and hamlets as we whizzed by. The landscape became a fleeting vision with a line of flickering lights as we passed through small stations. Then a more populous area as yellow streaks were more like solid masses of light. We were flying through the darkened countryside, engulfed by the night. A lonely visage appeared. I saw it was my reflection, like a waxen mask in the steamy window glass. I reclined in the arms of Morpheus to dream and plan for tomorrow, the music of the clickety-clack becoming faint, finally lost in slumber.

CHAPTER TEN
TO THE JUMPING OFF PLACE

It seems as if I had hardly fallen asleep before I was awakened about five-thirty in the morning, so I dashed into the tiny wash room at the end of the car to beat the rush. After performing my ablutions, I noted others were lined up and down the aisle. I returned to my bunk and made ready for breakfast. Looking out the window I saw we had reached the outskirts of Louisville, Kentucky. Soon after that we saw the city of Cincinnati sprawled along the railway. A few of the men were from this area and they pointed out some of the landmarks to us. The train wound its way along stretches of the river, and as we left the area of Cincinnati we noted the farms and beautiful cattle along the way. We saw cylindrical silos and corn stalks standing bare in the fields. We sped along the farmland and even past a few deserted mining towns. The tall, lonely, mine scaffolding in disrepair indicated that the bowels of the earth there no longer gave forth the wealth that man eternally seeks. All too soon the day slipped behind the rolling hills, and the night was upon us once again.

After a few hours of idle talk and wondering about our destination, it was decided we could not actually make specific plans because our hospital unit had been trained for many different types of set-ups and deployments. This talk however, helped to pass the time, and we were in Pittsburgh by evening. There we saw where the Monongahela and the Ohio Rivers join to make the Allegheny River. The huge area of Pittsburgh and Tarentum was a steel metropolis (Tarentum being the birthplace of my father, and the place from which he began his westward trek). Against the darkness of the night we saw the fiery coals from the thousands of furnaces, blasting their defiance to those who would believe we were not putting forth every effort to grind out more tanks, munitions, and material for all-out war effort. As we rolled by we also observed the tall and distinct shape of the huge smelters silhouetted against the fiery glow of the molten steel.

The darkness engulfed us again, and we settled back in our berths to allow the song of the rails to lull us into slumber. Occasionally looking out the window, I gazed upon the rolling hills of West Virginia against the darkening horizon as we swiftly passed by. We rolled on through Wheeling, but by this time, slumber had overtaken me. When I awoke we were rumbling into Washington, D. C., the so-called hub of the nation, from whence all our orders emanated. We were actually moving quite swiftly as we went through Washington, and we caught only a fleeting glimpse of the white Capitol dome. Speeding on from one city and town to the other, we were struck by the great sprawling space of our country. We rolled on through the industrial East, including the flat lands of New Jersey, and the countless suburban villages. The traffic all seemed to be traveling north to the mother city of New York.

We arrived outside of the little gray city of New Brunswick, New Jersey, and the train slowly came to a stop. This seemed to be our destination, and was the area called Camp Kilmer. It was named for Joyce Kilmer, the poet who wrote "Trees" and many other beautiful poems and sonnets. Here we detrained and managed to find our baggage. At this point, we were again cautioned that no letters or telephone calls were to leave this area. We were to speak with no strangers under any circumstances, whether about our particular unit or any other unit with which we were acquainted. After we picked up all of our bags and paraphernalia, we were shown to our barracks where we took our baggage and placed it under the bunks or beds which had been furnished to us. We slept fitfully. Finally reveille sounded and we fell out. On getting out of the barracks, we felt the blast of winter against us, with sharp, cold wind whistling past our ears. We were informed in our various groups or sections that this would be the beginning of our processing. This was a term applied to all troops who were making ready for some important move. Again, we repeated complete show-down types of inspection for clothing. Physical examinations were again carried out with all the necessary stipulations and regulations as required by the port examiners. Speed was constantly emphasized. The examinations were very much the same as previously described when getting into the Army, with rows of naked bodies and various port doctors pounding chests and examining teeth, much as one would examine a good horse just before being placed on the auction block. We had other drills, such as boat drills, in how to stay adrift in a life boat. We were given complete instructions on how to maintain ourselves and our lives in the event the ship was struck and sunk. We were also given lectures, along with the drills, for about ten days.

We were kept busy the majority of the time in Camp Kilmer, and at the end of the ten days we were advised that we were moving on, so our bed rolls were placed appropriately. Then we were marched down the hill to the railway station through the frigid wind and snow to the strains of "*The Stars and Stripes Forever.*" We didn't know where the music was coming from but frankly, it was rather warming to hear. As we entrained for the last time, we all took our places in the various coaches and roll call was made by some of the officers. The train slowly moved out of the station on the way to New York City and to the Brooklyn Port of Embarkation, which was a relatively short journey. The train then took us directly to a ferry crossing. We detrained again and went across the river by ferry to the dock where the ship was waiting to be loaded. We were met at the dock by a band which was playing and there were many civilians present, but we were fenced off from the civilian area. The Red Cross girls were there welcoming us and handing out donuts, which was quite welcomed on that very cold day. Our full dress included steel helmets and helmet liners. We were told to keep our helmets handy at all times.

Our ship was huge; small wonder, for it was the *Queen Mary*. We marched up the gangplank and were given directions as to where the various quarters were located. It was rather crowded, and the lower decks smelled like a zoo. I can assure you that the decks and various areas in which we were to be housed had not been scrubbed down, as the odor was quite pungent from the last group that had been on board the ship. Once I had my bearings and knew exactly where I was located, I put my duffle bag down and returned to the main rail which was lined with G.I.s fore and aft.

It actually did not take very long to get under way. The pilot boat came along and nudged us out to the open sea. The harbor began to disappear behind us and as we looked out to see the huge Statue of Liberty probably the same thoughts were racing through most of our minds; that the Statue of Liberty was beautiful and it stood for so much, and we wondered when we would see it again. Moving out into the open sea, the pilot boat captain took his leave and his papers. As the little boat was relieved of its duties, we opened up full steam ahead.

Once at sea, I repaired to my bunk and retrieved a book on emergency surgery from my bag, and proceeded to read the essentials of surgery as seen by those who had been in combat previously. I recalled a British doctor by the name of 'Jolly' who went into depth describing the types of surgery performed in the first stations and then in the evacuation hospitals. It was very interesting and I related the high points to my colleagues. I had long since formulated the format for the personnel in the appropriate stations; those who would be giving anesthesia, those would be first surgeons, and the types of surgery in the different surgical sections. To those who were interested, I went over the various procedures such as debridements, primary or secondary closures, and stressed that all wounds would be considered contaminated. This was gone over and studied because it was not known when or where we would be committed to a battle zone, and we certainly knew nothing of the conditions with which we would be confronted at this particular time. I had a fair idea, having treated and operated on some of the wounded from the Spanish Civil War.

Toward evening I walked down to the men's quarters. I must say, it reminded me very much of a cattle car, with everyone crowded together. There was an appalling odor of what seemed to be urine. I asked about this as it seemed to be coming from the mess hall. This all fell in place when we went to eat. One of the foods we were given was a sort of pie, and the men were arguing with each other over whether someone had urinated on or in the pie. They didn't exactly use the term, "urine," but we understood what they meant. We discovered later that these dainty little pies were British kidney pies. Since we were on a British ship, we were given British foods. The general question from the majority of us was, "Where in the world did the British get all of the kidneys?" It seemed as if we had "kidney stew," "kidney pie," and "kidney" in all forms possible while on the ship. As the days went on, the men complained that they couldn't possibly continue trying to push down the kidney dishes and the little hard sausages. In the mornings, they gave us cold gray looking wheat or "oat meal porridge," as they described it. Actually, it became a question of how hungry one was as to whether he ate it or not. The mess hall had been transformed from a ballroom. The movement of the ship caused one of our men to state, "I am sliding with my mess kit all around these slippery tables trying to spear a sausage and place it in my indifferent mouth without suffering an amputation of the nose, or a traumatic enucleation of an eye."

Following the dining hour, we would make long trips down, down, through the bowels of the ship to the "mess kit laundry" and attempt to swab our kits in the briny water furnished for that purpose. The ship traveled with a convoy in a rather zig-zag manner, in order to avoid any submarine activity, should it become apparent at any particular time. We walked around the huge vessel, exploring the maze of hallways and corridors, where sprawled soldiers lay against the walls. Whenever the ship rolled, considerable emesis was seen lying in little pools over the stairways and halls. The reeking from this was not very conducive to keeping your own cookies in place. In the words of one of our fine men, who incidentally was the chaplain's assistant, Charles S. Guynne, "With all the vomitus under foot I realize civilized people can suddenly become very revolting."

I remembered reading in some manual that fresh air would improve your condition aboard a troop ship, so I went up to the deck, out the little curtain doorway to the open deck, and stood at the rail in the early morning gazing at the wild and untamed beauty of the sea.

The third day out, there was a very sharp, spanking breeze whipping across the ship's deck, and at the prow of the ship I watched how it plowed into the water, marveling how it sent its sprays out and into the sea again, like a magical fountain of mist transformed into the most delicate of blues, purples, and whites, as if a rainbow speared the mist. The sharp breeze continued throughout the day and the sea was becoming rough, with white caps getting high. We were told that it was unusually calm for this particular time of the year and that we were very fortunate. I rather enjoyed the invigorating, stinging salt spray as it would strike my face. It was certainly more pleasant than the time that I previously described in crossing the North Sea. The fifth night at sea was rough. The ship was rolling and the rumors were spreading ominously that the subs were hunting this speedy queen of the oceans. The sea itself was wild. We had spent the afternoon watching the high waves of the sea from the open port-holes of the promenade deck, for no one was allowed on the open deck this day due to the ship rolling so violently. There was danger of being swept overboard and this majestic ship would not stop for any one human life when it might mean risking the life of the other fifteen thousand passengers.

At this time, I do not recall the precise day or the hour, General George S. Patton was announced as the principal speaker to inform us regarding the enemy. The officer making the announcement was British and spoke in flawless, impeccably correct English. We were all gathered in the large meeting room in the below-deck bowels of the *Queen Mary*. The general arrived on stage and attention was called; we were so crowded several fell over each other in snapping to erect attention. The next command was, "As you were," so we sat or sprawled according to maximum ease in the crowded facility. General George Patton boomed loudly in his bombastic, yet squeaky voice, with an occasional raucous laugh. His talk was heavily spiced with vulgarities and obscenities as he ranted and raved, but the talk was obviously made to incite and instill hatred for the enemy. It was interspersed with what we believed to be half truths and enemy action reaching back into the War of 1918. There were plenty of holocaustic horrors to describe, and he managed quite vividly. He was indeed stimulating, although seemingly pompous and overbearing as he strutted imperiously back and forth across the stage, stomping, kicking, and chair slamming similar to a dictator I had seen in action in former times. His pegged pants were precisely pressed, the boots and spurs shined to a sparkle, and the ivory-handled revolvers glittered from reflected lights. He also carried a shoulder holster with a .32 caliber pistol. The light colored pegged trousers reminded me of the ones I wore in my days in the machine gun company D2-1st Infantry Division as a sergeant.

General Patton warned, "These Nazis will try every trick known to man to kill you. The Nazi S.O.B. has been trained to hate and to kill since he was five years of age, beginning in the Hitler *Jugend* (Hitler Youth); always know this and be aware. A Nazi will smile and slice your throat at the same time. We (you and I) are going into glorious battle to kill these sons of bitches. You must kill the enemy, do not just overpower him: kill him. A true Nazi will always be a Nazi and the only way to eliminate the rats and prevent them from poisoning all people is to kill them. There is no other way. Remember this, my brave men, I will never show you into battle, I will lead you into battle. Know this also; there is no place in my army for a coward; know this and fight for your life, your buddies, your country, and your way of freedom for all." I add here: General Patton did exactly what he said. He led his army; he was always directly in front, standing up in the jeep, going into battle, and he was followed by a light M4 tank. I know he did not consider himself; he feared not, and in the end he seemed to want to die in battle.

If one listened carefully through the cataclysmic tirade, there was in reality, a wealth of sound advice for the soldiers. He advised never to dig a fox hole or slit trench under a tree because a shell passing overhead might strike the tree causing an immediate air burst and drive splinter fragments straight down, nullifying the advantage of the slit trench and killing its occupant; a dead soldier will never win the war. He further advised us to dig only when on the defensive or when stabilized in the final objective or when in bivouac, as protection from artillery fire and strafing. Basically the general was otherwise opposed to digging in, as he believed the fighting soldier should continually be on the advance, firing against fire and moving forward to attack. In other words, he should keep an aggressive attack moving forward, which would do more to neutralize the enemy fire power than waiting or advancing by rushes. His advice was to keep the gun blazing while walking, all guns firing; the light machine guns, the Browning automatic rifles, and the M1. Small arms fire was not effective beyond two-hundred-seventy-five to three-hundred yards. Courage was to be engendered by forcing yourselves forward in spite of fear. He stated one must have strong discipline, self-respect, confidence, and pride, not only for ourselves, but for those men with us. Discipline removes resistance to obedience and obedience becomes a natural reaction, subconscious and habitual. You are then fighting for yourself, your fellow men, your unit, and above all your great country, the United States of America. We were told also that practically all European ground plots and woods are intersected at right angles by lanes or hedge rows every thousand meters. Extreme caution was to be used in crossing the lanes; we were to never walk down the lanes, and were advised to use the utmost caution at all crossings, as the enemy had these areas zeroed in or mined. The areas of anticipated action were already spotted with machine guns and at intervals, the 88s. He further stated that hospital and medical units should be set up in the open so the enemy would know them for what they were. They were to be well marked and far away from ammunition dumps or air strips to avoid direct bomb strikes. Medical installations were also to have adequate, alert guards at all times.

The expletives of General Patton, with the vivid and dramatic revelations of horrors and crimes against humanity by the S.S. German troops were bloodcurdling. We all heard, but the reactions were different. Some of us developed a real hatred for the enemy, but others considered the expounding message as purely propaganda. I wonder how many knew that what the general was saying had actually already occurred. I realized that every word of the horror was true but was not able to convince all of the troops. The mass murders brutally exacted against the Jews or any dissidents were taking place from 1938 through 1944 to my own knowledge. Most of the soldiers would not believe the extent of the atrocities which were perpetuated by the sadistic Nazi hordes.

In September 1942, areas of Poland were gutted, hospitals were raided, the defenseless sick were murdered, and newborn, naked babies were flung from the third and fourth floor windows to waiting trucks below; some of the babies were caught on bayonets held by recent graduates of the Hitler *Jugend*, the newest S.S. members. This action was taken in full sight of the families of those being murdered and carted away; the screaming, praying witnesses were held and restrained by a ring of bayonets and guns held by the Nazis, who seemed to be eager to thrust them into the bellies of the innocent, agonizing families.

As I write this now it is 1981. In Germany as well as in our own country, we are tolerating the re-formation of the neo-Nazis—the cry of the jackal or the squeal of the rat has not been eradicated. Where has human dignity gone? Where has the morality of religions flown? The written word is cold, and grows colder with time, with the horror and evils often thrust behind us; the curtain falls, but let us part that curtain at times to remind ourselves. We must remember the crimes of the Nazis, the persecution of the Christians facing the lions in the early days of the Caesars, the Spanish Inquisitions when the entire populations of nations were murdered, the pogroms of the Czars. Do we negate this past and turn the page on the atrocities of yesterday in Europe, in Latvia, Lithuania, Estonia, and today in Viet Nam, Laos, and Cambodia? Is life really as cheap as it seems? We need not read past, when we see by the daily media of man's inhumanity to man. Can we walk the streets after sundown or must we too, exact the *Allegemeinegesoerre*—(the general curfew) or fight fire with fire? Our courts, our laws, our penal systems like much fundamental teaching in schools is decadent, archaic, and lowered to the level of the untamed and undisciplined for the decline and degradation of our society.

We clung to the port-holes and stared out, watching the waves slamming against the entire side of the ship to the top deck. We watched them recede to what seemed hundreds of yards below. The open sea was doing its best to cleanse the emesis ridden decks. That night, the waves and the zig-zag motion of the ship made chaos out of the crowded quarters. Mess kits, duffle bags, canteens, books, and countless personal items went zooming through the air, or slid noiselessly along the floor under the bunks. We crouched under our blankets awaiting a direct hit, feeling sure that this was to be our first taste of this war we had heard so much about.

On the night of 28 January 1944, a voice rang out over the PA system, which for so long had been telling us that everything was by order of the commandant, announced that a special broadcast was being given. The dry, close clip British accent was welcoming us to Scotland, and informing us that we were now in the Firth of Clyde, so our journey was nearing its termination. Now our life jackets that had become a part of us, could be removed and we looked forward to seeing a bit of land. On the morning of 29 January, we went up on top deck to feast our eyes on the beautiful landscape of Scotland.

The little village of Greenock looked something off a Hollywood movie set. The emerald hills reached down into the sea and the aquamarine blue of the harbor were picturesque balm to our eyes having been accustomed to the angry sea. We marveled at the array of ships in the harbor. Aircraft carriers were sticking their stub noses over the water, sleek cruisers were lying low and silver-like against the sea, dirty smoke smudge destroyers were snarling their defiance in their bristling guns, and among them all, the minute little harbor craft were drawing their foaming wake all over the blue surface.

The order sounded off to prepare to go ashore, so we went below decks, got our equipment and carried our baggage, trudged down the same long hall we had traveled when we boarded the ship; we walked around the perilous gangplank and aboard a small boat which took us ashore.

We went ashore in Greenock, which is just above Glasgow, in the Firth of Clyde. Whenever one goes ashore after rolling and rocking for several days at sea, one finds the meaning of "sea legs." The rolling motion seems to continue leaving one a little off balance as the centers of equilibrium are still not quite square with the world, and you feel as if you are still aboard ship. So you walk with a wide stance, and everything seems to rock a bit the way the ship did. This seems to last for a period of about twenty-four to seventy-two hours.

We quickly found what luggage we could, then boarded a Scottish train, or British train, which had all the appearance of a Lionel toy train. These types were unusual to us. We had tiny compartments each accommodating four to six people. All blinds were drawn on the train for strict black-out purposes. There were to be no lights showing at any time after dusk. Quickly loading into the train we started southward through Scotland; Glasgow to Carlisle straight south to Birmingham, England into Bristol. We noted here that Bristol had been fairly well battered by bombs. We rolled straight on through Bristol and into the green meadows and hedge rows of Cheddar which was in Somerset, the Southern part of England close to the coast. It was a quiet, picturesque village. We all thought of Cheddar cheese of course, however, in England it is known as Cheddar Gorge. This little town, nestled in the very depth of a huge gorge between two very large and deep stony cliffs, was actually to us a return to antiquity, as the history of the town itself, goes back for centuries. The church of Saint Andrews was partly built in the eighth century, and the other part built in the twelfth century. The old Market Cross was almost worn away at that time. There was the old dam present and the older houses in which we were billeted at the time. They were old when the British fought in Canada and in the wilderness of America. It was a clean town and rather quiet. The only noise made was by the "Yanks" from the United States and we were supposed to be somewhat uncivilized in the eyes of the British. The quarters were adequate and they were what we made them.

Our stay in the United Kingdom actually termed from mid–January, 1944 to early June, 1944. The people of Cheddar were quite hospitable and as pleasant as they could possibly be under the circumstances of having us "Yanks" come into their quiet little village. It took several days for the unit members to become accustomed to the change in the monetary system and the pronunciation such as the farthing, bob, florin, the three pence or *thrupenny bit* as they call it; the half penny, pronounced *hopney*. We learned that the guinea was not an actual piece only an amount along with the shilling, or a pound note. However, we soon became accustomed to the use of them and we established ourselves with the condescending townspeople. Our unit was quite satisfied there in the small town of Cheddar. There was a pub or two and the main complaints were that the beer was always hot or warm. There was no such thing as ice. The beer was either mild, bitters, or occasionally had some Bass Ale or Withington Ale. From what I understand, there was none or very little alcoholic content in any of their ale or beer.

The road, or the highway through the town, was fairly narrow and wound through the entire gorge on out to the next small towns of Axesbridge, and the coast of Weston Super-mare. The "Rock of Ages" cleft for which a hymn and lyrics have been written is located off the highway out of Cheddar, England. The cleft is high and into the side of a very high stone precipice to the right of the highway. The cleft is wide enough to hold the body of a large man and act as a shelter from storm. I stood back into the cleft and hummed the song of "Rock of Ages—Cleft for Me."

The British looked upon us with skepticism. They were quite querulous as to what type of individuals these "Yanks" were. They had heard so many stories about us that they wondered if we were actually as wild as they had heard. Actually, the British as a whole, were splendid people and very hospitable under trying circumstances although with reserve and understandable reticence. The British people impressed me as being resigned to the fact that there would be a war so they would make the best of it and give a good accounting of themselves, although they had already tasted the bitter parts of the bombing with the destruction of property and the loss of lives.

We often think of the Englishman as being somewhat aloof, monosyllabic, and rather cool to most strangers. However, we found the average Britisher on the streets to be friendly and a good conversationalist. In the pubs any reserve banished completely and we found them to be quite talkative. They would not speak of the war or the oncoming problems of the war. They would speak occasionally of the battles of General Sir Bernard Montgomery, who was commanding his troops in Africa. However, they seemed also to be just as interested in the cricket and rugby games that had been taking place the previous week. The outlook for the rugby team would be very poor that year because the men were going off to the war. The average British citizen seemed to see no reason for great alarm even though they agreed that this would probably be a very severe and long conflict.

A few of us officers stayed in the Curtain home, maintained by the Curtain sisters who were exceedingly lovely and charming. They made the place very comfortable for us in all respects. The heating system of England had not changed in centuries. Apparently, they did not believe in central heating. They did have large, lovely fireplaces, where you burn your "front" and freeze your "rear" or vice versa. It was generally a bit damp, and keeping the fire going all night was a task, but we managed it quite well. The enlisted men had fine quarters and they seemed to fare quite well also.

Guard watch was kept continually on all our areas. Every day and every night we would have considerable activity as we were in the center of the so-called "buzz bomb alley." Buzz or V bombs came over almost every evening. We could tell them by the rumble which was like that of an ancient street car. We also knew the V-2s by their unsynchronized motors. Whenever the bomb or buzz bomb hit we counted to ten before the tremendous explosion came. Of course we were always in total blackout. There were many nights when we had to seek shelter, as the buzz bomb would shriek over, or the sirens would sound for a possible raid by the Luftwaffe and all the anti-aircraft opened up. The screaming whistle of the bombs was almost a nightly affair, leaving in its wake the lurid lights from the fires that had been lit by bombs striking homes and buildings. We realized that we were the ones in shelter and the ones the Germans were after. I remember very distinctly a loud thud on the hill nearby, and the bombs landing in the Cheddar Gorge. A plane was shot down close by on the moor near Retmoor. The censors, however, did not allow us to make any mention as to where the bombs were landing or about the plane falling and all mail was censored in and out. Thirty-five miles north of Cheddar was the city of Bristol which had been badly damaged by the bombs. Before we left, Bristol was fairly well bombed out in spite of blackouts.

We had several side trips also, including a trip to Bath, England, to see the old Roman baths. They haven't changed much since the times of the Romans when they held Britain. The large round lead pipes are still used for the hot baths, and the ancient artesian wells are still functioning and used as a spa or a place for bathing.

I was sent to London to the Hammersmith Hospital for a six weeks extension course in surgery, which proved to be very valuable. While in London during the Blitz we were bombed every night and occasionally by day. I was staying in the Hammersmith Hospital and really not believing the Germans would knowingly and purposefully bomb a hospital. While having all this good faith it just dawned on me that the V1 Buzz bomb, and the V2 had no conscience and would drop their explosive charge whenever their time-clock so designated. While I was trying to rationalize, a huge bomb dropped in Saint Bartholomew's Hospital. It buried itself in the hospital courtyard where there was a twelve foot square of grass and flowers. The bomb struck and dug in exactly in the middle. The good Lord must have nullified the firing pin as the bomb was found to be a dud and never exploded. An explosion from this particular bomb would have devastated the entire hospital and a large area surrounding.

The following evening after my hospital surgical duties were completed for the time, I went to my room. The shades were drawn for the black-out and all cracks and crevices were sealed where light might be detected. I had a light late evening meal of kippers, fish and chips along with a spot of tea. I downed the lights and crawled into the sack and for once felt too tired to read. I must have slept a bit as I was awakened by a terrific blast. Jerry was on the prowl again tonight as I could hear the drone of bombers overhead. The motors were unsynchronized so I knew their origin. Then came another blast like that of a volcano, the hospital shook and shivered following the first salvo. The plaster split and fell from my room ceiling, cascading around my bed. I got up and peered out the window. The fires were raging across the way. A glance at my watch showed it was a quarter past midnight. I then went to the door expecting some excitement—it was as quiet as a tomb and as dark as the inside of a black cow. Not a mouse was stirring in the hospital so I closed the door and crawled back into my warm sack. Outside it sounded like an inferno, the anti-aircraft guns were now in action and the steady drone of the bombers continued. Now a swoosh of the British night fighter attack force was in action. The heavy booms were more distant now for another five minutes and the sound of engines disappeared. Then it suddenly came to me that someone across the way could need help. I bounded out of bed, threw on my clothes and buttoned them as I burst out of my room, down the hall and stairs, then out in the open. Two of the most antiquated fire engines were in action to extinguish the fire. The fire engines were actively spurting out the water as two men were pumping with all their might to force the water out sufficiently to quench the roaring fire. I asked a policeman what happened to the people. "They have all taken to subterranean shelter with the first warning and there were no injuries as far as could be determined." The sky was aglow like a summer sunset to the north and west to the sea. The ferries must have come from the south across the channel and left over the North Sea. It was a really fine evening other than the miserable devastating fires and the lurid color of the north sky over the city.

On finishing my tour of duty at Hammersmith, I returned to my unit where work continued. We packed and unpacked the trucks, making them waterproof, waterproofing the boxes, folding our tents, pitching the hospital tents, exercising, going on road marches, and doing general toughening-up processes. Our daily classes were in Alexandria Hall, where medical and surgical care of the wounded was reviewed. We simulated actual casualties and how we would handle them. All in all, Cheddar will always be remembered pleasantly. Some of the enlisted men enjoyed and appreciated their friendship with the lovely girls and several of them married the girls. It was a most pleasant interlude before the terrible invasion and loss of so many men at Normandy. We had always wondered what it meant when the words "Omaha" were stamped on so many boxes. We finally found out; it was Omaha Beach Easy Red, where we were to land. For five months, we had waited and trained for the eventful day of the invasion. The weather was always rather muggy and on that day there was the usual early morning fog, which lay heavy over the entire lower British coast.

We all knew or sensed that Cheddar, England was our last pre-invasion encampment. We knew we had been fully trained and had all the confidence in our ability to carry out our duties in a most expeditious and excellent manner. We fully anticipated a full fledged war with all the horrors and misery such a large scale undertaking entails. In my estimation, there was not a solitary member of our unit who had the slightest wish or thought of turning back. I talked with the majority of our unit on individual basis. Everyone knowing that some of us would be wounded and some would perhaps be lost. They all hated war. However, as a group they were reacting as a group of well trained and skilled technicians should, quietly yet impatiently awaiting our allotted time of D-Day.

I do believe the British are surely among the most, if not the most stoic peoples on this earth. Many went about business as usual during the bombing, others would queue up quietly without hustle, haste, or bustle awaiting their turn to get into the underground shelters. On questioning the people, their attitude was why run? We may run into danger from a bloody bomb so we are just as well off when and where we stand.

Wallace Harry Graham

CHAPTER ELEVEN
JUMPING OFF

Planning of the invasion was meticulous, one of the greatest assaults ever attempted. It had to cope with enemy defenses, tides on the coast, weather on the day of invasion, even the soundness of footing on sandy beaches. Much depended on weather. Enemy defenses were formidable: the coast was filled with an underwater system of foreshore obstacles, devised and ordered by General Erwin Rommel, Counselor of the Normandy coast. He had used this system in Africa outside El Alamein where he constructed the underwater, so-called Devil's Gardens. The invasion beach had been planted with railroad rails to point into a landing ship's hull. Beaches around Normandy, including Utah and Omaha where we were to come in, were filled with mines and explosives. There were sharp, steel objects to wreck all types of landing craft, pointed steel girders tipped with explosives, wires engineered so that the slightest touch triggered mines. Inland, fields and meadows were filled with Rommel's "asparagus," huge poles and stakes set into the ground to prevent airborne landings, gliders, or planes. The success of our landings would be due, in a great part, to intelligence gained by our underwater Corps of Engineers, the Frogmen and the Sea-Bees, the Royal Navy, and many long maneuvers before the assault date.

There had been concern about the footing of sand on Normandy beaches-its texture and compactness to maintain our vehicles. A British captain took it upon himself to find out. Taken by submarine to the Normandy coast, he took a core from the beach, whereupon plans were made accordingly.

The French resistance helped our cause by sending messages and by sabotage. They inserted substances in concrete mixers such as sugar which has a devastating effect upon formation of concrete by weakening the block so that some pill boxes were easily torn apart when shells struck. Usually the French evacuated their towns when the Germans moved in, as invaders took over and used towns as headquarters. The French would take shelter, go to the open country, or live with friends in towns invaded. The German counterintelligence, the Abwehr, knew of the messages of the French through spotters who would transmit over radio. Countless messages were coming over the armed services radio. Lines of verse from a poem by Paul Verlaine were used to alert the French of key steps in the invasion at the appropriate times. Transmission of the first three lines would put the French on alert, and transmission of the second three lines meant to begin their sabotage:

> *Les sanglots longs*
> *des violons*
> *de l'automne*
> *Blessent mon coeur*
> *d'une langueur*
> *monotone*

The question was where the thrust would be, and plans called for a mock army to sail from the English shore. We have held a slight advantage. Regardless of where or when, losses would be great. Channel waters would be bloody. There were moments of worry. I learned from General Eisenhower after the war that he had questioned where the attack should take place. He told a few of us as we gathered in a sitting room in the Sheraton in Washington. I was next to the General and across from President Truman. Others present were Clark Clifford, advisor to the President, Maj. Gen. Harry Vaughn, military aide to the President, and George Allen, friend of Eisenhower and Truman. "I used every possible bit of information in the determination of weather, winds, turbulence, and tides," the general said. "I knew there would be no one to blame but me if I made the wrong decision on the date and place to attack. My original decision was to attack along the coasts of the Cherbourg—Le Havre area, but this communique was never sent."

The Normandy invasion, with the code "Overlord D-Day," had been designated by Eisenhower to begin on the morning of 5 June, and if it were not feasible because of weather or if the movement had not gone too far to change, the general would change it to 6 June, early morning. The date of 4 June brought extremely bad weather with practically no visibility and high waves. Some units had put to sea, but the invasion was called off and the Navy rushed their destroyers to head them off. If troops had gone on assault in those high seas, they would have been seasick and lost their edge. Next day brought no relief, but it was set for 6 June. If that date failed, the operation could not begin for two weeks, and the prospect of keeping a secret with a hundred forty thousand men waiting would be slim.

The question of tides was of extreme importance, as the Normandy beach was flooded twice daily by mountainous, crested waves that rose about twenty feet from low to high tide. Defenses of the beach were exposed at low tide. At low tide, landing craft would be grounded between four-hundred and four-hundred-fifty yards offshore, a full quarter of a mile of open sandy beach for soldiers to cover, while enemy guns were trained on them: a costly landing. The time of assault was to be rising tide, which would give engineers thirty minutes to clear main obstacles and detonate explosives before the water became too deep. Assault waves would arrive on the rising tide closer to the sea wall through gaps made in the line of obstacles. The invasion was to attack 6 June in the early hours after daylight. Daylight would help the Navy spot targets and permit the Air Force to exact their bombing mission, and meet the tidal conditions. Daylight would allow troops to be seen by defenders. Even so, there was no choice. Prior to the assault landings, we had x-type midget submarines to guide our landing ship's course by light signals. Engineers spent many dangerous, fearful, cautious hours and days defusing and neutralizing hundreds of mines and underwater explosives prior to invasion, allowing us to drive in when a rising tide hit the obstacle line. The magnitude and ferocity of the Normandy assault was overwhelming in the initial thrust by allied armies of two hundred thousand fighting men. The objective was under the greatest of hazards.

Our ingenuity nonetheless was able to put allied armies in position with twenty thousand vehicles and hundreds of tanks. At the D-Day invasion the British went in on Gold and Sword beaches, in line with Caen. The destroyer *Augusta* struck out across the main-swept and rugged Channel, accompanied by multiple landing craft, all with a huge overhead barrage balloon. Our men were surrounded by several fast destroyers, screening them seaward into and across the rough Channel. The weather was miserable, and fog so dense it saved us from Luftwaffe attack. Because of winds and overcast, the enemy was sure nothing could venture across the Channel. The enemy had grounded Luftwaffe units, canceled naval patrols, and kept minelayers in port. The invasion plan had been discovered by Admiral Canaris, chief of the German Abwehr, who had reported to Admiral Henneicke that it would be on 6 June. Henneicke was in Cherbourg. Rommel had been there but had left to meet Hitler. When the invasion did take place, Henneicke was advised that heavy bombers and paratroops were striking the coast and inland towns throughout the peninsula. This caught them by surprise, since they had been sure the weather would have prevented the attack.

Two days before D-Day, the 101st Airborne had dropped north and east of Carentan and generally behind Utah and Omaha Beach. The

82nd Airborne Division was dropped Northwest of the 101st and was to command the crossroads to Sainte-Mère-Église, before dawn of D-Day. Both divisions had many objectives. As soon as a plane goes into enemy territory every paratrooper stands and is hooked up ready to jump. Then the C-47 bounces with repercussions of shells. The jump from the plane is hazardous enough, with the possibility of jumping into one another, or one's canopy not opening. The world is dark, the only light being from the blast of the anti-aircraft at the troopers and cross lights of the enemy switching around trying to find where paratroopers were dropping. Paratroopers oftentimes were caught in the searchlight. Then machine guns, mortars, and every mechanized machine was thrown at the descending trooper. Hundreds of brave men were lost before they had a chance even to show their firepower. The trooper cannot always see where he is jumping, but can see fires below, caused by the bombing raid that has just taken place.

Troopers depend on pilots to take them to the correct level and drop zone. Pilots are supposed to drop Airborne troops at seven- to eight-hundred feet because it takes five-hundred to seven-hundred feet for the chute to open. Many dropped from two-hundred-fifty feet and less, and with this drop zone being a deep-water marsh and not the chosen site, and with low height of this drop being two hundred to two hundred fifty feet; if the trooper's chute did happen to open, chances were he would be drowned. It is safer for the pilot if he goes under the radar, but this is at expense of the trooper's life. If the plane is going too fast, it throws the jump off. To jump at a level of two-hundred feet or anything less than three-hundred is nothing short of certain death: many chutes did not open. Many have reported how they saw their buddies chutes pulling out of the pack trays and just barely starting to unfurl when they hit the ground. In one special jump around twenty men hit the ground before their chutes had time to open. It was most unfortunate in airborne drops that some pilots were apparently fearful of getting shot if they were at the height where the radar could pick them up. Pilots also could see other planes hit and falling. Some planes came in too fast. It looked as if airborne troops were dropped from two- to three-hundred feet. Many who were injured were brought into our hospital stations, some of whom had been shot while hanging in trees where they had been dropped and tangled; many were shot in swamps. It was a miserable melee and many airborne troopers were vociferous about how a few Air Force pilots had scattered them along the peninsula. Some dropped as far as twenty miles from the zone of intention, where the area was heavily manned by German troops. If they escaped the Germans and mortal injury, they had to fight like demons through town after town, against great odds, in enemy strongholds, to get back to the rendezvous.

Several men were dropped in the English Channel. I talked with one who lived to tell about it and he said that nearly all of the men dropped in the Channel were drowned.

But it is amazing that many of our planes got through despite anti-aircraft shells, rockets, and tracers. If a plane was hit in a crucial area it would explode. I have seen many a plane trying to cripple home after many hits. One time I felt compelled to yell at the pilot, "Land in the field you are in." He was trying to get back to England. The plane then took a nose dive straight into the earth.

All troops dropped had been issued tin crickets; when pressed and released they would click-clack for identification. In event the metal cricket was lost, the passwords were "Flash-Thunder-Welcome." Crickets and passwords saved many lives, but lost a few. In one area a German found the secret, took the metal crickets he found, and when our men gave the return signal they were shot.

In hours of darkness on D-day morning any sound of gunfire was from the enemy. Orders were given in England that there was to be no sound, no firing from rifle, pistol, or machine gun. Our troops were only to use knives, bayonets, or hand grenades; the grenade, when thrown, would not reveal the position of the thrower.

Gliders could not land because of the so-called "asparagus tips," huge logs placed upright in vacant fields. One glider landed on top of a German barracks. A medical officer landed in this glider and was hit by machine gun fire. We counted thirty-eight bullets in his bowel. Oddly enough, this major lived.

Our day had arrived, and we were now to become part of the war machine flung at the enemy. We left our post. As we marched to the depot in the rain we were impressed by the lack of cheers. Could it possibly be a dry run? We had a short, uneventful train ride and reached our destination by mid-afternoon. The weather continued heavy; rainwater dripped from helmets. We were told this sort of weather was not unusual. Rain was always misty with heavy, low clouds, not a soaking rain. But, in the week prior to leaving for invasion it was a little heavier.

The morning of our arrival there was tension in the air. In the pre-dawn darkness, waves of British Royal Air Force night-time bombers saturated the enemy coastline defenses. The second attack was by waves of U.S. heavy bombers and medium bombers at dawn just prior to our landing. The pinpoint firing by big guns of the Navy gave support. Our landing began at H-hour, thirty minutes after dawn and was to be no later than one and one-half hours before the enemy could recover from the Royal Air Force attack. The invasion did not go so smoothly as anticipated. General Rommel had reserves ready to back coastal defense, making his so-called

Atlantic wall. The fortified wall would not halt an intruder, but it would slow him down enough for reserves to counterattack. Beaches were loaded with barbed wire and teller mines. Rails pointed to the sea so as to rip out bellies of landing craft, and like the beaches, bluffs were permeated with teller mines. The atmosphere was shattered by radios screaming of the long-awaited invasion. We were tense, but this was intermingled with a sense of elation and our esprit-de-corps was high. This was in part due to ignorance. We were ready, trucks loaded, and well on our way to the embarking area, called Land's End.

We boarded trucks to the marshaling area, called Truro, not far from Falmouth, on the southern coast of England, our port of embarkation. There we crowded into pyramidal tents, ten to a tent. We were issued D.D.T. powder, Halazone tablets for water purification, filled burners, and Dramamine tablets to prevent seasickness. We were all given K and C-rations and then went to the port of embarkation in Falmouth Harbor. Men from our outfit will never forget the USO group, established by the Salvation Army, our favorites, as they were the only ones we found who gave doughnuts and coffee free. They handed them out by the hundreds to all of us embarking from the Channel before the invasion. The USO had little buildings and trucks. In one was a small band tooting out tunes while cooks passed out coffee and doughnuts.

We waited in the yard for about an hour, had final roll-call, then at the crucial moment we double-timed up to the pier and waited along the small Liberty ship called the *Francis Drake*. We boarded it approximately an hour later at 2100 hours, and anchors were hoisted at 0215 hours 9 June 1944. We were shown bunks to be used while crossing the Channel. Breakfast was 0500, of 10-1 rations, D-rations eaten slowly, taking a half hour.

Nurses went over on the same ship and were an admirable, hardy bunch. Everyone of them deserves praise. There was not a weak one among them. They buckled down just like the men and proved their worth. They took all the rough and-rugged work like the best of soldiers with no complaints because they realized they were in it. Although the area where we embarked had been a favorite place for the Luftwaffe to bomb, weather was so heavy and fog so thick we did not hear any Luftwaffe planes and we were not the least disappointed. Fortunately we were not discovered. Barrage balloons were cabled to fly over ships to keep enemy planes from diving on us. Their pilots feared becoming entangled with the wires leading to them.

We cleared submarine nets as they opened into Falmouth harbor, and an armada joined our convoy as we steamed into the Channel. It seemed as if the U S. Navy was following the *Francis Drake*. Ships with balloons resembled small zeppelins because of their silver cigar shapes.

This sight as far as the eye could see followed to the farthest line of the horizon. The most gratifying display was the massive air escort as planes of all descriptions zoomed. We had several thrills as our ears detected loud blasting and our ship began to roll and heave. We were sure we either had a hit or near miss from a submarine. The speaker announced that the sudden upheaval was from depth charges laid by our destroyer escorts, as we were in U boat waters. If any U boat had been in proximity it would have been crushed. Time came to hit the sack or bunk, if one could sleep. We awoke before dawn, nearing the coast. Now we heard bursts of gunfire and heavy artillery. The great ships opened fire. The *Augusta* I recall sent volleys of steel into enemy lines.

An LCT [Landing Craft Tank] came alongside the *Drake* and Major Edwards came aboard—he was in our advance party sent ahead on D-day as reconnaissance officer. Our surgical section was to land immediately and proceed to the 51st Field Hospital to relieve medics there, who were at the point of exhaustion, They had been operating continuously, day and night, since D-day. Three trucks rolled out of the lower deck of our ship and were loaded on the LCT.

Our surgical section climbed down the starboard side of the *Drake* with full packs. We had been trained in going down rope cargo nets, holding onto the vertical rungs without getting fingers stepped on. Transfer was difficult as the sea was rough and the LCT bounding. We had to wait for the LCT to bound up as we let down, otherwise risk fractures. Wind and waves were fairly high, causing us to toss and rock. The LCT proceeded to pull into "Easy Red" on Omaha Beach. Its huge gate dropped down as we neared the beach; some of us jumped on the trucks, others walked through the knee-deep water.

I had never known why the term "Easy Red" had been designated for this landing area, but the thought soon struck. Here were half-buried bodies beneath the bloody sand. Easy Red had been attained at bloody cost, but was it easy? Bodies of our brave heroes, some of whom had fallen here, others washed ashore on the littered beach studded with debris of battle and grounded ships and tanks. Here on this small strip of sand seven thousand of our men gave their lives for the rest of our nation to live in freedom.

Over the beach, a tape-lined path had been placed, so we followed it, deviating neither side of a narrow roadway, as mines had not yet been cleared. Sporadic shooting sounded, but main sounds of war were five miles inland. We proceeded to our objective atop the sharp rise overlooking the beach. None of us will ever forget the realization that we were in France, but the sight on that stretch of sandy beach had been a horror.

Insignia on officers' helmets were smeared with mud to prevent snipers from recognizing us, because we would be prize bait for the fatherland. We went in on the beach in "Easy Red Omaha" where there were many reminders of what had taken place. Bodies of the brave had been taken over the beach and interred near LaCambe. We went into the area of pillboxes and climbed up the sandy hill. Assault troops of the 1st Infantry Division and the great 29th Blue and Gray Division under Major General Charles H. Gerhardt had taken the Omaha Beach, silenced the pillboxes and moved inland at great cost. It was nearing midnight, fog was clearing at that time, and suddenly it seemed as if all hell was loose. Occasional Luftwaffe planes hit the beach and anchored ships, along with an American airstrip. Antiaircraft guns opened simultaneously with big navy guns. Lead and steel split the air in great bursts. The ground trembled and shook. As I crouched, a 155mm shell "whooshed" over my head. It was then that I became acquainted with some of the sounds and sizes of shells. The 155mm "whoosh" was one of our own shells. The Germans were using the 88, which gave a distinctive whine as it passed overhead. We wondered how the infantrymen could cross an eight hundred-foot beach, crawl up the sharp incline of loose sand, and round the upright natural, high sharp ten-foot rise surrounding pillboxes, under enemy fire. Here the guns of General von Rundstedt's troops were on a rise, looking down on hundreds of running, crawling, zig-zagging forms. Machine guns and 88mm cannon protruded from openings below the rounded heads of concrete pill boxes, which were built into the ground for the most part, and with rounded concrete top above the ground; barrels pointed at invaders trying to take the beachhead. See the picture? Reflect, and you transpose yourself into a blazing, murderous nightmare of flying hot steel.

Our graves division accomplished a tremendous task in removing torn, lifeless bodies. Medics braved fire and shell to retrieve wounded, some having been treated by stopping the flow of blood from gaping wounds, others by binding in and pressuring open abdominal and chest wounds, and by dragging the injured back to receive more help. Every fighting man believes that once medics have him he will live. The beach was strewn with litter, belts, tattered clothing, and some equipment. We reached the top of the incline and crags, stopped a few moments to catch our breath, then sprawled on the slopes, and adjusted our loads. We reflected on yesterday, then looked forward to the flat ground ahead where we could treat new casualties with better facilities. Naval guns were blazing; projectiles of destruction were striking enemy positions five-ten-fifteen-twenty miles distant, with phenomenal accuracy. As we moved over the hard-fought ground, we heard battle sounds. We could not differentiate the sounds at this point—armor-piercing bullets, intermittent with tracers and flares that passed over us, then dropping like Roman candles. Tracers and anti-aircraft shells streaked skyward, then rockets blasted out and down like Fourth of July fireworks. The sky filled with this rain of death.

Wounded that we received were continually looking for and asking about buddies. One of the wounded from the 29th told us that within ten minutes after lowering the ramp from his LCT every commissioned and non-commissioned officer and all but five of the men had been killed or wounded: any in that wave who survived stayed in the water. They would move in slowly with the tide and just get enough air to exist by bobbing their noses above water occasionally. Assault company boats were blown to the heavens. Cries for corpsmen and stretchers rang out. The living sought shelter behind the dead. The machine-gun crossfire was deadly accurate. Pointblank anti-tank 75 and 80mm guns fired through smoke and machine-gun bursts. Men would drown from the sheer weight of equipment. Some were saved by being sheltered by the high steel defense barriers under water while others became entangled in barbed wire. Assault regiments of the 1st Division found it almost impossible to get beyond a hundred feet of the approximately eight hundred feet. They crawled, dug, or ran through loose sand. It was incredible that anyone made it. The plan was, however, to continue, wave after wave, regardless of casualties—the objective must be gained. Omaha Beach was about three to four miles long, and after six hours there were four thousand dead or seriously wounded. Armor tanks and vehicles were smashed. By tenacity and spot-firing of our Navy, Sea-Bees, engineers, Rangers, and infantry, the men managed to silence a gun at a time. By crawling to a pillbox and blasting it with fire, grenades, and mortars, each mound was conquered.

The German high command was convinced that the British under Montgomery would hit Caen for a big dash fifty miles to the Seine and one hundred twenty miles to Paris. Actually the British were to act as a decoy to attract the German army, which they did. The Germans sent their reserves racing to Caen, leaving the U.S. Army to advance more rapidly and engulf the enemy. The high command could not be shaken from belief that the primary landing was a feint: the actual invasion would come through Pas de Calais.

A few hours after our second group hit the beachhead they were sitting in a pouring, drenching rain. The sky was dark because of a severe storm. We wondered if the beachhead would ever be consolidated. We dared not walk outside the marked limits for fear of mines. About one hundred yards from the beach we saw a small group of tents, a few ambulances, and litter bearers hurrying with loads of injured. We found this a small Field

Hospital, the 51st, and personnel doing their best to care for wounded. The casualty load was much too heavy so we doffed our backpacks, unloaded, scrubbed, put on masks and gowns, and went to work.

Beds of the 51st hospital were full of patients waiting to be assigned. Wounded patients were coming in by stretcher. We saw wounded lying on cots, raising their heads, staring at us. Here were our wounded, still in the middle of a battlefield, the battle raging. At onset of the artillery attack, several of us newcomers hit the ground, not knowing whether percussion and shell bursts were from our artillery or the enemy. We were assured that most of the shelling was from our own batteries. We no sooner arrived than a large, high-explosive shell burst close by. Several men dived under tables for a few moments, knees shaking, until they learned how foolish their actions were, as tables could protect nothing.

Veterans of the two-day battle informed us that the barrage we just went through was all from our own guns and artillery, which they called "outgoing mail." It just takes time to learn. We learned that when we got to our tasks and kept busy, there was no fear. We were too busy to consider personal safety. We wiped sweat from our face, re-scrubbed, put on gowns, masks, and gloves, and began. Wounded areas were scrubbed by the scrub team in the holding area, and carried into the large surgical tent and placed upon the operating table. Wounded were administered the proper anesthesia. Captains Cake, Van Dyke, and Kuhndahl were at our side tables with anesthesia. Occasional "heavy mail" (large, high-explosive shells) would come in over our heads and crash beyond us.

In the not-too-far distance we could hear the rattle of small arms, to which we became accustomed. The Luftwaffe was out to bomb ships, and was hitting the harbor, the American airstrip, the neighboring airfield. Planes roared overhead as the sky lit with bomb blasts from our 90mm guns and ack-ack. Ground shook like an earthquake from artillery bombardment and naval guns fired at distant objectives.

We worked for the next two days and nights, never a lull. This was our first setup in the field. But, our operation moved efficiently and we carried our share for the 1st Army. On the third day we moved out past the 51st Field into an orchard where most of us spent the night. Nurses remained in the Field Hospital until the following day. Colonel Rylander and a few officers proceeded a few more miles where the advance party began setting up our hospital near LaCambe, where on we were admitting wounded for ten days. The advance party for the 24th Evac returned to the 51st on 12 June 1944, and we of the 24th moved out and set up our hospital there. Some of our group had stayed aboard the landing ship until 1 June. They disembarked at night on rope ladders and landed on the Normandy Beach from an LST (Landing Ship Tank). This was just the beginning. Little did they realize what fate had in store for them. After they cleared the beachhead they were taken to the first operating area and then met us. By 14 June we were functioning full blast, receiving casualties, some only five, ten, or fifteen minutes from the battle.

The 24th Evacuation Unit was in full swing. In ten days we had admitted and treated 1,146 wounded. After the second day the 45th Evacuation Hospital landed and gave us help. The 45th Evacuation joined us and we all did double duty for the heavy load. While I was operating, an officer came up to me and asked a question—I looked up and here was a long-time friend, Captain Stoughton White, urologist from Kansas City, who came over the beach with the 45th Evac. There had been a gale and heavy storm, and landing craft could not get onto Omaha Beach because of the high waves and sea, so the 45th held off and operations delayed three days. Equipment of the 45th Evacuation Hospital came in a bit later. Captain White's unit had to clear out a mine-field before they could set up. Infantry that had just passed through failed to clear the field and it was up to the medics. The 45th Evac helped us for a short time before we both moved on.

An Evacuation Hospital, one should relate, is a hospital for immediate care and evacuation of wounded. Patients from our unit would pass to General Hospitals away from any battleground. It is doubtful if our hospital functioned as a true evacuation hospital. The man who was wounded on the field would be seen and cared for within minutes by the aid or corps man, or by fellow soldiers. Walking casualties were directed to the nearest aid station. If incapable of walking, the wounded would be transported by litter or jeep. At times wounded would go to the clearing station if closer to the line of battle. The clearing station would evaluate the condition of wounded and send the casualties to the Evacuation Hospital. More often than not, however, we received casualties direct from the battlefield as we were so close.

Our hospital had highly qualified surgeons in the specialties. We received and treated wounded in every category. As soon as their condition was stable they were evacuated to the General Hospital, often in England or the United States by plane. We attended immediately to wounds. Teams reserved clothing, kept the wounded warm, and evaluated, cleansed wounds, and sent wounded to x-ray. A tag fastened to each casualty noted the type of wound—caliber bullet, mine, high explosive, bayonet, or small arms fire. Parts injured were noted for x-ray and surgeons. Vital signs were noted. X-ray reports were immediate, with name attached. Each wound was noted separately, except multiple wounds on chest, back, head, or extremities.

Our organization worked well and always with thought of improvement. We altered our arrangement of big tents several times, to find the best, two large ward tents sewn side-by-side. The regulation ward tent gave fifteen by sixteen feet, room for three operating tables. We opened the side flaps, giving us a large operating theater an expanse of fifty by forty feet, and length of one hundred twenty feet. We kept nine surgical tables busy with every influx of casualties. Our surgical theater formed a large letter "H". We placed tables according to:

1. Neurosurgery (head, spine and nerve wounds)
2. Maxillo-facial
3. Orthopedic surgery; adjacent with Hawley table for body casts and hip spica casts
4. Two tables for minor surgery, interchangeable; three tables for general surgery

Two shifts worked daily from eight to eight, one shift starting in the morning, working until evening, and the second shift picking up in the evening, working through the night until the next morning. Each had eight to ten operating surgeons, five anesthetists, ten technicians, and five to seven registered nurses.

In the adjacent area was the entry and preparation room, attached to the main surgery tent. Here eight wounded men on litters were made ready for surgery. This setup ensured a flow of casualties. One man controlled traffic to and from surgery. Three technicians were in the "prep" areas for surgery, cutting casts after application in the operating room.

Attached to the large amphitheater was a central supply room which provided sterile materials, instruments, and trays, with one nurse and three technicians on each shift. Another arm of the letter was the dressing room and scrub room for surgery, with one section for records. Completing the fourth arm of the "H" was the separate operating tent for infected wounds admitted with gas gangrene or obviously purulent wounds and with potential of spread. This area was under supervision for decontamination, never allowing one to leave this tent and enter a clean area without new scrub and change of clothes.

The compact arrangement of our mobile Evacuation Hospital was excellent for care of wounded—the arrangement with the receiving tent adjacent to the X-ray and shock wards on one side and post-operative and evacuation ward on the other. This formed a large ring, with our big tent the jewel in the center. Our average operating daily load was one hundred twenty casualties in twenty-four hours. Average surgical procedures were much greater.

Practically every wounded soldier had multiple wounds. Rarely did we find only one wound, as our casualties were from machine-gun and mortar fire, land mines that splattered fragments of steel into a man at every angle, antipersonnel shells, high explosives, the dreaded and accurate 88-caliber cannon the Germans handled like a rifle, hand grenades, and skull crushers from tremendous concussive blasts. All these instruments of the devil contributed to multiple wounds. Every one we investigated, cleaned, and debrided of foreign bodies.

We surviving members of our hospital unit have been sickened by the display of foolishness and horse play in the television account of MASH unit hospital. We treated every wounded man with dignity.

Blood and plasma bottles were hanging by each litter in the shock ward; dirty, bloody clothing was cut off, tourniquets removed or applied, bleeding vessels clamped as prepared for surgery. The wounded were sedated, prepared, and scrubbed by efficient personnel. In contrast to the serious and quiet atmosphere of the shock ward, #4 was always buzzing like a hive.

Less seriously wounded patients in this tent would be talking and comparing experiences as they waited for surgery. Some would lie there with legs and arms in splints, quietly staring at tent poles, thinking of home and thanking the good Lord that their wounds were not too serious. Many were wanting to get back to their units, as they were badly needed, others were hoping their wounds would take them home. Post-operative tents were set up rapidly to receive patients brought by litter from surgery. The quiet was broken only by a moan here and there as patients became restless and aroused from anesthesia. They were attired in fresh white plaster casts or large gauze bandages, awaiting evacuation to general hospitals or to England.

Medical wards had their share of medications and shots to be given. Here and there a lad sounded hysterical. Men sat under blankets having malarial chills, to remind them of days in Sicily or North Africa. I recall one patient who was a deep yellow color, which could have been secondary to atabrine medication for malaria, but he happened to be a victim of infectious hepatitis contracted from combat days.

The operating room of the 24th Evacuation Hospital was the center of activity. Surgery tents meant work day and night. Operating rooms were analogous to a three-ring circus. All departments worked smoothly: I have never seen such efficiency. Internal medical problems were taken care of in another section, where consultation made surgery possible when needed.

A patient would not be brought to the operating room unless all X-rays were ready, so x-rays were taken in that section adjacent to surgery with laboratory procedure including blood counts, blood reports, plasma protein determination, and other essential or special reports ordered by surgeon or internist. Tests taken there were a guide to our difficult and seriously wounded patients.

Final check on our surgery came with the work of the so-called Ward Thirty, where surgical Aesculapian meetings took place. Good surgery is useless without vigilant nurses and care by ward men. Infectious conditions and contagious diseases were kept in isolation.

CHAPTER TWELVE
INITIATION INTO BATTLE

The group that took care of the American bodies was the "graves registration team." They followed a division into battle also. After the battle had been fought and the area practically cleared of combatants and it had quieted down a bit, the graves registration team moved in and would gather the bodies all at one point to take them back to a central cemetery.

One very large cemetery was out of LaCambe, France, a little beyond where we had set tents just over the Normandy beach at Easy Red, Omaha Beach. Within fourteen days, more than 16,000 of our wounded were evacuated from the Omaha Beach area. A cemetery just over the beach was ready to accept several thousand more.

The psychology of the wounded varied considerably; a few were bitter, some sincere in wanting to get back to their units as soon as possible; some even demanding to return when their wounds were closed and they could stand after coming out from under the anesthesia. Some were imbued with the fact that they were such a skilled and integral part of the fighting unit that the unit could not survive without their individual help. They had learned about the enemy and they knew how to kill. Others were happy to be out of it; they had not learned how to deal out death and would rather have accepted it themselves. That is how and why many have been wounded or killed. It is no easy matter to negate the so-called Christian precepts or the ten commandments, or to forget that every human life is sacred. Those who had not been properly indoctrinated and imbued with both hatred for the enemy, self preservation, and knowing they must kill or be killed, ended as objects for the graves detail. Survivors learned by hard experience, (battlewise seasoning), and some by a practical attitude that they were fighting as an integral part for the ideal of freedom. Most fought as men have fought since time began—for survival; and the fittest survive.

In the LaCambe area, we received numerous unusual types of wounds. Many projectiles would leave only bruised marks on the skin, while others would penetrate. On retrieving some of the projectiles we found they were hollow, wooden bullets, some of which splintered and caused considerable damage to the lung tissue and other tissues. This was particularly difficult to control from the standpoint of secondary infections. Retrieval was difficult as the wood could not be defined or visualized by our x-ray.

It was learned from the German wounded that some of their soldiers had exhausted their live ammunition and were reverting to wooden bullets which they had been using in this area during their maneuvers (war games). The Germans would fire between hedge rows with these wooden bullets, but the velocity with penetrating power would frequently be lost. It could, however, be used effectively at close range, firing on the troops advancing through the open space between the hedge rows.

The hedge rows in Normandy, France are similar to a farmers field in the United States, however they are much smaller in Normandy. In the United States, the boundary of a man's farm is surrounded by a fence, whereas in France the small square plot is surrounded by high banks of earth with a dense growth of roots and trees along the embankment which acts as a boundary between similar square fields.

The Germans would dig into the hedge rows and use them as underground pits to leap in or dig their gun emplacements in solidly such as mortars, machine guns, or an 88 cannon. Between each square bit of land and the hedge row is a small roadway adequately wide to pass a small car like a jeep or cart. The other farmer's plot then begins with another hedge row on the opposite side of the roadway.

One major factor I neglected to note before was the vigor and ferocity with which our fighting men attacked. Another great advantage was our obvious, overwhelmingly continuous supply and reserves. The enemy casualties were also very impressed with the above, as well as the knowledge that our wounded were taken care of so efficiently and fast. They recognized the massive air power which was ever present. All were amazed at the tremendous fire power of the navy with their guns hurling explosive projectiles many miles right on target.

The 29th Division was moving on down on the Cotentin area while Big Red of the 1st Division went north to meet the British and while on the way the Big Red 1st Division soldiers knocked out small enemy pockets, and we were collecting their casualties. The destroyers, *Augusta* and *Texas*, were continuing to slam in the shells.

We were also getting casualties from the 29th Division when they were in Isigny and Carentan; some continued to come from the 101st Airborne.

We were told that evening that the 101st had smashed Carentan and the Navy and the 29th had smashed Isigny. On 13 June, the Germans threw a counter attack against Carentan. Our German casualties would often sneer and tell us they would massacre us at Calais—the Germans continued to be convinced that the Normandy beach landings were only a diversionary thrust.

Our troops fought exceptionally well, even though it is really a severe mental shock for new or green troops facing death. It is real terror at first to face the wounded with their agony and the horror of wasted life. After a few days of advance battle, the stark reality of war and death is learned. They knew they were there to fight and that it may be their time to be sacrificed. At this time the majority, if not all of us, had steeled our minds and had psychologically adjusted our morale. We knew our duty and set ourselves accordingly. We were determined to fulfill our tasks and that absolutely nothing could daunt our efforts.

Neither my unit nor I, ever at any time looked upon war as a thrilling adventure as depicted by some movies. The real soul suffering, agonizing pain of not only the wounded, but the abject loneliness from loved ones. The mutilation of mind and body followed by silence, with days, weeks, and months of depression. Only the battlefield soldier and the war-worn weary know and understand. We were now living in a world of constant pressure, terror, and fear.

Almost every man out of battle wanted to know how the battle was coming along, where the advances were, and where the weakness was evident, as well as the overall picture. These are men from civilian life never wanting the ferocity of war. They know about Hitler and his hordes, the atrocities and murdering of millions of people who want to also live in peace the same as anyone. They have been thrust into bloody battle. They know that every attempt has been made to reason to bargain for peace, not however, for the loss of individual freedom. They know that force is now the only way to neutralize the powerful and ruthless demagogue.

On 18 June 1944, several of us had been in surgery for a continuous forty-eight hours. The orthopedic team of Captains Hogan, Van Dyke, Kuhndahl, and Sergeants Horrell and Thalberg and I beat a retreat to the field about thirty-five yards from our back tent where our slit trenches were ready for us. They were fairly close, being about five yards apart. We flopped in them and I snuggled and dug around a bit until my hips fit. We were nearly asleep when we heard the intermittent sound of firing of small arms fire followed by occasional snap or whine of a bullet. Captain Dan Hogan raised up and said, "Some son of a bitch is shooting at us."

I looked over to one side and said, "I doubt that."

Sergeant Gordon Thalberg shouted out, "Some G.I.s shootin' squirrels."

Sergeant Horrell answered, "Hell, we're the only squirrels out here; just dig in deeper, and keep your tail down."

At that time, I looked up and heard a snap of a bullet, and saw a divot of grass popping up, which the bullet caused. I knew then someone was shooting at us, so instead of staying quietly in the slit trench where it was safe, I thought I would get back to the tent to warn them and notify the military police. I told the others to lie quietly and I would report it, so I jumped up out of my slit trench and started to run, but was stung in the posterior medial aspect of my right arm. It didn't actually wound me seriously, but it certainly scared me when it penetrated my clothes. I ran into our casualty ward, but discovered there was no injury other than a flesh burn. The report was made, then I took a Tetanus booster shot and went to another slit trench where I caught a few hours of needed sleep.

Later in the evening, we were told the sniper had been caught. The sniper was found to be a young French girl, nineteen years of age, who had been in love with a German officer who had taught her to be a sniper. She had been there in a tree the entire day with her food, rifle, and ammo. We were told she had killed seven men. The Military Police mopping up operations caught her, had a summary court martial and that ended the problem.

Snipers are trained to be skilled marksmen, be they he or she. They are also experts in the art of camouflage, and are usually so well concealed they are not found until they at least have accounted well for themselves. Many victims are killed before the sniper escapes through a well planned route, or are themselves spotted and killed. They are usually found to one side of where individuals frequent, whether it is a watering place, crossroads, gateway, or where a straggler would be found.

Every hour we were busy with the wounded. The major dirty wounds were treated by meticulous cleansing, debridement, dusting well with sulfa powder, then layering with antiseptic gauze. Some wounds were closed primarily and drains left in place. Abdominal wounds were opened and thoroughly inspected, then the wounds were closed, drains placed, and the abdomen closed, or a colostomy established as a temporary safety measure. All wounds were carefully handled and the wounded men were flown to England, often for secondary closures when the wounds were primarily infected. The majority of wounds were considered infected when over two to three hours had expired since infliction or when obviously contaminated.

Injuries from land mines were notoriously infected, and we found many unusual foreign bodies embedded in the wounds. I found another man's hand in an open abdominal wound from a land mine. Often we found cow or horse manure, clothing, mud, and scrap iron embedded in wounds. All were treated with sulfa drugs internally as well as externally.

The area around LaCambe was particularly hazardous due to the many land mines which were placed about five yards apart. Many of these spots had been taped off, but due to the fast movement of the troops the mines had not all been cleared out. There were several types of land mines that were a considerable hazard to us, but one of them was particularly devastating. It was called the "Bouncing Betty." When this was triggered, it would be thrown into the air and explode tremendously to about the height of the abdomen and would tear men completely apart. The explosion would send the steel pieces flying immediately in all directions with a tremendous velocity, and flare out like the spokes of a wagon wheel with circumferential range. I have seen many soldiers who were almost torn in half by these explosive-type mines. We went through the mid portion of the hedge-row and an 88mm cannon would often be located in the corner of the hedge-row or in a strategic position, but impossible to see, and one couldn't judge if the enemy was on one side or the other; as the area had been sprayed with machine gun fire before our soldiers started through the middle. The 88mm (shell) cannon of the enemy was used with straight-on fire rather than being a long range missile, and being used as short range fire, it was extremely devastating. An 88mm shell would tear the body asunder, completely disintegrating half the body with a direct hit.

One of the most devastating types of fighting was through the hedge-rows. Another tremendous problem which caused the loss of many of our men was that when we fired our arms or rifles from the hedge-rows, the enemy could see the smoke curl up immediately. The Germans used a smokeless powder so that it was impossible to see exactly where it came from, and our men could not zero in accurately on the enemy.

The hedges were at times so thick it was impossible to tell an enemy was there, even if he were only five feet away. Several times we found helmets which had been pierced completely by a shell, but had not pierced the lining of the helmet. The velocity of the shell had pierced the metal helmet and had gone between the plastic liner and the metal helmet and made an exit from the back. We often found the bullets had just gone through the helmet and then simply dropped out. My own helmet had been struck by a piece of flying shrapnel and jarred my head back considerably, but it only split the front protrusion of the helmet. It jarred me so that I was sure I had been struck in the head. I began talking out loud to myself and giving myself a few mental tests to be sure I was all right. However, there was just a scratch mark on my forehead which was bleeding. As far as I was concerned the helmet had saved my life.

The Military Police always warned us to be very careful passing any clump of trees, because there were German snipers or German sympathizers who had been left behind and were very highly trained sharp shooters. They were often young girls. I told the MPs that we had a foray of this type just a little over the beach and he very well understood and knew of the incident, as he was still bandaged from action from the same nineteen-year-old girl who had taken shots at us while sleeping in our slit trenches. We found also returning and going into small towns that there was practically no town in which the church steeple had been left, as we had bombed them level. There was no tall edifice of any type in any town, because the German snipers were usually found in the towers of the church steeples or other areas where they could easily observe our approach and use this elevation as a fire direction center.

A very interesting facet in our setup out of LaCambe was that in one of our forays, I found quite a stand of horses that the American Army had taken over. I discovered that they were horses formerly owned by White Russians, and had been either conscripted or taken into the German Army where they were used in fighting by the German cavalry units. Several captured, wounded Russians were with the Germans, but we could not understand at first why they were with them. They were White Russians, some of whom had come over of their own volition; however, some had been captured and taken along with a division or two of the Mongols. The Mongols were with the Russian Armies who had been conscripted to fight for the Germans.

An incident occurred when we were encamped in tents and taking many casualties in the area of LaCambe along the Normandy coast. We were under heavy shelling and a few of the homes close by were smashed out completely. We picked up some wounded and dead civilians in the field and among them was a grandmother who had been killed along with a mother and a father, but their two young children were alive. The mother and the father had been killed by shell fragments, and we discovered they were both medical doctors, Dr. Bernard and Mrs. Dr. Hue. The two children were Bernard and Marie Louise Hue. They had both been slightly wounded, so I treated their wounds and brought them back to our encampment. I had hoped to adopt them and keep them with me as long as I could, but the order was given that they must be transferred back. We sent them back to a convent nearby with some of the other civilian wounded, but I later went back to the convent and tried to get papers to adopt them. I also worked through our French Ambassador in this attempt. It was a very difficult time and we were still under fire, but they had no one to protect them other than the nuns at the convent. I had made clearances for the two children, and it was quite satisfactory with my family to adopt them and to keep them in their religion. I told the nuns that I would sign all papers to that effect. However, it didn't seem to register very well, and sadly the adoption was not allowed by the nuns. I often wonder how the children fared.

Often our energies were taxed as the fighting intensified and we saw many of our brave young men who were practically torn apart. The battle casualties came in by ambulance, jeep, trucks, tanks, half-tracks, or by any mode of conveyance available at the battle lines; fifty or more at a time, and over four hundred on some days. In times like this our splendid nurses revealed bravery, compassion, kindness, and superb professional care, with words of encouragement to these young men, urging them to hold on to life and look forward to better tomorrows in spite of the tragic situation confronting them. Many times have I heard them reassuring the wounded with the words, "You will be well and healthy again." In the evening occasionally in the so-called off hours, the nurses would come back and write letters for the wounded who could not do so themselves because of their wounds.

We don't often hear of the nurses in a battle situation. They generally are unsung and unrewarded for their many deeds of heroism, but all of us; the hospital personnel and patients alike, appreciated them and admired their great qualities. If the wounded reached our hospital alive, we all had confidence along with the wounded man, that they would be treated and all would live, but to just have faith.

We had expert and highly qualified surgeons, anesthetists, nurses, internists, technicians, skilled assistants, orthopedics, neurosurgeons, eye, ear, nose and throat surgeons, genito-urinary specialists, general and thoracic surgeons, and the best of available equipment. Eight to ten surgical tables were usually busy continually from the moment the casualties arrived. The first large tent was the receiving tent, where all wounds were expertly and expeditiously evaluated and assessed. Captain Harry S. Freidman and Captain Harry A. Beckenstein were in charge of the admitting triage ward to assess every casualty with type of wound and begin treatment and emergency care. First, the individual was thoroughly examined, bleeding stopped, the blood for agglutination taken and cross matched, and plasma administered, and the patient's shock treated. All dirty bloody clothing was then removed, the person scrubbed, and all wounds were cleansed. The wounded man was then moved when the vital signs were in normal range.

Surgery was performed upon our own troops first with those most in need receiving the most immediate care. German casualties were treated, also following care of the American wounded and according to severity. For instance, eye and facial bleeding, intra-abdominal wounds, perforated viscera, and central nervous system wounds all were first kept warm and comfortable and then were evaluated by skilled medical officers and placed appropriately on the surgical table with the list of all wounds in sequence of importance and necessity. They were re-evaluated by the surgeon, and the patient was re-scrubbed with sterile solutions, appropriately positioned on the surgical table, and properly draped. He was then placed under the proper type of anesthesia and carefully watched throughout the surgical procedure.

On completion of surgery, the wounds were dressed and the patient sent to the recovery ward where the vital signs, fluids, electrolyte balance, and the cardiac status were all taken and corrected if necessary. Intravenous infusions, with all necessary ingredients, were administered. The patient was always reassured on awakening, and proper and adequate hypnotics and sedatives were administered. Every medical and surgical team worked efficiently and expeditiously and continuously until all wounded were properly attended. Proper surgical approach and care of a gun-shot wound is related in a good history of the wound. It is well to know the position and physical attitude of the man at the time he was hit. It is also good to know about both ours and the enemies' weaponry-caliber, and from what direction. We always searched for a wound of entry and co-exit.

A sad commentary was provoked when we and our fighting men were told that our weapons were the best, absolutely dependable. However, we were disillusioned to learn that many of our casualties were due to our faulty weaponry. The carbine was found to be nearly worthless; it lacked the fire power when it was desperately needed. It would jam at the slightest provocation, with any dirt, a grain of sand, or with poor shell ejection. These guns were later replaced. We were told that the Bazooka was an armor-piercing weapon which would pierce a tank. The actual report from the men who carried the Bazooka was that the trajectory would glance off a German Tiger tank like a cork from a child's popgun and was no more effective than a BB gun. Actually, our army had no gun comparable to the fire power, mobility, and destructiveness of the German 88mm. Also, our Sherman tanks were smaller and carried five personnel counting the commander, whereas the German Mark IV or Mark V Panzers carried seven personnel including the commander. The German 63 ton-Tiger E Mark VI, and the German 50-ton Panzer Mark V could all out-gun and generally out-duel any allied tank we could put in the field. The German tanks did have more mechanical failure, however, as their tank was too heavy for the 650 horse-power engine. Our 75mm tank guns were absolutely ineffective against any of the German tanks, so the 75mm was replaced by a 76mm gun, firing HEAT (high explosive anti-tanks shells). Although the change was made, it was quite rare to out-gun any German Panzer tank. We had to rely on our more maneuverable Sherman tanks, with the revolving gun turret with a 360° range, and the cleverness of the tank commander and crew. The British 17 pound gun was the only tank-mounted gun which could penetrate the heavy armor plate of the German Panzer. I did witness a tank battle in which our Sherman completely out maneuvered a German Tiger tank by blasting the treads, then giving a slanting to right angle barrage of 76 HEAT shells. The Sherman tank which knocked out the Tiger Panzer, however, was itself lost to explosion and fire.

We had no land mines with the destructive power that any of the several types our enemy was using. When there is lack of proper equipment or inadequacy of equipment, it means many lives are needlessly lost. Our greatest asset in battle, according to the wounded men and officers, was due to our ferocity of attack. The main factors in our approach being our method of deception, engulfing the enemy in pockets, our extreme aggressiveness, and spot ingenuity. An example was cited from a soldier, "When we found that our fire power was ineffective against the German tanks we made so-called molotov cocktails with a bottle, gasoline, and a rag which we would burn the treads off the tanks and set them afire."

Late on the evening of D-Day plus eleven, our fire power increased considerably. Then in an effort to take back the beaches, the German counter attack with artillery tore the earth apart. First Sergeant Dunn's voice rang out in warning, "All personnel not on duty better crawl in your foxholes or slit trenches and pull your puckering string up, because those darn Jerry krauts are throwing everything they got at us." Thank the Lord almost everything was flying over our heads. The black sky would light up and a shell would land occasionally with a sickening snarl, a red flash, and a crash. The shelling and explosions ceased as suddenly as they had started. Most of the artillery fire from both sides was long range, although we were continually aware of dangerous possibilities. We could have a short-fuse high explosive shell hit immediately over us, which could be very damaging. This, however, did not occur in this area.

Many of our patients became quite uneasy because of their inability to seek cover in the fox-holes, and many of the fighting men seriously requested to be discharged from the hospital and returned to duty on the front line where they felt a little safer. Work under constant shooting was difficult to become accustomed to at first, but we soon became inured to the danger potential. All personnel, including our nurses, however, performed their duties with admirable courage and fortitude. They worked, apparently undisturbed, notwithstanding the trying circumstances and dangers. The nurses contributed much to keep the morale at a high level. No individual let it appear that he was more afraid, or less eager to work than those young women.

In the fighting around Carentan it was my understanding from one of the Germans who was shot and brought to us as a wounded prisoner of war, that two American Medical Officers had been taken prisoners and they were helping the Germans to treat both the Americans, Germans, and all other wounded, including the French civilians. I was told the American doctors were doing a marvelous job. They were using an old cider mill and store outside of Carentan as a hospital. The American doctors had organized this along with the German doctors. It does seem ironic when the opposites are operating in time of war, we strive to kill, destroy and eliminate, yet as doctors of medicine and surgery we strive to save whether or not the injured is one of us—friend or our enemy.

Carentan fell on Sunday the 11th of June, 1700 hours. The Germans fought valiantly and they were very tenacious, determined, and extremely difficult to get out. Our troops proved to be more aggressive, and attacked with more ferocity and determination and without any let-up in their continuous push. Our troops captured the city although we had a very rugged time trying to hold it. Hold it they did, even though on 12 June, the Germans came back again, counter attacked, and nearly recaptured the town. However, we held it and maintained our position from that time on. Carentan was on national highway Route #13 which was the road that we took for most of our movements.

As the battle lines advanced farther away, the evenings were reminiscent of a prairie summer storm out in Kansas, with occasional flares and thunder rolling around and over the horizon with increasing activity. It was also similar to the northern lights with crackling and shooting of bright colored spears as I recall them when we were in Northern Canada. That is where any comparison ends, for we were very aware of the cause of the noise and the lights.

There were times of lull when our battle lines moved forward. Our patient load continued, as many of our wounded were in much too serious a condition to be sent to the rear. They could not tolerate transporting in this early phase post-operatively. Lieutenant Col. John E. Smaltz and Major James J. Coll were constantly busy in their medical wards, particularly after the first month of combat as we had an increase in general medical illnesses.

When under fire during combat operations one does not contemplate death particularly if busily carrying out his duty. We took complete care of our own brave soldiers first and above all. When our duties were completed we would then turn to the enemy wounded. They were treated with the same care and kindness with skill and efficiency. None of us ever carried any hatred or rancor for any, whether foreign, civilian, or enemy. It was difficult at times when we could see hatred gleaming from the enemy wounded or hearing and understanding the pungent remarks spewing from an occasional S.S. man's lips. The latter was actually rare. When the enemy was subjected to surgery and wound care, they were fearful and frightened that we would take their lives. Generally the enemy wounded were quite grateful, happy to be out of combat, and thankful to be alive. Many volunteered to help us in any way possible when not severely wounded to the extent of complete incapacity.

It now seemed that my greatest happiness was being so busy with the teamwork with our great surgeons, enlisted personnel, nurses, and corpsmen technicians. This was the answer to my actual explosive energy, and to every team member, to extend our technical skill until fatigue compelled us to rest.

Mail call was always filled with anticipation for a word from home. I watched the hopeful faces as they awaited their name to be called however, I was saddened when a face turned to gloom because of no word from someone who cared. It is amazing the joy and happiness a few words can engender and too, some were saddened when the letters carried only the trials and tribulations of despair at home. Perhaps a letter would come, "Dear John, I just met the cutest fellow named Joe, I am sure you will understand."

In Normandy, it was interesting to see the small prayer stations along the main highways and roads with crucifixes along the way noted at most of the intersections. The signal companies would string the crosses with wires for our communication system, the crosses being used as telephone poles. We would receive articles of the press from home describing the war and some of the battles and the fact there was no Luftwaffe. The German planes, however, would frequently bomb our areas and one reconnaissance plane would fly over our unit every night without fail. There was not the least comparison of the few Luftwaffe and the tremendous armadas of allied bombers and fighters which would fly every clear day.

Our reconnaissance group was always on the move to advance our hospital at the appropriate times and places to keep up with the battle lines. Our motor transport section of the hospital performed superbly at all times in keeping our supplies in constant readiness. Many times they were on duty both day and night, and we never had any accidents or serious vehicle breakdown while in convoy. It was very enlightening to see the efficiency and expediency of our men in unloading the various trucks. This included the very heavy x-ray equipment, two complete generating systems with all electrical material, operating room tables, and our heavy kitchen gear. They could move our huge ward tents, beds, and entire equipment in two hours' time. We were readying to close down the hospital and move to a forward area on 5 July, and found we had a bit of time. Captain John Van Dyke and Captain Dan Hogan requested to go up the road a bit out of LaCambe and asked me to go along. I alerted Major Vesper that we would be gone, but would return by dark at the latest, and asked him to check any problems if they arose. Captains Hogan, Van Dyke, and I then took a jeep driven by Private James Walker. When we were about eight miles from our base we crossed the Vire River. At this point, we heard heavy artillery bombardment ahead of us between Isigny and Carentan. Not knowing whether the artillery was ours or the enemy, we decided to turn back. We made a turn to the left instead of to the right and came upon a T crossroad where several bodies of German soldiers were on the banks of the Vire and near the crossroads. It was somewhat unusual to come upon an area where many dead or wounded were lying unless it was at the time of battle or at its immediate cessation. Bodies were usually removed on cease fire, although following a fast over-running offensive, counter-offensive, or retreat they could be left. Often a lull or cease fire was requested by one side or the other, at which time the bodies were removed by a special section of men, and the wounded were removed by medics, corpsmen, or litter-bearers. A body would often be found in a fox-hole, slit trench, hedge-row, or in a more obscure area not readily seen.

We were suddenly under artillery fire, but we saw some pill boxes which we hoped were empty so we could take cover in them. We stopped the jeep and I ran to the one on the right. Captains Dan Hogan and John Van Dyke took the one to the left. The pill box I ran into was partially dark with an observation area of squares of heavy glass to see the surrounding area. Private Walker, in the jeep, drove to the left into a clump of bushes and trees.

The average hedge-row was about four feet in depth and five to eight feet high with the base elevated from a narrow roadway between the hedgerows. At times the road was only a path, but was generally wide enough for jeep travel. The area, however, was not in the true hedge-row section but was more of a very large field on a ground elevation. With the change of bright sunlight to the darkened, rather shadowy pill box, my eyes had to become accustomed to the change as I bounded down the few steps, half stumbling. I saw the light coming in from the front to my left and ahead a few feet, and ahead there was a three quarter foot step-up. On closer observation, I was shocked to see a moving figure. It was an S.S. officer peering out the pill box window! He probably saw us coming up, as he was looking around for us at that time. On hearing me, he swung around grasping a shiny object in his hand. He turned toward me and I saw the glint of a pistol in his right hand. I lunged toward him and slammed into the gun with my left hand as the gun was being fired, twisting his body to his left. I smashed into him with my right fist as I shouted, *"Was sagen sie?"* Without waiting for an answer I ended up on top of him, retrieved his small pistol, and noted he was a Hauptman (the equivalent rank of Captain), and was bleeding from a scalp

Wallace Harry Graham

wound. I shouted out for Captains Van Dyke and Hogan, or Pvt. Walker, but received no answer. While sitting on this officer who turned out to be from the 17th S.S. troops, I learned he was a forward observer. Most of his unit had withdrawn and he was preparing to leave when I interrupted his departure.

I asked that if I let him up would he try to kill me, and he replied in German, "Certainly, I must. It is my duty."

My reply was, "I am a doctor and will probably be the one to sew your deep scalp wound."

He replied, "*Ja wohl,*—that is your duty." I told him then it would be healthier for him to remain quiet.

His reply was, "*Ja, Ich verstehe*—I understand."

We conversed about our families and he mentioned that he also had two children. I was wondering what to do with him when I discovered that the blood on my left hand was not the German's blood but my own even though the wound was painless. I said, "I think I have been hit."

His reply was, "*Gut*" (good) and stated he would not be taken prisoner. My reply was that he hardly had any choice when the gun was in my possession, and that if he tried to escape, I would have no regrets about eliminating him.

He replied, "I understand and will be very quiet."

Again, I shouted for Van Dyke, Dan, or Walker but there was nothing but silence. Soon, to my great relief, I heard voices speaking English so I again shouted louder for someone to come into the pill box. They entered and I discovered that they were infantry men from the 29th Division and from the 116th Regiment, I believe. They were quite surprised to see the duo in the pill box and then said they were the clean-up squad. They took the officer as prisoner and I came out of the pill box.

I then saw Captain Van Dyke with his arms filled with bottles about sixty yards away unloading them into the jeep. Van and Dan were as happy as if they had found a cache of gold. They had found a good sized supply of Edelkorn Schnapps, and both were arguing about looking around for more, even though they appeared to be in the near-stumbling stage. They saw the G.I.s with the German officer and Dan was all for giving up the bottles and starting his own private war with "that German bastard," so the two argued over what they would use for a persuader. They both grabbed a bottle of Edelkorn to use but, I pushed them into the jeep and headed back to the main road, returning to our bivouac area. Van swore all to secrecy, as he wanted to keep the bottled joy juice, and he was sure we could catch the devil for being in enemy territory.

Van wanted to know where I found my "buddies" and I tried to explain, but he garbled back that one of those guys looked like a Jerry Kraut but that something was wrong with him.

Dan's only reply was that the character in the kraut uniform was in one hell of a place. He stated further that the kraut should be a dead duck just like the two he had seen and stumbled over before he found his treasure of German Edelkorn Schnapps which they called "Irish Whiskey." Whatever the liquor was, they both agreed that the newly acquired joy juice was better than Calvados and that the afternoon off was a great boon to them. No more was ever said about the incident.

When we were driving back in the jeep from Carentan, we saw a plane coming at us and thought it was possibly a German dive bomber or *Stuka*. We stopped the jeep and jumped to one side, hitting the ditch along the roadside. This plane dove at us spitting out 50 caliber shells. It didn't hit our jeep, but it hit a truck traveling down the road, which was ablaze in a moment. Another plane came along immediately afterwards, opening up with 20 millimeter shells and hit along the same road. We were lying as quietly as we possibly could in the ditch with our faces pressed into the sod.

This reminds me of the cartoon by Bill Mauldin I saw in the *Stars and Stripes* paper: Willy and Joe were lying flat under enfilading machine gun fire. Joe yelled, "Get flatter, Willy." Willy replied, "I can't, my buttons are in the way." If you have never been through these fighter bomber attacks you have no idea what war is, or what it is to be blasted by a fighter bomber. We looked up and were dismayed to see our own Allied British planes strafing us. We had no way to signal that we were friendly troops. We felt so utterly helpless there lying in the ditch, our faces pressed in the sod with these blazing planes roaring down on us, and wincing at the whistle of the bullets splashing to one side. Although the Red Cross insignia was on the jeep hood, we didn't know if it was going to come back again or not, so we waited anxiously. Finally we realized they probably were finished with us so we went back to the truck where we helped two French farmers put the fire out.

Going back to our unit, we had to make detours through the fields to get by, as the road had been blasted. There were huge bomb holes and other vehicles that had been smashed in the roadway; the majority of them however, were German vehicles. A G.I. convoy guide was now at the crossroad directing; he told us they had just knocked out an enemy artillery piece and the Germans were removed, and urged that we should hurry through, as his unit was moving on through to Cherbourg. We turned right at the crossroad to get back to the main route where we first made a wrong turn, and below where the gun emplacement was entrenched. Here there were several enemy soldiers that had been killed around the hedge-row. There was a miserable, sweet, sickly smell, which by now we had learned was the smell of death. Naturally this becomes even stronger and more pungent as the bodies of men and animals lie for a while in the sun.

There were other odors of war which we learned. For instance, whenever we went into a pill box or a dugout where the Germans had been, there was a very typical, sour, leathery smell; not obnoxious, but quite different from the others.

We left the area near Carentan and went into an area where a large group of Mongols had been captured. The Germans were using them as their own troops which had formerly been captured from the Russians. We also had several casualties who were White Russians, also some Hungarians. The Russians had been fighting in the 439th East Battalion, but when the Americans came up they all threw down their guns and surrendered.

At one area near a crossroad, the roadside was littered with dead humans and animals so close together that some had to be pushed off the roadway so that we could get through. It appeared as if tanks had come through this area as there was one of our Sherman tanks in a field off to one side about twenty-five yards that had been hit with enemy fire and had been completely burned with the charred bodies in their respective positions. The scene at this particular area gave us even more of an idea of the meaning of war and sudden death, and how far the war could reach in depth and misery. Here congealed blood was still thick and clotted on the pavement at the crossroads. In the hedge-rows there were dead cattle, horses, and some of the enemy. They had been absolutely torn asunder. It was starkly obvious that there had been a heavy battle between our airborne troops and the Germans. Some of the Germans had been hit by their own mines. This particular area was on the road from Isigny to Carentan. I was later told that a little farther down the road past the crossroad was the so-called "battle of the bloody gulch." The sights I have just described were absolute slaughter.

We then continued back to our unit, and on the way, we saw the home where we wanted to pick up the family whom we had seen when going out. Sadly, the area had been blasted apart and all of them had been killed with the shell fire. While riding in the jeep, we could hear an unusually deep whooshing sound of explosive shells going overhead. We later found that the Germans had a 240mm mobile railroad rifle, similar to our 240s. These tremendous shells were the cause of the unusual whooshing sound. They had been fired from fifty miles distant and toward the beach.

Before we reached our hospital area, we sighted another plane which was very definitely a British Spit-Fire. He probably recognized that we were

American or he may have seen the red cross painted on the hood of the jeep. Captain Van Dyke said, "Let's get back the fastest way possible and get the hell out of here; I have had the pants scared off me. Man, I am too old for this foolishness. I'll never listen to this crazy 'Orshman' again. Step on the gas."

The clouds were merging into twilight as the blazing red sun was setting in the West hiding behind the world that found it necessary to settle differences in such a disastrous way. Other than the jeep's hum and the bumping over and around the pock-marked areas of shell holes, the world seemed to be ghastly silent. Suddenly it seemed there were no sounds of guns or artillery, and no birds were flying.

South of Isigny and east of Carentan we came to another crossroads area. It had been hammered and blasted, as the deep holes stared open and blank at the silent vehicles. One Panzer and three of our Sherman tanks— mute evidence of a disastrous and uneven battle. A few tree stumps stood stark and shredded. Pfc. Walker stepped on the gas, as we knew our tents were only a few hills straight on according to the map.

Captain Dan Hogan broke the silence by saying, "Well, I did want to get a bit of fresh air and clear my mind from the misery we had been facing, but I am not so sure I am happy about what we saw and just missed. We are just plain lucky, and I am staying close to my tent and trench from now on. I got a belly ache."

We arrived in our area and tents in good time. Our casualties were being transferred by plane to England for General Hospital care. We were to move on the morrow or by 7 July 1944, and the trucks were nearly loaded, ready to move by noon at the latest. There were many comments about my bandaged left hand; but I gave no answer. We had been in an area where we probably should not have been, and happy to be back doing our duty.

We received move orders, referred our wounded to the other hospital moving in our area, folded our tents, and on the 7th of July we began our move to Saint Lo in a downpour of rain. On arriving at the first major crossroads intending to make a left turn, we were directed by Military Police units to change our course. We were to continue across the Carentan Peninsula to Mortain, as there was a concentration of troop movements and a battle in progress from the Vire river to Saint Lo. We understood that there had been fighting in and around Mortain, but that our forces held the area at the present. Our convoy rolled along the shell-pocked highway which actually was not nearly as bad as we had been told.

We moved toward the town of Mortain, which I will never forget. Mortain was built on a hill overlooking the surrounding flat land for over twenty miles around. It was in a very commanding position to watch the enemy from any direction. The Germans held Mortain, as it was a place of advantage or high territory to watch all troop movements many miles around. General Hodges' VII Corps fought hard, certainly to our advantage, although it was a hard battle to both gain and to hold. The Germans tried valiantly to hold this position. However, our troops captured the area after a very hard-fought battle.

Much of the battle had been in mud and drenching rain. We moved in before the graves section could remove those killed in battle. However, we did not see any American dead. We arrived on the outskirts of Mortain in the darkest part of night; the moon was not shining, and there was a steady curtain of rain. We were slogging in mud when we turned into a farm area close to Mortain, at the base of a hill on the outskirts of the town. I was with the group that walked by the side of the house and to the barn. Several dead soldiers and animals were lying around, which bespoke the heavy fighting that had taken place the preceding day. We were told to bivouac in this area. We were all extremely tired, and welcomed the respite. We went into the barn and climbed up into the hayloft to get some rest. I thought it smelled a bit foul, but thought it was from the bodies in the yard below. I laid down and fell asleep.

Early the next morning I was aroused by a buzzing and hissing sound every so often and a heavy stench filled the loft. Dawn was just breaking, and as I looked over within an arms reach of me was a dead German soldier. I remember seeing bodies under gray coats, along with bloated dead cattle and a horse or two down in the barn yard during the heavy cloud burst. Through the night I thought that I had heard occasional sighing, whistling noises which probably were the same noises which had awakened me a few minutes before dawn. My feet were cold, and Van Dyke was snoring off to my left, as he was in the far corner. Sergeant Hoffman was somewhere close by, and whenever Van Dyke let out a loud, gasping, sonorous roar, Hoffman would moan and mumble about a noisy someone being more nuisance than the dead cows. He thought the snoring was from his friend, Frakas, the former mess chief. I turned on my belly to bury my nose in the straw, and in so doing I struck something cold and wet. Hardly awake, another sigh and whistling sound was emitted followed by a very foul odor, which intensified the odor already permeating the loft. I looked over, and facing me was a bloated Jerry with his belly splitting his loosened uniform. The eyes were open and glassy without sight, the mouth was open, and the tongue swollen and protruding over blood-stained teeth. It was a ghastly sight.

Our clothes were still wet from the slashing rain of the preceding night, but my socks were dry. Hogan and Van Dyke were pulling out of the straw cursing each other. Van Dyke was holding his head, as they both had a self-treatment of Edelkorn to warm the cockles of their hearts and for "circulatory stimulation" the night before. Van Dyke swore he couldn't sleep because that damned saturated "Orshman" talked in his sleep. Hogan then insisted that Van Dyke snored and gurgled the Edelkorn Schnapps so loudly he could not sleep. Actually, they both did quite well. I looked at the dead German again and saw he had been hit in the head, causing a bloody but fairly superficial wound; also there was a small gaping wound in the right anterior abdominal wall which he evidently treated himself as there was a packet of sulfa beside him and a pack bandage around his body. It was obvious that the liver, colon, and a large blood vessel had been hit. I rolled over and sat up, laced my boots, and saw Sergeant Hoffman sitting up. I told him what the smell was and he said, "I thought Farkas had stuck his stinkin' feet in my face." Farkas had already left the loft and we could hear pans clinking from the mess truck. Sergeant Hoffman started down, saying, "I've got to watch Farkas or he will have Arthur Keith or Sergeant Muska barbecuing those dead cows."

Dawn was just breaking as we alighted from the ladder of the barn loft. The sun was beautiful to us as it peaked over the eastern horizon. Arthur Keith and Charlie Chan had collected the wax coverings from the K-Ration boxes for fuel. There is no smoke to be seen from this fuel. The water was heated and we enjoyed the aroma and taste of warm coffee from our canteen cups. We used our helmets to dip water from a shell hole for washing.

Others in our group were stirring, after which they got their hand spades and retreated to the rear of the barn. We washed and shaved, then broke out the C-Rations and munched away, as this section of our unit was now up and about. When we were leaving our bivouac a few miles outside of Mortain, we noted that one German had probably been milking a cow at the time he was killed. The cow was bloated until its skin was stretched tight, with the legs stiff and straight up, and the German's head was against its belly. The German had been killed probably by the same explosion that killed the cow while he was trying to milk it.

Our Airborne troops had taken all this ground first prior to our infantry coming through. The infantry came through at an exceedingly rapid pace, once they broke through the beachhead. Charred Wehrmacht trucks, tanks and other enemy material lined the roadway where our bulldozers had pushed them off or rolled them over. Marked lines directed our line of traffic, and mine fields were also marked. However, many areas had not yet been cleared of Teller mines. The heavy rain of the night before had slackened to a stop to let the sunshine through and there was now only sporadic heavy-artillery fire in the distance. We moved forward then into the town of Mortain.

We were receiving reports and reading the old papers from the United States on how all the German Luftwaffe had been wiped out of the air. At 2300 hours a German Stuka plane with an unsynchronized motor would make his evening rounds without fail. We called him "Bed-check Charley." He never fired a shot; only made a turn at our hospital and flew back. On entering the town of Mortain, it seemed as if all inhabitants were either asleep, exceedingly quiet, or vacated. Nothing was astir as though the town were dead. Mortain had obviously taken a fair amount of shelling, with resultant heavy destruction. We did not stop there, and our trucks rolled on over hill and dale as we traveled the muddy trail. An armored division had preceded us and tore up some of the road. We speculated and hoped it was not some retreating German Panzers.

An occasional high explosive shell whined over, and we prayed we were not the mark, but our helmeted heads did a turtle retraction into our chest. Captain Harry Friedman sounded off, "Are you scared ?" I thought about it and realized that most of us were tense to a degree, but not outwardly afraid at that time. We all knew that we could not allow fear to impede us or interfere with our duty. Depending on the circumstances, we all have some degree of fear and alert awareness, although I have yet to see a single corpsman, nurse, or any army personnel who would allow it to govern their assigned duty.

The day was clearing and our convoy rumbled on. Some of us were nodding and some were talking, planning, or thinking as we sat on long seat benches facing each other from both sides of the truck bed with canvas covering the top. The canvas covering the round hoops over the top protected us in event of rain. However, the back of our truck was open, which allowed some dust to fly in when the roads were dry. Even so, it felt better to be able to look out to see where we had been, although not seeing where we were going. The opening also served as an escape hatch in the event of emergency. We moved through L'Epinay–Tesson, France, then to the high bluff overlooking the entire area of Saint Lo.

General Karl Wilhelm von Schlieben, the commander of Cherbourg, had been directed by Hitler to fight to the death of the last man. "Withdrawal from the present positions is punishable by death." This ultimatum was broadcast by the BBC (British Broadcasting Corporation), 21 June, 1944. It was a great thrill when we learned of the fall of Cherbourg. At approximately the same time that Cherbourg fell, our tent unit functioned on the side as a sort of hotel for the 45th Evacuation Hospital, which was just moving in at this time. We also took in the 2nd Evacuation Hospital, the 4th Convalescence Hospital, and the 10th Medical Laboratory group. We welcomed all these wonderful people and they helped in the management of our casualties, while getting first hand information and experience on the spot. It was quite obvious what tremendous fighters our soldiers actually were, when we could see the ground taken even though it was often at a tremendous cost. The various fighting divisions; the 1st, the 20th, 101st, and 82nd Airborne divisions with whom we were associated and assigned, along with the 30th and the 2nd infantry division. Also the 2nd Armored division were in immediate contact with our hospital when needed. We were working with all these divisions of men in an area where everyone of them were actually fighting heroes. The 82nd Airborne troops were dropped around Ravensville and Montebourg. These areas are in the Cherbourg Peninsula up to Saint Mere-Eglise. The 82nd was there near the 101st which followed and was dropped more around Carentan and deeper into France just behind the German lines.

We had many interesting casualties among the Americans, Germans, and civilians. On one occasion a seriously wounded, young S.S. trooper asked for water. Captain Hogan knelt down, lifted the German's head with his left hand and gave him cool water. The S.S. trooper flushed the water around in his mouth, and with burning hatred in his eyes spit it all out in Captain Hogan's face. We watched the man as he cursed us saying, *"Schwachweich, einfaltig Amerikanen,"* meaning weak, soft, stupid Americans. His head rolled to the right and he died with a sneer on his face, detestation in his eyes, and hatred in his mind. He was no doubt a thoroughly indoctrinated Nazi S.S. man up from the ranks of the Hitler *Jugend*. There was another instance I remember of an S.S. trooper who pleaded and begged to have the S.S. tattoo (of Runic lightning bolts) ⚡⚡ removed from his left arm. He said he had been mislead and disillusioned and wanted no part of the Nazi S.S. He refused anesthesia, as he was afraid we would kill him with a shot. Many of the enemy soldiers had been told that if they were hospitalized in a Yank hospital, we would give them a "shot" and kill them. He knew, however, he would be killed the moment he was caught out of the hospital with the tattoo. The tattoo was removed, without anesthesia, while he moaned, groaned and ground his teeth through the entire procedure.

A few instances of torture were found, as on two occasions three airborne paratroopers were found with their genitals having been shot away. We knew this was purposeful and fiendish, as all three had been shot in other vital spots and their jumpsuits were down. Both the enemy and we were guilty of occasional atrocities; however, we like to think we were guilty of much less. Our findings later seemed to verify this.

Near Saint Lo, our tents and equipment were unloaded and erected and soon our generators were working and supplying adequate lighting facilities. We were ready for action in a two hour period on the 8th of

July. The battle of Saint Lo was a critical turning point for the Americans, just as Caen was for the British. Saint Lo was strategic significance as a communication center and because it was at a road-junction of a national highway. Including the Saint Lo sector, about twenty roads came into Saint Lo from around the hills and the Vire valley. Over the Vire River was a large bridge which was near the railway station for the city.

Saint Lo was once a beautiful city, and at one time a beautiful cathedral could be seen from many miles around, but it was transformed into a flaming inferno by our bombers and the attacking forces. Saint Lo was over flown by heavy, friendly bombers on the 24th of July. Five hundred bombers of the first formation found the visibility almost zero, and accurate bombing was impossible, so the attempt was aborted. A second group of thirty-five bombers flew in later through the overcast and dropped their bomb loads through breaks in the overcast. Following this a third bombing formation of three hundred heavy bombers dropped seven hundred tons of bombs. This was a miscalculation caused by the lead bombardier who had difficulty with the bomb release mechanism causing the load to drop prematurely. The subsequent planes in formation then dropped their loads, assuming the leader was correct. We had sent our infantry in before the bombing took place, thereby losing a great many of our good infantry men in the battle.

This miscalculation, coupled with the failure of the bomb release mechanism, and the lack of communication resulted in the killing of twenty-five, and the wounding of one hundred thirty soldiers from our own 30th Division. The fighter bombers again began striking the morning of 25 July. Again, there was no communication between the air and ground troops. The resulting total of bombing errors was 111 Americans dead and 490 wounded. We also lost heavily in equipment. An entire artillery group was decimated, and the enemy artillery was never struck. This was one of the most demoralizing occurrences of the war.

Involved in this battle of Saint Lo were the following American divisions: The 2nd, 9th, 28th, 29th, 30th, and 35th and elements of the 63rd, also the 19th Corps. The Germans, who held Saint Lo, put up very stiff resistance, but our very heavy bombardment of the city took its toll. One day I remember looking outside our hospital tent to check on a tremendous roaring noise, and saw in the air an incredible spectacle. The sky was filled with our huge bombers. Over two thousand of them were roaring overhead in a continuous wave to raid on Saint Lo. A British group of bombers followed our own bombers on the attack. This was a most sobering and awesome sight. The concussion of the eight thousand tons of bombs they dropped shook the very earth for miles around and was nearly continuous for four hours. The concussion caused by our bombing in Saint Lo practically bounced our patients out of their beds or off their cots. The tents shook with the sides flapping, and you could hear frequent screeching tears as the steel fragments sliced through the side of our tents. It was in such fire power as this that our nurses continued to work, our officers continued to demonstrate skill, and everyone of the enlisted men did their utmost, not a one shirking their duty at any time.

The pattern or carpet bombing in Saint Lo was massive, rendering all life, equipment, buildings, and homes asunder. I thought, "What horrible destruction, all because of one evil contemptible man and his ideology." This was truly their Armageddon and I could mentally visualize the galloping Four Horsemen.

For many miles around us the air was super-saturated with the aftermath of battle with smoke powder, fumes and dust. We could smell the gunfire over the completely ravaged earth and up into the hill where we were. We could also see the dead and the wounded from our placement. On the ground the devastation was almost unbelievable, and we realized even more the helplessness of man against the machines of war. Shells continued to go in as our pilots thought there were more German tanks in the far corners or the perimeters of the hedge-rows. There was the sweet sickening smell of death spreading over the area; this is a typical smell which occurs soon following the kill and before actual degeneration and necrosis begins. As soon as the bombardment stopped, we received large groups of casualties. Sadly some of our casualties were from some of our own bombers, as our ground forces had advanced farther and faster than the bombers had anticipated.

General McNair was in Saint Lo on 20 July at that time, as he was inspector of the Land Forces. He was killed by our own planes during the Saint Lo bombing. The fighter bombers of the United States were repeatedly great life savers to us, however and on occasion one of our tank divisions was hard put against the heavier German tiger tanks with the terrific fire power of the 88s mounted on them. Our fighter bombers came to the rescue and an entire Panzer division was completely annihilated and was left without any obvious operational Panzer tank. The S.S. Panzer division and the Hitler unit was completely decimated. The latter had been made up of former members of the Hitler *Jugend*. In one day's bombardment, point firing from the fighter bombers knocked out forty German tanks.

A deadly tank battle was witnessed by some of us. One of our American tanks was coming around and down the hill just below our hospital to our right on a road going into Saint Lo. We assumed he was trying to

Wallace Harry Graham

escape. Neither tank could see the other, as the road was a transverse "S". around and below our hospital.

The German tank was a Mark IV, or Panzer, and the American tank was a much smaller Sherman, normally no match for the powerful Panzer. The German tank rounded the road to its left, at the same time the American tank rounded into the straight-of-way. Both tanks were nearly facing each other. The German tank, however, was at an angle to our tank—leaving more of a broadside open to our Sherman tank, which was facing it directly. The Sherman fired a volley of shots, which apparently had no effect on the German tank. We were at close range at this time when it seemed that both tanks were firing simultaneously. Our "76" cannon was, we were told later, firing armor-piercing HEAT shells, which blasted into the Mark IV turret-track. The guntracks on both tanks began to burn at the same time. The German tank with the "88" cannon began to burn at the base of the turret. Our tank then moved to the right, and again fired a volley of armor-piercing shells. The German gun-turret could no longer revolve, so their shots went wide of their mark. The hatches on both tanks were now opened. Two men from our American tank escaped from the front, but evidently three could not get through the turret. Some of our corpsmen ran down and pulled out the three badly burned men from our Sherman tank, while the other two who had escaped, opened fire on the two Germans who were firing at our men as they were escaping from the emergency exit. The German tank commander tried to get out through the tank turret, but couldn't make it. The two Germans were killed outright by our men. Our soldiers went to the German tank to drop a grenade, but instead they found all four in the German tank dead except the tank commander, whose left foot was caught in the track, as he had missed a step. With considerable struggle and the help of two trench-knives, the German's foot was amputated at the ankle and he was thereby extricated.

After all had cleared the tanks, except the four German dead in the tank, both tanks exploded and burned completely. Our tank commander (the gunner) and the radio man were the ones who were burned; whereas, the driver and assistant driver escaped with relatively minor injuries. Later more of the technicalities of this tank battle were narrated to us by Captain Henry E. Curtis, Tank Commander, 3rd Tank Battallion, 10th Armored Division.

We brought all of the living casualties into the hospital and started to work on them without delay. The one American officer had been very severely burned over his entire front and it had charred the skin completely. We knew that he had very little, if any, chance to live unless we could keep his electrolytes and fluids in accurate balance. We immediately removed all of the charred blackened, hard tissue, which was devitalized through all layers. At the same time we were doing this, a dog fight in the air between a De Havilland Mosquito English plane and a German fighter plane had been taking place. The English plane fell immediately adjacent to our hospital, almost striking our receiving ward tents. Both the pilot and co-pilot were killed instantly, shearing off their aortas. We took their bodies out of the cockpit, and brought them into the hospital, but their demise had been immediate. Thereupon, we took the normal intact skin off the pilot, skinning him almost completely in front and placed this on the denuded raw area of the American. We realized that the homogeneous graft most probably would not take, but our idea was to suture this large graft in place in order to retain the fluids and the electrolytes until his body could maintain itself, if at all possible. We continued to keep his electrolyte and fluid balance up to normal by steady inflow of intravenous infusions. At the same time we sutured the remainder of skin. We kept him in good balance for the first forty-eight hours until we could get him aboard a hospital plane and send him back to the Fifth General Hospital in England.

We later followed this case up and were very pleased when we were told that this man did live and that he was having grafts from his back placed on his front with great success. There were hundreds of other heartening incidents where we had saved precious lives and repaired their wounds. However, the heavy and dreadful toll of war damage to humankind is incalculable and even incomprehensible.

The U.S. 47th and 120th Infantry regiments were severely hit and the U.S. 12th field artillery unit was completely annihilated at Saint Lo as I recall. The early casualties came in and a twenty-four hour period of steady heart-aching work began, caring for our own injured men. The casualties on both sides were tremendous during this battle of Saint Lo.

The Corpsmen did their best to retrieve the wounded and get them back out of the gunfire. Our unit was close, so we received the wounded within a minute's time. We also cared for a few wounded German soldiers. The Germans from the Saint Lo battle whom we had in our wounded group had been generally under the S.S. or Schutzstaffel General Obergruppenfuhrer. He had been in charge of the German armies along the Normandy front, and was called back from there to the Saint Lo area. However, he was relieved of his command on the 2nd of July and General Von Kluge took his place. We knew this from my talking to wounded German prisoners. We obtained all the data we possibly could.

As I mentioned previously, there were large divisions of German armies held in reserve, as the main commander, Hitler himself, or the so-called "Arm Chair General," was giving commands from the inner-circle. He still believed the allied invasion was only a fake, and that the real push was coming through Pas de Calais which was the narrowest place on the English Channel. The German high command was definitely obsessed in their belief that the invasion was no more than a diversionary maneuver. This may have been fostered by the fact that in England at the Port of Embarkation a huge camouflage had been made up to look like an entire army was encamped there. The wooden tanks were set up to look as if we had a tremendous force waiting to cross the Channel. The Germans were observing this area with their reconnaissance planes, and they would report the tremendous build-up of troops that were waiting to take off. We also had dummy ships. The British prepared this very cunningly with a huge armada of battleships, making it all look as if we really had a tremendous navy to make the real invasion. Therefore, the Germans held back on many of their main divisions.

To return to our activity from the battle of Saint Lo—our hospital unit had 2,749 admissions from 8 July to 5 August 1944, and 70 deaths, with an overall mortality of 2.5 percent. On 30 July alone we received 333 injured. The days and nights were filled with the steady thunder of artillery, and the German bombers continued to make night calls. We were almost constantly caring for the injured during that period of 8 July to 5 August.

I must say, our hospital unit actually functioned as a very splendidly efficient mechanism under the direction of Colonel Carl Rylander. It was certainly in keeping with the grim, fast moving and hard hitting army divisions that we supported. During the time of the Saint Lo battle on 20 July 1944, a bombing attempt was made on Hitler's life by his own officers in their attempt to save what was left of Germany. Unfortunately, it failed, and the many German officers implicated in the plot either committed suicide or were executed by the Nazis.

Also on Thursday, 20 July, when we were still on the bluff overlooking the area which had been Saint Lo, a tremendous storm of rain, thunder, and hail hit us hard. This storm raged throughout all Normandy. It seemed as if God wanted to wash away the terrible carnage below.

After the initial heavy activity and our casualties were cared for surgically, we had some time, so Major Vesper and I went into the destruction of Saint Lo the day that Saint Lo capitulated and the Germans were cleared. The rubble and the dust had settled, but we could smell the destructive odors of war. We gazed in disbelief at the incredibly pulverized rubble of former buildings which covered the entire former city. It was late evening when Major Albert Vesper and I made the reconnaissance. As the night was closing in I recall seeing a full moon arising from the horizon. The Major and I remarked, "Such a beautiful moonlit night to look upon such horrible devastation." This was the worse destruction we had seen up to this time. I might add here that Major Vesper was assistant chief of surgery, and he was one of the most efficient officers that I have known. He was exceedingly, kind and good to the patients, very alert, and an outstanding surgeon of great skill.

Later, on another of our reconnaissance trips, I happened to find and pick up a series of graduated bar bells and weights which we took for the officers and men to use to keep in good physical condition. They were utilized later when we were in rest areas, when we were kept inside in inclement weather, and when we were not so busy. I carried these weights around the entire war to good advantage.

The area of Saint Lo was still in the Calvados sector of Normandy. I have mentioned before, that when some of our men were off duty they would nip or sample the Calvados wine that tasted like gasoline. Calvados was the name of a section of Normandy, France, as well as a type of wine or alcoholic beverage made from apples. The abundance of this liquid and its effect of killing off much of the grass in this area was quite apparent. The Calvados had been given to some of our men by the French in Normandy. As a matter of fact, the Calvados could be used like gasoline, as it burned well in alcohol lamps. It is amazing to me how it could stay in the stomach of any individual.

The splendid performance of our surgeons and all personnel was representative of their splendid technical ability in civilian life. The conformance and ability to work together was excellent. Cooperation was perfect between specialties as from the radiologist with the surgeons, as well as the internists, ward, and triage officers. We were subjected to periods of furious activity with every imaginable type of serious body wounds. Practically all casualties were taken to x-ray. Close liaison was observed between our evacuation hospital and the rear zone general hospitals either continental, England, or direct to the states. The wounded were evacuated to allied hospitals—both military and civilian. Some civilians were sent to hospitals that had the capability of giving continued casualty recovery care.

Our litter bearers were constantly on day and night duty shifts and worked with kind and gentle handling of casualties at all times. They would often help in clothing removal and the cleansing of wounds. We would often use prisoners of war to act as litter bearers and other ward duties for their own wounded. The enemy wounded were under our general attendance with constant nursing care and supervision, both of the best quality.

CHAPTER THIRTEEN
FOLLOWING THE FRONT LINES

Members of the 24th evacuation hospital kept a unit diary, and I have used part of this diary in the present chapter.

On the 5th of August, we moved to a field near Percy, France. This move took us through piles of rubble, dust, and masonry which was formerly Saint Lo. The ruins of that great city were so impressive, that they became a persistent medium of comparison for damage done to all of the cities until we got to Germany. Around Percy there was a large apple orchard which had been cleared from mines and booby traps, and the majority of our personnel slept there when they could. However, the first night, we had a battle royal, not with the Jerries [German soldiers], but with millions of bees, flies, and mosquitoes. This battle soon ended with proper placement of the mosquito bars. These insects were also a problem at mess time where we would eat with one hand and flag our anatomy with the other.

We were in full operation on the 6th of August, 1944. At this point in our forward advance, came General Eisenhower's order to the troops to pound the enemy into total defeat. At this point also, the well-merited promotions came for Vesper, Edwards, Coll, and Distefano, who were all promoted to their very deserving and long awaited promotions from Captain to Major. To date, Percy, France was the quietest area we entered and received wounded. Even though we were busy, the artillery was not so heavy, but according to the type of wounds we were treating, there was more hand-to-hand fighting. There were many bayonet wounds, and as horrible as some were, the great majority of the men with these wounds were saved. It seemed as though our troops far excelled the Germans, as our enemy load from hand-to-hand battle was far greater than our own. This fact was admitted by many German soldiers. They hated everything about hand-to-hand fighting. One German officer asked if we spent most of our training time with hand-to-hand combat. I told him that we had trained very well in this, and that we were particularly adaptable because of our sports programs in football, boxing, wrestling, and many martial arts with physical contact.

I recall quite vividly a wounded German soldier by the name of Dahl, because it was a most unusual case. An American bayonet had been thrust through his back and entirely through the left side of his upper chest. The bayonet protruded approximately two inches from the anterior chest wall. I was surprised that the bayonet had not been shot out, but Dahl could speak English and made a plea for his life. It apparently had either gone through the heart or immediately above the heart. He survived this, to the present, either due to the effect upon the large vessels, or it could possibly have missed the heart and vessels and gone to one side of the aorta and the other large vessels that are present in this particular area.

The heart sounds and pulse were rapid but not particularly abnormal. The bayonet had been thrust through the third and fourth rib anteriorly, and we prepared for immediate thoracic opening. I recall he was having only some minor abnormal chest sounds from the pulmonary area and there was some blood in the diaphragmatic area. We removed all clothing, scrubbed him and the bayonet throughly, and placed him on the operating table. Under anesthesia we very carefully and slowly removed the bayonet from the back, almost a millimeter at a time until it was entirely out. It was done with considerable difficulty for it seemed to have been fastened to one of the ribs. This was probably the reason why the American soldier could not remove it. So the soldier apparently took the bayonet off his rifle and continued on. We waited then, but there was no change in his blood pressure and no abnormal heart sounds; only some acceleration of the pulse. We kept him on the operating table for thirty minutes awaiting a possible change. We were afraid to move him for fear that the bleeding would start immediately. Following this, we very carefully removed him from the table to the stretcher so as to get his hospital bed clothes on. Again we listened to the cardiac action and took all the vital signs; they were unchanged and normal. We inserted a nasal gastric tube to possibly prevent vomiting post operatively. We kept him in the hospital for our stay in this particular location, and he progressed remarkably well, with absolutely no deleterious or untoward effects whatsoever. The enemy soldier said he went to sleep praying and awakened saying the same prayer.

Another unusual bit of surgery was performed by Captain Phillip Morrison. His patient was an American soldier who had blood in the pericardium according to our x-rays, and further revealed a fairly large piece of steel shrapnel in the heart muscle; protruding through the entire ventricle and acting as a tamponade. Captain Morrison carefully removed the high explosive fragment and skillfully sutured the cardiac muscle. The patient progressed remarkably well with no change whatsoever; no more than if he had had an appendectomy or other simple type of operative procedure. These were some of our many remarkable instances of unusual surgery.

On our stay here in Percy from 5th to 22nd August we handled 1216 total admissions (435 patients on the 7th of August alone), 24 deaths, and an overall mortality of 1.97 percent. Activity around Percy was part of the campaign sweeping through Brittany just prior to going on into Paris. The army was moving, and we were following them right on their heels. While in Percy we received word that at one o'clock on the morning of 7 August, the Germans launched an attack on Mortain which was disastrous for them. Five Panzer and S.S. Divisions smashed head long into their first massive offensive in France. Their objective was to gain a commanding position which was only 20 miles east of the Mont Saint Michel bay. This move by the Germans drew armored troops from Gen. Montgomery's front and took some infantry reinforcements from the Pas de Calais front. The Germans had kept the 3rd army around Pas de Calais for two useless months in anticipation of a main allied thrust over this easy beach head. The 30th Division of Major General Leland S. Hobbs had moved into the area of Mortain to relieve the 1st Division, and both divisions battle weary.

The past several days we were receiving another large group of the injured men. Some of them were tired and agitated beyond measure. They were just beginning to let go and release some of their frightful tension they had gone through. One of the wounded men had been machine gunned across the pelvis and both lower extremities had been badly wounded. He gave the story that the first two companies, Able (A) & Baker (B) were attacking an enemy strong point but did not realize the Krauts were loaded and waiting to launch their attack at the same time. We were attacking with everything we had after our own artillery had laid down several rounds. The Jerrys open up with firing point blank fire of anti aircraft guns, 88 millimeter guns and every type of small arms fire know to man. Our men were plenty mad knowing about the point blank fire power of the enemy.

They charged yelling, cursing madly in the face of heavy enemy fire. It seemed as if the whole earth was seething and heaving with high explosives. The very air was filled with screaming *shells & whining metal. There was a blast through A company causing a night-mare of flying debris raining down arms, legs, flesh, blood & guts of our own men. At this point all reasoning seemed to leave. I figured I was already dead and was so mad it did not bother me, there was no more fear, my only desire was to kill. We were all screaming cursing mad and not considering our life or death struggle. We were probably too confident as we were running standing up firing & not giving a damn for anything except blowing the enemy off the earth. A couple of the fellows were crying & firing, one was laughing while firing his BAR—the enemy were falling and others were filling in. "Sir, I was making one hell of a dent in their lines when I guess a Burp gun or something hit me. I didn't feel it but here I was lying on my belly & couldn't run. Sir, I was more than mad then. I kept firing, but could not move my hot legs. I blacked out I guess while I was hitting those bastards. Perhaps I should have jumped in a shell hole and blasted the devils as they came at me, but it wasn't in me. Every muscle and brain ached to get at them the fastest & the best way possible."*

"Kevin over there said we pulled back till our Shermans (tanks) came through and Charley (C) company and what was left of Able & Baker companies took over."

"Phil over there said he was in Charley (C) company with the tank & they were doing great—they knocked out the 88 & the anti aircraft batteries in a counter attack. He got hit in the face & gut. He can talk so I guess he'll make it—won't he sir?" I told him we both were confident he would make it fine.

Many such stories I could narrate on the miserable state of war and its fateful and disastrous impact it has on our lives.

The Germans were successful in cutting off the 2nd Battalion of the 120th Regiment, and called for surrender of the 120th Regiment after having surrounded it for six days. The 120th held on though, and fought back, but they desperately needed medical supplies. The air force was notified, and the answer was immediate. The air force sent C-47's over, dodging enemy anti-aircraft fire, and parachuting the supplies into the besieged battalion, even though much of the parachuted medical supply was inadvertently dropped in enemy territory. The 30th Field Artillery then packed the supplies in semi-fixed artillery shells and lobbed them over the enemy lines into the isolated battalion. After two weeks, the 120th (which we called the "lost battalion") was liberated from behind a large mound of dead Germans who had ringed the position. The above battle cost the enemy an entire 7th army and gained France for our forces. Winston Churchill called this the most daring and decisive battle of the war. On 22 August 1944, we started our longest convoy trip to an area in a harvested wheat field near Senonches for a rest and critique for a few days until we were to hit the battle zone again.

Our hospital unit moved and operated as smooth as fine clock-work. The many hours, days and months of training and the work on maneuvers were paying off. Each individual knew precisely what their duty was, and any who had not been acquainted with our capabilities marveled at the efficiency of our unit. Each primary surgeon and every stationed nurse had his or her special team who functioned automatically without fuss and hardly a word.

Major Albert J. Vesper, Captain John O. Vieta, Captain James E. Lewis, Jr., Captain Phillip Morrison, Major Edward J. Marshall, Major Chimera and I had our General Surgical teams. Captain John J. VanDyke, Captain Paul C. Kundahl, and Captain Margaret Cake were assigned as anesthetists. Captain John W. Teahan was the Neuro Surgeon, Captain Daniel F. Hogan, the Orthopedic Surgeon, Guy A. Myers, Opthomological Surgeon. These officers and their teams were unexcelled in their specialties. Captain Harold L. Wilt, Pathologist, skillfully managed his unit with all the laboratory technicalities, transfusions, cross-matching blood studies—all on immediate notice.

Major Warren H. Enders and his team gave constant support day and night with the X-ray department. They were always on duty and were expedient at all times. Major Enders proved himself to be an outstanding Radiologist. The medical management under Lieutenant Colonel John F. Smaltz (now deceased) and Major James J. Coll were continually busy with their division of duties. They both deserved honors for their superb direction and care. The hospital management was carefully and expertly attended by Major Clifford N. Brown and Captain Walker G. Reaves, now both full Colonels, retired.

At one gathering of the men, I attempted to acquaint them with some of the customs that they may find in France, when on leave during rest period. The following instructions, cautions, and admonitions were given to better acquaint those who had never been to France or had not known certain customs. Some of the soldiers were given rest passes to visit the beautiful city of Paris or some other interesting cities of France where, for a short time, they may not be actively engaged in the misery of war. I stressed that they should not make an issue or act embarrassed or vulgar about physiological functions, as the French are quite open and take these things matter-of-factly. Along the French avenues were small stations to one side just off the sidewalk, by the street, where full bladders could be relieved. These stations may have one's entire back covered as is usual in the cities; however, often there is only a horizontal board about twelve to twenty-four inches wide across the area to cover the hips of a user of the station, revealing only the feet, head, and shoulders. In small towns there often times were not even such conveniences and I have seen either party of a couple just depart for the side lines. The party not involved perhaps stood by nonchalantly, or even greeted a friend and tipped his hat, as I saw on occasion. This is all a matter of what is accepted as normal behavior as one is growing up. (I have previously mentioned about toilets but will take the liberty of repeating some of it.)

Many of the off-street toilets throughout Europe were marked "W. C." (from the British), meaning water closet. Some, where German was spoken, were marked "*Damen*" or "*Herren*" (Women and Men). It was not uncommon to find a buxom female sitting on a public throne knitting or reading while you anxiously paced; trying not to be obviously obtrusive.

I learned also to be cautious in the French hotel bathrooms, as when the average Frenchman washed or bathed, he splashed water like a duck in a pond, consequently, the floors were built accordingly, with the drain in the center of the tile floor. Above all I cautioned that, when using the shower, "*Chaud*" meant hot, and "*Froid*" meant cold so that if a faucet had "F" or "C" on it they could remember this and would not be surprised by cold water when they were expecting hot. I also reminded them that if the French sign "Douche" was there, to take heed, as the meaning of that term is "shower." In one section of the bath some had a pear-shaped, open stool with a spout in the center. Caution again—as this was not a fountain, but a "bidet." Turn the water on slowly in investigating, as there could be a forceful blast of water. This diminutive stool or fountain which drains constantly on use, is actually a bottom washer and cleanses other parts as well. I told them that paper may be found in the bathrooms, but that after one used the bidet, there was usually a towel available. I cautioned that they should be sure to remove their clothing before attempting to use this contraption or their clothing and shoes would be thoroughly drenched. I overheard a French guide for tourists explain the bidet, "A very necessary fixture; it is for women to wash "zere poozies" and your American women who do not have them must be avoided."

The tormenting challenge of a Parisian so-called "Turkish" toilet is one to unruffle the hardiest stomach. I ducked into a restaurant hurriedly and requested directions to the toilet. After passing a few coins to the outstretched tip-begging hand, I was shown a door in the corner of the room. If I would have only walked past the door, it would have been quite obvious where the toilet facility was kept. On opening the door, the ammoniacal fragrance hit full force. A very tiny closet was dark except for a tiny yellow light. There, in the middle of the cubicle, was the glory hole surrounded by a slightly slanting floor super soaked, wet, and slippery. On either side of the hole was a deep imprint of a shoe sole. The idea was to place both feet in the imprint and stand or squat. Only the most demanding necessity would allow one to gain relief. It took a masterful stance to avoid slipping into the foul abyss. There was no wall hook, nail, nor ledge to hang a coat, camera, or any carried item. Paper or cleansing material was non-existent. On near completion of relief a buxom lass entered—I was near the terminal point in more ways than one, and said, "Pardonney-moi, uno momento." The reply was, *"allez, allez, depechez-vous!"* meaning go, go, hurry! I was then rudely and forcefully pushed to one side so made my exit. I wanted to wash my hands so I re-entered the main restaurant and requested water. Instead, I was given wine. This was the first time I ever washed my hands in wine, and the waiter mumbled something in pigeon English, which sounded like, "Those crazy Americans." Some of these so-called "Turkish toilets" are found in the passage-ways under certain streets of Paris. One is the Champs-Élysées. They are also scattered throughout France.

On our way to Senonches we moved through a convoy of heavy French artillery forces and across the rolling green fields with quaint and picturesque thatched roofed houses in the old villages. It was saddening to see the total destruction of war and death going in some of the small villages.

We passed burned-out tanks which had been blasted by artillery fire. The debris of war was scattered in the fields and was a common sight. Everywhere we could see the terror and misery of war. Finally, we understood the gratitude of the French people. The villages were lined with people cheering us. Liberation of Paris was imminent and the French were delirious with joy. Our convoys moved slowly through the villages between lines of people laughing, waving, crying, shouting at us, showering us with gifts of tomatoes, flowers, fresh eggs, and even an occasional gift of wine or cider. Flags were fluttering and Mademoiselles waved gaily from the balconies and upstairs' windows. We felt wonderful, and tipped our helmets and at a more jaunty angle and sat up a little straighter, acting as if we alone were responsible for the liberation.

All did not go completely well with the convoy. We split up because of the advancing troops along the roadways. I was riding in a jeep with Major

Vesper. The convoys were split into three different sections by armaments moving to the front. Our convoy got lost and we arrived in Senonches in three sections. While enroute to a rest area our convoy became entangled with some of the German's armored divisions. Two sections of our convoy crossed through a German convoy and a few hours later through a French armored division, our second encounter with the French. The sirens on these tanks kept blasting through the night giving all the personnel a good case of nervous exhaustion.

At this time, our hospital convoy was moving into a rest area zone while preparations were being made for our armies to move into Paris for necessary action. Several of our divisions were set and posed, hoping and waiting for the order to move into Paris. Many had looked forward to the enjoyment of throwing the enemy out of this great city. General Omar Bradley chose to have the French divisions re-take their own city. Commanding the armored division was the renowned General Jacques Leclerc who had been a P.O.W. of the Germans in 1940. General Leclerc was a *nom de guerre*, as his family was in German-occupied France and he feared retribution on them. He later escaped and performed brilliantly in the Libyan campaign of 1943. General Leclerc was chosen because of his outstanding ability and his prior leadership in Africa. General Bradley issued the order to General Leclerc for him to move his French 2nd Armored Division immediately. His duty was to re-capture Paris and take command in the elimination of the enemy. General Leclerc however, was very slow in getting started. Over twelve hours were lost and General Bradley was exasperated when he learned of the loss of time as he had a commitment time to fulfill. The French divisions were finally underway twelve hours later than ordered by General Omar Bradley, and were further delayed along their route by admiring French citizens. When they rolled into the small village of Moyteux, they wined it up in the local bistros as the villagers inundated vehicles and personnel with wine, song, and flowers. There were toasts to de Gaulle, the Cross of Lorraine, and the Maquis. The French officers succumbed to this praise.

A U.S. Liaison group came upon this scene, and realizing that several American divisions were waiting impatiently outside of Paris to allow the French the honor of liberating their capitol. Its members were understandably disturbed. A sergeant with the liaison group fired a telegram to General Bradley, describing the situation. The revelry of the French armored division abruptly ceased as if a bomb had been dropped when General Bradley sent a message to General Leclerc telling him that unless the French divisions moved forward immediately, all aid to the French would stop and the U.S. divisions would move on Paris within the hour. General Bradley then told General Allen, commanding the 4th arm to slam into Paris—General Leclerc understood when General Bradley gave orders to act immediately. There would be no toleration of delay for any reason. General Leclerc was told of General Bradley's orders to General Allen. He then dropped all frivolity and moved his armored divisions into action immediately. The French, now more than twelve hours late, burned up the tank treads racing for Paris. On 24 August at 10:00 in the evening, Captain Drome of the French 2nd Armored Division arrived at the Hotel De Ville with his tank squadron and a company of infantry.

In the meantime, on the morning of 24 August, while on a rest period at Senonches, Major Vesper, Major Marshall, and I took a short trip to Paris. As we traveled along in the jeep, bumping and bouncing without notice or care, I was reminiscing through my tunnel of memories trying to reflect on all the areas we should see in Paris. Major Vesper would write, taking notes on the sequential order of sites and places of history to visit. Beginning at the Eiffel tower, then trying to jog my memory of the exact location so we would not spend time in retracing our steps or travel.

The day was pleasantly warm with a cool breeze which made our Eisenhower jackets just comfortable for all purposes. There were now only distant sounds of war—this we suddenly realized and felt quite relieved. Arriving in Paris, we felt excitement in the atmosphere. It may have been from spontaneous shouting of the citizenry, or it may have been from the occasional flurry of small arms fire near by—too near, yet far enough for our welfare. It was on the 25th of August that the commanding German officer of Paris, General Dietrich von Choltitz placed his name in history honorably for not carrying out a direct order from Hitler to completely destroy Paris. He was ordered by Hitler to bomb the entire city and burn it to the ground. General von Choltitz had stated that war had been thrilling with their many victories, but that now it was one humiliating and tragic defeat after another. He did not want his name to go down in history as the one who destroyed and ravished the beautiful and historic city of Paris. It would be a far greater disgrace for both him and his family name to be the German General responsible for the plunder of this great city even though he realized he would be labeled as a traitor to Hitler and his staff. It was at this time also when he recalled that "Karl," the great artillery piece of destruction, was rolling across Europe from the Russian front, and was to be used for the destruction of Paris.

The Germans had several railroad rifles—I recall my father used to tell me about "Big Bertha" in the first world war which could send a huge shell seventy-five miles and be on target. In this war, the Germans had a huge railroad gun called "Karl" which was supposed to be zeroed in on Paris.

It was never used for this, although it was threatened. The barrel carried a two ton shell which, when fired, could hit on target also. It was the most powerful artillery piece ever made and was carried by railway from the Russian front. Upon the surrender of General von Choltitz, he informed the French General about "Karl." Von Choltitz was dumbfounded when he was told that we knew about this fact and that the U.S. Air Force had bombed "Karl" and the railroad network near Soissons early this day, 25 August. One of the officers under General von Choltitz had unwittingly divulged the secret to a French paramour, who in turn, related it to the proper French underground authorities. The U.S. Air Force was then notified and appropriate action was taken immediately.

The American divisions had been closing in on Paris, however did not enter the city until after the French division had gone in first as liberators of Paris. American General Gerow was standing by with the V corps at Argenta (a town close to Paris) with many other divisions and the 3rd army of General Patton, to drive into Paris. Now, with the French finally moving forward, our troops went on with the war, generally bypassing Paris. Then, on 25 August, a platoon of French arrived at the Hotel Maurice. Smoke bombs were thrown in the lobby, and the Germans, with General Dietrich von Choltitz, commandant of the German garrison in Paris, came out with hands up. The Germans were then taken to the Gare Montparnasse where the surrender formalities were carried out—General von Choltitz to the French. The loss of Paris was a most serious blow to the Germans. This loss was commensurate to the loss of all France and was a great morale loss to the entire German staff.

CHAPTER FOURTEEN
PARIS

Riding in our jeep down the Champs Elysees we turned left into the Place Vendôm, then off the circle to 13 Rue Capucine. This was the hotel where Velma and I had obtained overnight accommodations in 1936. It was also where our German acquaintances stayed. We unloaded our small bags and ration boxes, then went into the streets looking for excitement. We roamed the city, visiting more places and areas than I knew existed. This was a surprise, for I thought I remembered the city.

As we drove around on our tour, I recall passing down Rue Reaumur where we saw the early residence of Josephine de Beauharnais, who later became Napoleon's Josephine. It was here that her son was born. He was to become Viceroy of Italy by appointment of his famous stepfather. Rue Reaumur is a street filled with history. In the fourteenth century it was traveled by Chaucer. Then there is the theater which was closed by decree of Francis I; in his judgment it had displayed poor taste by exhibiting a picture of the emperor with a large red nose. Further on we chanced by 4 Place des Victoires and noticed a sign, "Le Roy Gourmet." I remembered having dined there years before. We agreed to stop and have dinner. We then enjoyed a delightful multiple-course meal. By American standards it was tiny portioned, but the price was modest. The rickety lift (elevator) in the hotel had not changed in my nine years' absence. It clattered and creaked as it rose slowly to the fourth floor. We then clanked the iron gate closed and sent it creeping, with subdued screeching, back down to the lobby.

Next morning we awakened refreshed, completed our ablutions, and had a meager breakfast. Butter was among a multitude of other luxuries not available. We did have supplementary C-rations, which helped. Since we were all non-smokers we traded the cigarettes and candy bars in the ration boxes for things we wanted that the natives could supply. (Not an original practice, but highly successful.) Lucky Strikes, Camels, etc. were far more valuable to the French than money. They rarely wanted our paper currency, which was understandable, since they recently had suffered a costly experience with Reichsmarks.

In the morning we returned to the city, looking, talking, and listening. We frequently encountered French troops; some of the most colorful were the Moroccan *Spahis* in crimson garrison caps and white baggy breeches. We came on a crowd of civilians watching French soldiers marching a group of German prisoners. Most of these captives were terrified, red-eyed and exhausted with hands behind their heads, and being prodded by guards. They showed no sign of arrogance—some recently had been slashed across the face. The French people hissed and threw stones or any other missile at their former tormentors, now being moved for incarceration and judgment. Shortly after this encounter, we saw a group of eight women with heads shaved, marched through the streets. They were being called horizontal collaborators by the crowd. The French were so happy they were hysterical, but they did take time out to vent their wrath. Hatred now boiled over.

The three of us then returned to tourism. To appreciate Paris one should know the city's history. Without the background it is little more than a collection of colorless, lifeless buildings, resembling the description of Victor Hugo; that it was a teeming of thieves and prostitutes, filthy alleys, and intertwining pathways reeking of decay and beset with dens of iniquity. But the eye of the beholder must reckon with beauty. All cities are interesting, but those in Europe have the flavor of antiquity, and passing years have left tales of love, war, travail, and rapture. The world is rife with the history of civilizations. Some have declined and some have crashed, but most cities do survive. Paris is a survivor. And so we enjoyed Paris, relishing the present, but recalling the past.

There were noticeable differences since Velma and I had lived there for a short time before World War II. We found then, the average Parisian was reluctant to respond to any request for directions. It was a rare exception when one would listen to our school French. They were usually rude in explanations or demand that we hurry. *"Allez, allez, dépêchez-vous, vite vite!"* As a subtlety we would thank them for their courtesy and do the best we could with map and guidebook. People appeared uninhibited. In 1944, however, in the aftermath of another war, attitudes had changed. Major Al Vesper, Major "Speedy" Edward Marshall, and I found the average Parisian more willing to give directions and a bit more kindly disposed. The last of the Germans were leaving—replaced by Americans. In a sense we were invaders.

Despite bursts of gunfire the street traffic was resuming. It was subdued, however, as our invasion forces were a calming influence. Among interesting sights were girls flying down the streets, steering their bicycles with one hand and using the other to keep their dresses from billowing over their heads. We continued to drive slowly down the Champs Elysees—a wide avenue of beauty, divided by a park lined with shrubs and trees, and leading to the Arc de Triomphe. We saw the parish church for the Kings of France at the time when the Louvre was the Royal House and its grounds served as a burial place for artists. Farther, there came into view a white edifice on a hill, the Basilique de Sacre Coeur. On the way we passed the iron-fenced Grand Palais.

After parking the jeep near Sacre Coeur we walked across the cobblestone to the corner bistro where we sipped on light wine. Meditating, we saw in our minds' eye the diminutive Toulouse Lautrec, painting a few ladies of the night. Fortunately, the spot is still alive through the work of Lautrec. The colorful life of Paris that he committed to canvas lives on, to be admired by millions.

Since our time was limited, we shifted our attention from the past to the present and we moved on to the southern foot of the hill. Pausing only for a brief look at Place Pigalle and Place Balanche, we then went on to Boulevard de Place and quickly past the ancient Montmartre Cemetery, to Rue Canlaincourt. We then found ourselves before the massive and ornately carved doors of Notre Dame Cathedral. Outside Notre Dame we paused to stare at the Gargoyles; their grotesque faces seeming to mirror the agony of the many wretched inmates they had seen below them in the prison yard across the street.

We then went to the flea market where it was once the scene of a mass of humanity and the din of bargain hunters. It now had become the victim of troubled times and an uncertain future. There were more people selling than buying. The majority were fumbling over clothing fitting, and haggling over prices. The stalls of arts and jewelry were vacant. We wanted nothing there; only to see the changes brought about in a few violent years.

As we strolled on down the streets, we saw many idlers and café generals mapping war plans, strategy, and battles. Much of their time was spent staring in bewilderment, wondering how the great Maginot protective line with its deep underground bunkers could have fallen into the hands of the Germans.

The benches in the parks prior to the war were usually occupied by lovers; entwined in each other's arms, with the rest of the world obviously locked out. This time the occupants of those benches were elderly people idly reading the daily paper or simply staring into space. Possibly, they were wondering what would happen next to their beautiful historic city.

On Boulevard de Palais at the corner of Quai de l'Horloge, still stood the first public clock in Paris. Installed in 1353 and restored in 1574, it continued to run and keep perfect time. It was elaborately decorated with gold *fleur-de-lis* on a brilliant blue background, and surrounded by fruit and flowers, rams' heads, royal crests and shields with angels guarding the highly ornamented arch. There was still a bell overhead which had been rung for royal and festive occasions. It was so overwhelming we almost forgot to check the time.

Some of our unit could never understand how part of our convoy got so completely lost. At this phase it seemed as if some of us ended up in Paris, accidentally on purpose. We did not know when there would be another chance to visit this fascinating city. It took us a long time to get there and the best excuse given was to say we got lost because of both friendly and enemy convoys; and that we had to stay in Paris for a few days.

While in this area, promotions for several of our officers came through. From Captains to Majors: Chimera, Endres, Marshall, and Colpoys, also promotions came through for Lieutenant Van Gundy to Captain, and a few of our nurses received promotions including our chief nurse, Captain Crawford to Major.

After return to our group, by then at Senonches, we rested. We supplemented our 10-1 rations by tomatoes, carrots, cucumbers, and eggs from the stores and neighboring farms. We had a few softball games with the 5th Evacuation Hospital, also in this area. Evenings, we spent at the 51st Evacuation: some from the units went on a trip to Chartres. We also made expeditions to the Hotel de Foret in Senonches where meals were excellent if one could get in. The culinary art of the French was the best. Days of our so-called rest in Senonches we spent time patching tents, repairing and replacing damaged equipment. Weather was poor with a steady wind, frequent rains day and night and little sunshine.

After about two weeks we received orders to move to La Capelle, France and then to Belgium. We spent miserably cold nights moving in blackout.

We left Senonches on 6 September, and at La Capelle slept in trucks and ditches cleared of mines and any other place we could find. On 8 September, we left for Dinant in Belgium, not far from La Capelle. Again we moved in the middle of the night, cold and miserable. The scenic drive along the Meuse gave a glimpse of orderliness of Belgian villages. The people received us very enthusiastically. Our convoy arrived near Dinant and set up tents and began receiving the wounded by air. Our duty was to prepare patients from field hospitals and clearing stations, and treat wounded surgically or medically. Then we were to get them off to clearing stations for evacuation to the General Hospital away from the zone of action, some to England.

We were fogged-in almost every night, and the one night with heaviest in casualties we had the most dense fog. The fogs lasted until noon every day. We had a great number of German wounded and Key words on the ward were, *"Wie Gehts? Gut?"* We found it a better policy to keep wounded Germans in one ward tent and Americans or Allies in another.

Nights were cold, we had no stoves, and we were caught in the middle of a battle. It was miserable. Germans in the hills next to us were close to our encampment and would infiltrate at night, coming through our tent area, for battle with Belgian resistance fighters. Generally we laid low, in foxholes and slit trenches, and some patients had to stay in the trenches too. We gave all the blankets to the wounded, and by the fourth night mustered up a few stoves. We were located by the Meuse River close to Dinant. The river seemed to flow slowly only a few inches below the grassy meadow.

The Germans were entrenched just beyond our encampment in the hills, and Belgian resistance fighters were coming up from the river area. They would have brief battles, usually at dusk through our hospital grounds. We collected many bullet holes through our tents. Our canvases looked liked patched quilts from our necessary constant repairs. Our guards had to do "flat duty," crawl instead of stand, for if they did stand they could be mistaken for soldiers. The small arms fire between the enemy and the Belgian resistance fighters were shot at random and made it very unhealthy to be a marching guard. We certainly did not want to lose any of our hospital guards with "lead poisoning," regardless from which side it came. Many people of Dinant told us that their city in World War I was totally ravished and burned to the ground by German troops. This fact had been fostered in the Belgian's memory and their fighters wanted to avenge this atrocity.

One cold morning I was lying awake in my sleeping bag and a heavy fog rolled in from the Meuse a few hundred feet across the highway. On this morning sleep was impossible as I was worrying about one of the wounded men. I shivered awake about five o'clock finding myself half out of my bag. The coffee had not been put on, so I thought I would go out to the supply tent and get some. The distance was about one hundred fifty feet from our kitchen and the main hospital tents. I thought I could possibly get the mess sergeant to start a bit of early coffee or an early breakfast. I went to the tent where I heard someone moving in the food supply area. I saw a German officer picking up cans of beans. I spoke to him in German and told him I would help him, and said he was up rather early and should go back into the prisoner-of-war section with other casualties in the wounded area. "You must not be wounded very badly or you would not be out here," I said. "Where were you wounded?" I looked down and saw he had a luger I said, "You have that pistol on you. You should have turned that in as soon as you were taken in the hospital as a casualty. One of our troops is liable to see you with side arms and it might be a bit rough on you. You better give that to me. I have a special place for that in my own equipment and you have no further use for it."

He became a bit direct, and said in broken English, "No, I came down here from my battalion," as he pointed to the hills, not very far from our organization and where they had been fighting with the Free French.

"Well," I said, "it certainly is absurd for you to be trying to carry a little bit of food back there to them." I tried to convince him to bring his battalion down to the hospital and turn them in as prisoners. I tried to convince him that he was in the midst of a pincer in which Patton's army had him surrounded. The Free French and Belgians were cleaning up the pockets. I told him he should surrender and that we would keep them until our troops came through and took them to a special camp. He refused again. I admonished him for doing it this way and told him that if he changed his mind, to bring his troops on down. He said that they had orders not to surrender, and that was final. I was not about to argue because of his side arm, and I'm sure he would have been willing to use it. I saw it was unbuckled and ready. He proceeded to fill a box with food, even stuffing some into his shirt and went up into the hills in the heavy dew of the morning.

Late that evening, after another skirmish, we were told that most of the Germans were killed; some were so badly wounded they could hardly be saved. The officer was not among the wounded; I had considered this incident to be another closed chapter until 13 September. There had been heavy fighting in the hills at eight-thirty in the evening, and soon after that a German officer presented himself to the nurse on duty, Lieutenant Cornelia B. Pound from Birmingham, Alabama. He clicked his heels, nodded, and asked for the chief of surgery. Lieutenant Pound pointed to me in the far end of the large post-surgical ward where I was changing a dressing on a colostomy of a German infantryman. Lieutenant Pound brought the officer to me and left. I looked up, and he clicked his heels and gave me a salute which I returned. Then I recognized the officer who had been in the supply tent taking canned foods. He appeared exceedingly pale, was trembling, and had difficulty breathing. I asked how he was, and he explained that his entire command had been killed or seriously wounded and we had many of his men. He reminded me that I had wanted to disarm him before, so he removed two sidearms from the holsters on either side, a Luger and a P-38. He handed them to me, butts first, saying, "I am Waffen S.S. Captain Walter Von Funck. I have been a good officer." He coughed and blood appeared. He wiped his mouth with his handkerchief and asked to sit.

I told him to sit on the next cot which was empty. I attempted to open his jacket and he raised his hand and said, "You, Colonel, are a good officer and I am honored to present my sidearms. I will no longer have use for them. I pray I shall be sent home to Giessen. My children and my wife will understand." His face tightened and he grimaced in pain. I laid him out on the cot, opened his jacket, and opened his blood-saturated shirt. I saw he had two holes of bullet entry and both were bleeding. I called for Lieutenant Pound and a corpsman. The captain whispered in a weak, hoarse voice, saying, "There has been no pain until now. Do nothing, it is useless. This is my destiny." All too soon he lost consciousness. We administered intravenous fluids but his respiration wheezed and bubbled until it ceased.

Inspection of the wounds of exit revealed his heroic determination to reach our hospital alive, as the wounds were massive.

At this station near Dinant we treated 1,810 admissions, with 462 on 14 September, and 363 on 15 September. We had seventeen deaths all together, with an overall mortality of 0.94 percent. All wounded, both American and German, were sent separately to the rear echelons for continued care and assignments. We had difficulty transferring all the patients at the stipulated date, as some were post-operative only one day. On 14 September, we received orders to move on 16 September for a secret destination, and we were assigned from the 9th U.S. Army at this time to the British 2nd Army.

CHAPTER FIFTEEN
HOLLAND

We were glad to break camp and move on, as each move forward was nearer the end of the horrible killing and crippling. When we moved we could not take our wounded or prisoner casualties with us. So we sent them back to general hospitals or England, although it was always with difficulty. We often wondered what had happened that they turned themselves in to us as prisoners.

Having received secret orders, we left in sections; and were told that our officers were to rendezvous with another unit and that our duties would be the same, but in a different area. On 15 September we left for a destination that involved our meeting outside Louvain, Belgium. We detached from the 9th Army, but were given orders to be attached to all under the overall command of General Montgomery of the British 2nd Army along with the British 1st Airborne. We were the only U.S. medical group chosen for this mission. We discovered later that the reason for transfer was that we were to support troops ordered to invade Holland, actually for the eventual move on Berlin.

We were under command of General Edward Phillips and our division commanders were Major General Maxwell Taylor of the U.S. 101st Airborne and Major General James Gavin commanding the U.S. 82nd Airborne. The 82nd was to seize the main bridge over the Maas (or Meuse) River at Grave, Holland and it was their task to hold the high ground around the area of Groesbeek. They were then to take at least one of the four bridges over the Maas-Waal Canal. Finally they were to take the big bridge over the Waal River at Nijmegen. In Germany, the Waal River is called the Rhine, but as it enters Holland it becomes the Waal. The 101st was to take the area around Eindhoven, Hertogenbosch, Uden, and Vechel. British troops were to take the bridge at Arnhem and its surrounding territory. Our airborne troops were to consolidate in the drop zone. The entire mission was to be done simultaneously.

Wallace Harry Graham

The 1st British Airborne Unit was commanded by General Urquhart. The British also had the excellent Polish Paratroopers Brigade commanded by Major General Stanislaw Sosabowski. This general's command was highly trained, rough and tough, determined and dedicated. The code name for the overall operation was Market Garden. The plan was for a sixty mile frontal attack by the three airborne divisions. The 21st British Army Group was to attack south and go around the Siegfried line.

In September 1944, the Germans stopped their tanks at the dragon's teeth of the Siegfried line. General Hodges, in command of the 5th Corps, smashed his way through Belgium to the Reich border, opening a path through Liege and beyond to Aachen. Our 1st Army broke through the Siegfried line, followed within six weeks by the fall of Aachen. Its fall was a decisive blow to the German command, and their disciplined troops fell into confusion. It was here that a German general was captured in his staff car driving north as part of the American convoy. The general had passed himself off as a RAF officer. He almost got by with it, until he got to Aachen. One of our sharp military police asked him where he was going. The general had been ordered to the Sommes sector to organize and command the entire German defense of the River Sommes sector. He had been informed that the British had crossed the Sommes two days before, so he inadvertently crossed the path of the invading army in his command car, made the wrong turn, and was in the American convoy. The German Army had become quite a highway hazard and was mixing with our troops. We considered they were retreating prisoners and gave it no consideration. The general's identity came out as the advancing American division cleared an intersection. A French farmer had pedaled up breathlessly on his bicycle and screamed, *"Le boucher, le boucher!* [the butcher]" This, incidentally, would have been a logical time for the German Army to have surrendered, as the Germans suffered their heaviest casualties during the following eight months of war.

When the Germans thought they were winning, they stomped hard and talked big and brave. When they were hit, they sagged like a spent balloon. On 10 September, the British Guards Armoured Division had reached the bridge over the Maas-Scheidt Canal, in the north of Belgium.

General Montgomery's plan was that the offensive airborne attack would begin on 17 September. This was the first section to block the northern route of the Germans, giving us a faster way to Berlin. The British were to advance to the Zuider Zee and cut off German troops just west of Holland, then outflank them in the east around the north end of the Siegfried line. This airborne drop was part of Market Garden. Where this name was dreamed up is anyone's guess. It must have been a garden of the devil's own, filled with bombs and mud.

The British Airborne's venture into Arnhem did not achieve the surprise anticipated. The brave British Airborne Division composed of the Polish Parachute Brigade and Canadian troops was dropped into heavy enemy resistance (the 11th S.S. Panzer Corps happened to be there) and was pinned down by counterattacks. The British held under this fire. They had 9,000 troops, and were reduced to about 2,400. The survivors infiltrated back in to our lines. The battle raged from eight o'clock the night of 17 September until the morning of 25 September. This attack is partially shown in the movie, A Bridge Too Far. The British had no alternative but to retreat or be annihilated. Therefore, General Montgomery ordered their withdrawal back across the Rhine.

The crossing of the Rhine was not made until six months later, fifty miles north of the Arnhem Bridge. Our campaign continued with heavy weather preventing supply replenishment or dropping of reinforcements. Enemy counterattacks were overwhelming because of sheer numbers and heavy weaponry. During this battle we received orders to move along, but keep as close to firing lines as possible so as to receive casualties in minimum time.

We knew our mission would be difficult and hazardous. Our move took us from Louvain over the Albert Canal, and from there into Leopoldsburg on the Dutch border. There we pitched tents in heavy rain during the night of 16 September in a large, marshy field of heather where we landed. Everything was wet and we spent a seemingly endless night in mud and water. We were surrounded by Germans and knew our work was going to be rugged. All roads had been closed and blocked by the enemy, but we received casualties as soon as our hospital had been set up. Our hospital was a large ward tent, fifty by sixteen feet, in which were ten operating tables. The early morning skies of 17 September were dark with rain and the aircraft of the allied airborne army. Our casualties soon got through due to our troops opening an area south of Eindhoven and in the first twenty-four hours we had received 512 patients. We worked steadily for two weeks with little rest. We built our own supply depot from materiel parachuted in to us flown in by C-47s. The Germans were repulsed and reinforcements of our tanks and men proceeded down the road.

During heavy fighting when I was operating in our massive ward tents there was a dogfight between a Luftwaffe plane and a British fighter. The British plane veered over the hospital tent and the Luftwaffe pilot roared into a dive, one of the planes firing a 50-caliber machine gun and peppering a path across the operating room. A fine nurse, Lieutenant Agatha Kurth, was in the line of fire and was struck by a bullet that plowed through her right shoulder, upper right chest, and wrist, avulsing all tissues and some of the bone in her right wrist. She made no commotion. She simply said, "I have been hit." After treatment she was sent back to a general hospital for plastic revision of the avulsed segments. We had many casualties of our own people, even though we were a hospital and marked as such.

In Leopoldsburg after the German plane strafed the hospital we could send no casualties by ambulance to the rear. It was frustrating to try to get ambulances past the British vehicles obstructing the highway, which refused to move or could not move. The ambulances were large and roomy, but clumsy, sluggish, top-heavy, and unsafe on roads. We called our attempts to go through as rides down hell's highway. The British did not or would not understand how to control a blackout, although they had been conducting them long before we entered the war. British trucks flashed blinding lights during blackouts, then suddenly extinguished them. They would get out of the slit trenches or foxholes, build fires, and have a "spot of tea" in spite of hell or high water or flying shell, large or small.

On the last day of heavy casualties an auxiliary surgical team came in but was not needed, as our wounded had been cared for and we were preparing to move. The army gave them an invasion arrow decoration but did not award the arrow to *our* troops. As a matter of fact, this omission may have been unknown to the army headquarters. During twenty days of operation at Leopoldsburg we had 3,432 admissions, with thirty-seven deaths, a mortality of 1. 07 percent which was a remarkable record for the serious nature of the wounds and the proximity to the battle lines.

By 1 October, our troops had consolidated the southern wedge of eastern Holland, from Brussels across the Maas River into Nijmegen. The British airborne venture into Arnhem had been a costly loss, and the overall mission of rolling back the German right flank for a dash into the Ruhr had been successfully stopped by the Germans.

On 8 October, we received orders to move to another drop zone in a muddy field near Uden, Holland. There was some question as to whether this was a field or a river bottom. Rain was heavy and we were over our ankles in mud. On 9 October, casualties poured in, and during the next twenty-four hours we received 512. We were surrounded by the enemy and had no help from auxiliary teams. We worked day and night, for two weeks, and most patients were major casualties.

There was a steady roar of artillery, supplemented by a continuous barrage as the British drove into the lowlands. Our casualty list continued, but was lighter. We were here for twenty days, until 27 October, handling 823 admissions, with five deaths—an overall mortality of 0.6 percent. In Uden we received casualties from the immediate area including Eindhoven, Son, Hertogenbosch, Nijmegen, and the lower third of the Netherlands.

We had only one surgical operating table for neurosurgery, one for maxillo-facial surgery, four to six for general surgery, one for orthopedics with an adjacent Hawley table for Spica plaster work, and two for minor surgery and burns. This proved enough for our teams and one or two auxiliary teams. Personnel worked surgery in two twelve-hour shifts. Each had from eight to ten surgeons, five anesthetists, ten technicians, and five to seven nurses.

There was an interesting occurrence in Uden where we slept in small pup tents. We placed boots to the front of the tents and hung uniforms on the mid-front pole. I had acquired a boxer dog, so at night we tied him to the rear tent pole. Early one morning when it was cold enough to see my breath the dog became restless. Suddenly the tent fell over me and I realized the dog was trying to jerk the tent along the front way. He was having trouble, since I was trying to get out from under the flattened tent at the same time he was tugging. I thrashed around in my scanty and breezy pajamas trying to get out, and at the same time trying to find my clothes and boots. I got my head out of the tent in time to see two of the Free French liberating my clothes and boots. My dog got loose and tore after the pilfering characters. I was running after them in bare feet along the muddy road, and was reluctant to yell at the marauders as it would awaken all the others. Fortunately, they dropped my boots and I retrieved them. Several members of our unit had articles stolen and we often saw our clothing worn by the Free French. We were not too pleased, as the young Frenchmen were freeing the wrong items. I slept lightly after this episode and tied my dog to the front of the tent.

One unusually dark and cold night the dog again was restless and I heard a rustling sound. I saw a moving shadow and grabbed a trench tool; I had a plan in my mind, and exploded from my tent and hit the moving object. I thought I had struck Niagara Falls, as I was suddenly drenched with cold water. I got my flashlight and saw that someone had placed our large canvas lister bag of drinking water outside my tent probably during the evening, and I was unaware of it. The wind had caused it to sway and I had attacked it in the dark, full force. I was silent about it when everyone wondered what happened to our drinking water.

The movement from Uden on 26 October took us through Hertogenbosch and over the Maas on the way to Nijmegen. Here we ran into enemy fire as we settled on a hill a few hundred yards from the Waal River. Our hospital and our troops were in a position similar to that of an island, surrounded by dikes with wide ditches on either side, where all roads to the city ran on top of dikes. This terrain would have been ideal for defense except that our advancing tanks or artillery pieces would have to follow along the top of dikes, silhouetted perfect targets for the enemy. By this time the Germans had proven themselves battle-wise, disciplined soldiers, but no match for our airborne forces.

All the while the 101st and 82nd Airborne were capturing objectives and holding operations east of Nijmegen. They had attained and held their objectives since 7 September. Our Airborne operations were driving the Germans back and keeping the Nijmegen bridge. On 26 October, we left "mudhaven" to occupy a modern hospital set up on a hill in the eastern outskirts of Nijmegen.

Our unit was set up in a new, modern hospital where living conditions were ideal except for the enemy barrage over our heads. The hospital was beautifully built of glass and steel. We found, however, that glass was not impervious to flying steel from the enemy bombardment of high explosive artillery shells. We were surrounded by batteries and so close to the Jerries that, with a minimum of error, they could have wandered into our mess hall at any time. We found it much safer to remain in slit trenches or foxholes when not performing our duties.

For the next thirty-four days we were subject to constant fire aimed at artillery positions immediately around us and at the Nijmegen bridge behind. The barrage was sporadic, day and night. German planes were active, and the entire area was practically blown apart. The site was an excellent area to garner wounded within minutes of injury, and the hospital facilities were excellent, but not one window was intact in our entire hospital: steel and shrapnel crashed into our area and we wore helmets at all times.

The Germans bombed a reinforcement depot, which resulted in death and injury to many men we had returned to duty. Those who were injured were again our patients. Replacements were coming through, looking fresh, but very quiet. Their uniforms appeared new. Soon a shell burst blasted out and there was the whine of a 155mm howitzer. New replacements hit the ditch and slowly crawled out, faces blanched. They were dry-mouthed with fear as they re-adjusted their weapons. The sergeant leading them was a battle-worn trooper, weathered and rugged. He stood in the roadway shouting, "Get the hell back in line, you damn chickens: that firecracker was a mile high."

One reason we were bombarded so heavily was that the hospital was so near the Nijmegen bridge and the Germans were trying to knock it out. They would skip bomb at times, and some of the skips hit our unit. The Germans were trying to miss our position: they would not intentionally hit us if only because we had some of their wounded. A problem developed when we found that a British artillery piece and battery was too close to the hospital, inside a two hundred yard limit. It should have been outside this limit. The German commander sent a message that the British were not abiding by the Geneva Convention. The British replied, "We travel and fight by the rules of war," and refused to move. There later was a tremendous barrage and the British artillerymen were forever silenced.

I went out on the dike to show Captain Crawford where a shell had blasted a deep hole. I was looking for shell fragments to determine the type of explosive or anti-personnel missiles, when suddenly a terrific barrage hit us. I am not sure I heard the explosion and was not sure I had been struck, but did know there was a tremendous concussion and that my body was lifted up and thrown through the stubble bushes, which knocked the wind out of me as I smashed into a tree. My back slammed into the trunk and I dropped to the ground. After I got up and dusted myself off, I felt all right, except a bit dazed, and walked back down the dike toward the unit. I could hear nothing but bells ringing in my ears. I was asked by one of my unit if I knew I had torn my trousers. I said, "No," and then looked to the side of my right upper thigh. There was a large right-angle split in my trousers, just in back of my side pocket. I still was not sure I had been hit. My ears continued to ring, but there was no pain whatsoever in my right leg, thigh, or foot—even though the entire leg was numb.

As I walked I became aware of a sloshing in my right boot. I thought I had been perspiring, but on looking back to my thigh and hip area I realized I was losing blood. We hurried back to the hospital unit where I talked with Major Vesper, my executive officer and second in command of surgery. He ordered the anesthesia readied and instruments set up, and had my right lateral thigh x-rayed. A shell fragment was eight inches from the point of entry. It hit the femur bone and was driven down near the knee. Major Vesper then skillfully removed the fragment and other pieces of steel. The following day I realized I had been slammed against the tree with much more force than I thought. Intermittent pain was present in the lumbar back, with numbness in both legs and thighs. I found some fiber splints, wrapped them in cotton and gauze, and had my technicians strap the splint to my back. This abraded my skin considerably, so Sergeant Gorsky fixed a perfect splint for me. He took a small section of a two-inch tree limb, split it, wrapped it in cotton, then bound it with gauze. It fit beautifully when plastered down with adhesive. The following morning I felt beaten and stiff. Sergeant helped roll me out of bed and stood me up, then helped me dress and I was able to function from that time forward, back pain being my only problem. When my back felt better it was x-rayed to see why the pain continued. It was then that I found two vertebrae had been fractured, but were healing. My legs did not track perfectly for three weeks after the injury.

Our commanding officer, Colonel Rylander, awarded me the Purple Heart. Many years later, and while in private practice the back injury led to resection of a portion of three lumbar vertebrae and removal of three complete inter-vertebral discs. This injury finally resulted in paralysis from my third lumbar vertebrae down, causing both legs to be useless. Fortunately it was temporary. A myelogram study found the problem, and surgery corrected practically all of it. I continue to have numbness in the left leg and three toes on the left foot, but it is no real problem. My recovery has been speedy with no debility except soreness across the back and a numb area in the thigh. My ears continue to ring constantly and the lateral strip of thigh remains numb.

The functioning of the hospital unit was not hurt by the shelling even though the building became a shambles. Cleaning up damage inside began after each shelling and then we continued our duties. If there were an individual star for courage, heroism, and devotion to duty, everyone of our unit deserved it.

One of our many unfortunate casualties was Private 1st Class "Rosy" Rosenbloom from Brooklyn, who came to us with both feet, both hands, and both eyes gone, and with other multiple head and body injuries. He told me he had stepped on a mine, which may have been of a "bouncing Betty" type, which usually tore a body in half. After treating him for shock, cleaning him up and caring for his wounds, he was interested in only one thing, and that was whether he would be able to see. His story went something like this: "Doc, be sure and tell me what gives with these glimmers because I don't need to have these feet or hands, but got to have them eyes. My brother-in-law is an interior decorator, and I don't need feet or hands. All I have to have is one eye, and I can sit in a wheelchair, and I can get some home-made feet and hands, and I can tell them how to decorate, because I am really good at it. So please, tell me about my eyes, and if they are both out and I can't see, I'm not going to stick around anymore." I believed that when he would be in better physical condition I could tell him about his eyes. I told the ward personnel about his condition and asked that he not be told about his eyes. It was obvious he was blind, as when I first saw him one eye was on his cheek and the other was an empty socket.

It was necessary for me to leave for a few hours, and when I returned new people were on the ward. Inquiring about Rosy, I was told he had died in an unusual manner. One of the corpsmen had been talking to him and told him his blood pressure was good and he was doing fine, and his wounds were doing well. When Rosy asked him about his eyes he was told they were gone. Rosy's reply was, "Are you sure?" And when the corpsman said yes he said, "Well, I'm just not sticking around this place and am going to leave."

This story sounds incredible, but amazing as it sounds I have seen it happen several times when a patient willed to die. When the corpsman returned to check him in a bit less than an hour he saw that Rosy had fulfilled his wish.

We had a few differences with the British, but for the main part got along even though we did not always understand each other's humor. I remember the frustration in trying to get ambulances to the rear zone. We resented the lack of consideration as British lorries took over the roads. Many "Tommies" or "Limeys", as we called the British soldiers, looked upon Yanks as their not-too-literate country cousins and tolerated our presence. The average G.I. was sensitive to any rebuff regarding prestige, pride, and soldierly bearing. The Limey was individually a fine man—tenacious, and stubborn. It was often said that once a Limey gets in his foxhole he is the best defensive fighter in the world and nothing can move him except a bag of tea at tea time.

An ill fated episode struck our unit as Captain Dan Hogan became extremely ill. He had fallen and injured his abdomen. The problem was twofold in so far that Dan had been having a problem with his liver for the past two months and the fall caused increased pain. The gall bladder was also involved with an enlarged liver. The complications were so manifest and symptomatic that we considered it would be for the good of the service to send him back to a general hospital. The time involved with probable surgery and prolonged therapy was not justifiable to hold him in a battle zone hospital. We had depended upon his splendid orthopedic surgical care and we hated to lose his skills. Captain Dan Hogan appeared to be burned out and ten years older when he left our unit. The past two years had taken their toll; his shock of black hair sprinkled with gray had turned gray to white. Dan slowly got into the ambulance. We saluted and the thought struck me solidly that this was our last goodbye. Dan knew it too. He gave a fast glance, and looked straight ahead.

Instances of tetanus were rare. Three were enemy troops and one a civilian, all found in the field, having been wounded for over forty-eight hours. Two died, two lived. I do not recall having seen any in our troops. Rarely did we see gas gangrene, for wounds were treated very soon after the injury. All gross wounds were treated by thorough debridement, cleansing, and loose packing. Infection was controlled, anti-toxin administered immediately, sulfonamides, penicillin, correct blood and plasma volume was maintained and fluid was replaced along with good general nutritional and supportive measures. We had practically no amputations, except from initial trauma. Amputations were only performed when agreed in consultation by three surgeons. We saved all tissue with any blood supply to the part not totally devitalized. Bleeding vessels were controlled by ligation or cautery.

The wounds of the airborne troops were varied: the men were seasoned and trained in deplaning, falling properly, and landing. Conditions, however, were less than ideal. Injuries were from leaving the plane, such as being blown into another chute. The first unusual injury could be caused by the parachutist's opening shock if not correctly positioned. The taut suspension lines would tear ligaments or muscles, necessitating surgical repair. From their landing there were some fractures of feet or ankles. Ligamentous injuries and sprains were usually treated by the unit surgeons. We received few such ligament injuries as deltoid or tibio-fibular tears except when complicated with malleolar fractures.

The Nebelwerfers known as smoke bombs and Screaming Mimis came in sizes: 150mm, 210mm, 250mm, and 300mm. The 210 had a range of about six miles, but its effect was not great from the standpoint of penetrating artillery or tanks. The screaming, terrifying noise was frightening. The Germans usually set them off around nightfall when we had to crawl into our foxholes or slit trenches and try to get some sleep. They were fired similar to mortar shells, from an in-ground or placement of a missile thrower that looked like a mortar. They would last fifteen to twenty seconds and sounded like a woman's wavering screams at the top of her voice. You could hear them for miles. When they struck they made a horrendous explosion. I do not know how devastating they were, but they did what the Germans expected and that was to work on our psychology. I doubt that they were the most devastating explosives. They were more of a concussion type. The tremendous sound and the earth-shaking, ear-splitting explosion jarred nerves. Muscles tensed up as the shells shrieked.

The most effective shells were smaller millimeter, faster than the speed of sound, with a range of one to six miles. It was well known that an 88mm shell was faster than that of a fire rifle. When an 88mm was fired pointblank the target does not move, because the sound of the explosion follows after it strikes its victim. The Germans were master gunnery experts in handling the 88mm. They did so with the speed of a rifle, and with the same agility as handling a BB or air-pressure gun, and very accurate. When one is battle-aware and knowledgeable, he can distinguish the size of shell by sound and origin. He knows the angle of fragmentation and splash and whether he should run low or high, or crawl. Knowing from what direction the missile entered the body was important to the surgeon. Blast fragmentation may be inches or feet from the ground and is difficult to avoid. Our armamentarium philosophy differs from the German. Many of their explosives were meant to injure or maim, the philosophy being that wounded require much more manpower and time in care than do the dead.

One S.S. trooper, wounded seriously and believing he sustained a mortal wound, confided in me that we were more kind than he would have been. He said he always put the wounded out of their misery by using his bayonet or a gun butt, and in this way did not waste bullets. He said he was saving the Fatherland food and costly care of its enemies. He added that if dead they could not shoot him. He continued on in this barbaric manner stating that it was easier to kill Poles and Russians because they were so stupid: many would just stand in the way. He ranted on that it was more difficult to kill young girls, but it had to be done, as he knew they would produce more enemies for the Reich. He tempered this point when he said, "I felt bad at first." Another S.S. trooper said he only killed when he had to, but that S.S. units could not take prisoners even when in large groups as "all must be killed without pity." He told us that war brought his comrades together and gave them strength to resist and kill. He said, "Might is our supreme right. On the eastern front we left nothing alive, and burned everything to the ground." On asking a former teacher and ardent S.S. trooper how he would feel when his country would be overrun by enemies of Nazism the reply was that war could not be a matter of sentiment, as General von Hindenburg had taught. The more merciless, the kinder, because the war would end quicker. The Poles, Russians, English, and French have forced the war upon us Germans. They have lied to the whole world. Hitler, der Fuhrer, had begged for peace."

Few storm troopers were taken prisoner or became casualties. The ones with whom we did come in contact were arrogant, even to the death, during the first phase of the war. Later, their attitudes changed dramatically, particularly when wounded. With pain and time for reflection, along with knowledge that they were not omnipotent, their minds became confused, and their bodies sagged, with no semblance of the former snap and arrogance. They wilted when their finger was no longer on the trigger.

On the Sunday before Thanksgiving, 27 November, we had more artillery overhead than usual. We had not paid close attention, but the Germans were trying to regain lost ground and shells were raining over and around us. We had just received a group of casualties, six with eye injuries. Our ophthalmologist, Captain Friedman, said it was essential for the eye surgeon, Captain Guy A. Myers, to see these wounds. Heavy casualties were coming in including several facial and eye wounds which were incurred by mines and hand-to-hand fighting. One was a bayonet wound where there was a possibility the eye might be saved.

I went to Captain Myers and acquainted him with our casualties. He looked up and said, "Colonel Sir, I have found that I am not the bravest officer in this army, and for the time being, I am going to stay here until this barrage lifts because I am one officer who is probably going home undecorated, but surely intend to go home unperforated. Sir, if you don't get off the edge of this hole you are going to be splattered right on top of me. Only a wild man would be walking around up there at a time like this. I am frozen in this hole and sir, nothing in heaven or hell could get me out now." I told him I agreed thoroughly and suggested that when the shelling stopped, do his best and I would attend the wounded in the meantime. It was within the hour that I heard that Myers had been in the ward taking care of casualties when a shell hit our hospital, wounding his head and face, which led, within a brief time, to his death. We were grieved at the loss of this fine gentleman and outstandingly brilliant opthamological surgeon upon whom we depended greatly.

The same shell wounded other members of our unit. One of these was a superb nurse from Marmaduke, Arkansas, Lieutenant Kathryn Foster. She was with us from 1 October 1943, and was efficient, very brave and quietly professional. She was struck in the legs, and sustained fractures of both major bones. Sergeant Albert L. Horrell, my first assistant, was wounded, but not seriously. He was a skilled surgical corpsman. Lieutenant Ann Jenkins and Captain Joel Woodburn were the only personnel at this particular area where the shelling took place and both received certificates of meritorious work for their extremely cool and efficient handling of casualties during this intense emergency.

Captain Friedman was attending wounded in the adjacent ward, but fortunately was not hit. The unit had to depend on him solely at that time to treat and operate on eye injuries. Even so, it was imperative to send him forward with airborne troops who had landed with the gliders. These troops struck obstacles so hard that their protective glasses broke and caused many injuries, especially in one area where gliders struck German barracks. Firing and shelling died down.

At this time Major General Taylor, commanding the 101st Airborne, came in via ambulance and cart as one of our casualties, having been struck by a high-explosive shell. He was anxious to see the shell splinters and fragments to determine the type of explosive. I removed large fragments from his right thigh and hip. He responded well, as he was in superb physical condition. The day following debridement and removal of the splinters, Taylor was trying to rest in his bed and shells began flying thick and heavy. The general rang out, "This hospital site is worse than the front line. The entire place will blow up soon. I assured him we were only catching a few short rounds of premature bursts.

The Germans had an artillery piece on a tank down a valley in the environs of Nijmegen, aimed and zeroed in on an elevated dike near our hospital. This area afforded good visibility and was a good target. Our position was not shelled directly, but the air was loaded with missiles and we received an occasional short misdirected shell burst.

It was in this area that we first saw the German Komet planes, the Messerschmitt 163. They seemed experimental at the onset and as they neared the Nijmegen bridge the afterburner usually fizzled out after they had done their destructive work. Several planes dropped in this area because the afterburner or jet thrust would not last long enough to allow return to base.

While operating in Holland our supplies were excellent. They were flown in to us and dropped by parachute or later brought by supply truck. I recall the excellent tasty and hot dinner we received on Thanksgiving day with turkey and all the trimmings. A more delicious meal could not be served anywhere, and we certainly appreciated it. The only complaint was that we could have been more relaxed to digest our meal better if the Krauts had stopped throwing the high explosives with their resounding blasts. In this particular area in Holland, Generals Montgomery, Kirk, and Hawley, visited our unit. Some of the movie stars also came up later to try to cheer the wounded. They were all great morale builders after the battles had quieted down considerably.

In one of our lax times the British came through with a tremendous show given by their armored soldiers at the Red Cross tent. The British Airborne also had a fine band that entertained us toward the end of the campaign. We enjoyed all this very much, especially since the firing was quelled. Corporal Charles Gwynne, the Chaplain's assistant, did his bit too, and put on a great show which gave a great deal of pleasure to everyone in our outfit.

At the close of the campaign in Holland, we received the greatest and finest letters of commendation from Brigadier General Phillips of the British 21st Army group and General Maxwell Taylor, commanding officer of the U.S. 101st Airborne. These letters speak for themselves, but most of all we had the pride and satisfaction of a tough job well done, as well as the friendship and respect of our Airborne Divisions. We thought that we should have been awarded the invasion arrow or battle star. However, the War Department probably did not receive word to that effect from our commanding officer. We had been on the Holland invasion for nearly three months, and five weeks of that time we sat directly under the heavy guns of the German artillery at the bridge of Nijmegen between bombings, strafings, and Screaming Mimis.

We lost Lieutenants Raus-Kurth and Foster, Captains Myers, Hogan, Lieutenant Colonel Huey, and Sergeant Evans during that long campaign.

Lieutenant Colonel Thomas F. Huey, Jr. left our hospital unit 10 December 1944 because of dual problems—a wound in the foot which had never healed adequately coupled by compassionate leave. His loyalty and duties as Executive officer were sorely missed having been with the unit since 15 July 1943. For three long months, we worked with the airborne troops. Our admissions were 5,349 and mortality totaled fifty-four, or 1.0 percent.

On 1 December 1944, the 101st and 82nd were ordered to withdraw, and were replaced by British and Canadian troops. Our orders were to move to Saint Trond, Belgium to rejoin the 9th Army, regroup, repair, receive replacements, and rest. We had evacuated all nurses and casualties on 27 November because of the increasing barrage and the hazardous gunfire. The remaining section of the unit loaded equipment and personnel and left the night of 1 December. Immediately upon our withdrawal, the buildings we had occupied were again bombarded and nearly leveled. The lowland area we had just left was flooded, leaving Nijmegen a virtual island.

After a cold convoy trip we arrived in Saint Trond on the morning of 2 December. The nurses rejoined us, and we all found the area pleasant and interesting. The townspeople were pleasant, generous, and kind. Enlisted men were quartered in an industrial or vocational school, and said their accommodations were good. The nurses were in another school building, but for some reason they never appreciated the outside latrines. Emmy Ware, one of our more vocal and morale-stimulating nurses from South Carolina, was particularly sensitive about those. They did admit their quarters otherwise were functional.

Major Colpoys and six other officers moved into the Saint Joseph's Clinic, and became the envy of the rest of us. Most officers were housed in a count's chateau, shared with the count and countess. They were quite cordial, and we enjoyed their company and that of their children as well. This was an interesting house, built as a large square around a cobblestone courtyard, surrounded by a ten-foot stone wall, almost like a castle. The kitchen was near one end, and adjacent was the stone barn for the cattle, horses, and other animals. The barn was actually the next room. We had odors from the kitchen and farm animals. One of the chateau's several niceties was cold running water, as well as hot running milk straight from the cows.

We were sent to Saint Trond for a rest, but soon after our arrival we heard a tremendous buzzing and roaring overhead and discovered that moving from Nijmegen (hell's half-acre) we had come into "buzz-bomb alley." The German buzz bombs flew over us; and in fact, were taking off just two miles away. Along with the bombs, we had occasional and probably misdirected high-explosive, long-range shells. The V-1, V-2, and V-3 rocket (or buzz) bomb launching pads were close to Saint Trond and we could almost see each other on a clear day. The rocket bombs were aimed to explode in three areas: Liege, an industrial center of several hundred thousand people; Antwerp, with its excellent harbor; and England, including London, Bristol, and other cities. We were told that the Germans had found out from the French that Americans were in Saint Trond and that we had aggressive weaponry around us. The Germans withdrew from the V-2 pad nearest Saint Trond, as the rockets could not be leveled or used for close targets. Two of our unit members took a short jeep ride to the pad and reported many V-1 and V-2 pads on the Cherbourg peninsula. The pads were like a section of concrete road and were the color of the surrounding earth. Each slab was the width of a four-lane highway and approximately five yards long. Rockets were kept in dugouts and caves on either side of the slab. Rockets were pointed at an elevated angle, set to explode in specific areas in Belgium, England, and other targets. The entire pad could be easily camouflaged and was very difficult to see from the air.

V-1 buzz bombs made a rattling, rumbling noise similar to the sound of an old streetcar, like those that went by my house when I was a boy. The noise seemed to rattle around in my helmet like a sounding board, and I thought of all the destruction and death it would wreak in a few minutes. We thought it odd that our Air Force had not zeroed-in on the launching pads. V-1 and V-2 and V-3 each more powerful than the one before, were first made by Dr. Wernher von Braun, who later became a naturalized American scientist. In Germany he was director of the Pennemuende rocket station. Goering named the V-2 the Vengeance Weapon.

While I was in Saint Trond, a supply truck came with five non-commissioned officers and Captain Frank Ross, who had never been in the combat zone and had only heard far-distant shells. We were talking in a courtyard of the chateau surrounded by the ten foot high stone wall, and there was a little dining area where we had put a small table with folding legs. We had coffee on the table, which had been boiling a while, and we all poured ourselves a cup. We were sitting around reminiscing about the war and what we were headed for, when shells struck just outside the chateau. One came whistling over our heads; another smashed down nearby, causing a tremendous blast. The shelter shook and the earth trembled, sprinkling a few flecks of dust and rock around. The frightened visitors threw themselves under the table, knocking out its legs, spewing scalding coffee down Captain Ross's back. He let out a scream like a banshee: "I've been hit! I've been wounded! My back is split and blazing! Tear my shirt off!" He was positive his back had been torn apart. Frank and the others looked up at me as if to say, *Haven't you got enough sense to duck?* I laughed and said they would get used to it. I knew that if you hear a shell hit it's too late to duck. To the best of my memory, that episode was the only shelling when we were in Saint Trond. They had no desire to eat, nor stay any longer than necessary. We took Frank's shirt off and applied a burn salve to the large splotch on his back. It was hard to convince him a shell had not ripped his back open. That happened to be the Frank Ross who owned a restaurant in Kansas City. I knew him as a good football player. His family owned an excellent restaurant, Il Pagliacci, specializing in Italian foods. I had forgotten all this until I received repeated letters from Ross asking why he couldn't receive the Purple Heart on my recommendation because he was scalded by coffee. Some of our men did not seem to mind bombs overhead and an occasional bursting shell, as the townspeople were generous with wine, champagne, and cognac, and there were many beautiful girls to benumb rationality. The unit thought they had found a paradise on earth in this little town. Several members volunteered to remain for the duration if there were no further fireworks.

Saint Trond contained a splendid museum housing a magnificent clock that had taken six years to build. The town had received the gold medal for clockworks in 1935. It was thirty feet high and twenty feet at the base. Carved figurines had been placed around the base depicting life and death, the four seasons, and people of various occupations. The clock told hours of the day in areas throughout the world. In spite of the rockets we did greatly appreciate the rest.

Our unit had a grand party before we left Saint Trond with help of the 404th Fighter group which was billeted close by, for a rest period. It was here that Captain Distefano and Lieutenant Jenkins made their bid for world championship jitterbug artists. Captain John Vieta, that well-known surgeon and field soldier, awarded the prize. Kathy Macon, R.N. showed her first and probably only inclination to associate with the stars, and General Nugent turned an attentive ear, much to the surprise of bystanders. It was here that certain elements of our unit so exerted themselves that the call back to duty came almost as a relief. We survived the Battle of Saint Trond, never to be forgotten. We received orders on 17 December to set up in Bardenburg making us the first evacuation hospital to move into Germany.

SPECIAL TRIBUTE

I have not adequately mentioned the nurses who had been with us in the majority of our areas. Our unit, our army, and our country should pay them the highest honor and tribute. They were real troopers. They came in on the beaches like the rest of the soldiers did: none of us ever heard any of them complain at any time. They had very difficult duties to perform under extremely hazardous conditions and never had I heard them complain or shirk their duties at any time. It is impossible to measure in adequate words their absolute devotion and the extreme amount of work and long hours they gave in caring for the wounded, always with compassion. The nurses were under command of Major Ensor-Crawford, who proved to be a very capable leader. They were not only indispensable in rendering help to the ailing and torn bodies of these young men, but they aided in dispelling the barriers of dark despair of many our wounded men by replacing it with renewed courage and hope. For many it was just a kind word, a kidding joke, or a comforting reassurance and reaffirmed the faith that was needed in the wounded men. I cannot name all of the nurses who were so extremely valuable in this organization. There were many who were decidedly outstanding throughout the heaviest bombardment we had received. I recall that Lieutenant Cake continued to administer anesthesia when our operating rooms were struck with shell fragments and high explosive shells, and Champam continued to work under fire at all times. Lieutenant Helen Hanrahan, Lieutenant Ann Jenkins, Lieutenant Dorothy Lucken, and Lieutenant Betty Munson, our assistant to the chief, also were courageous in their selfless performance of duty. In this same category of heroism were Lieutenant Josephine M. Pescatore from Philadelphia; Lieutenant Henrietta Piccirilli of Bethlehem, Pennsylvania; Lieutenant Doris Donofrio of Troy, New York; Lieutenant Emma Ware of Orangeburg,

South Carolina (who kept up the morale of the entire unit); Lieutenant Lillian York of Baldwin Long Island, New York; Lieutenant Ruth Young of New Freedom, Pennsylvania; Lieutenant Rhonda Richards (surgical nurse), Bluff City, Tennessee; Lieutenant Cornelia Pound of Birmingham, Alabama; and Lieutenant Dorothy Luchen of Savannah, Georgia. Our Red Cross personnel also gave their utmost. They were Eleanor Priest of Augusta, Maine and Emily Logue of Waterman, Illinois, and were very helpful at all times.

Our great officers, under the command of Colonel Carl M. Rylander, were splendid, and were some of the most outstanding doctors we could possibly have had. Captain Harry Friedman, (Eye, Ear, Nose, and Throat) of Minneapolis, Minnesota was in charge of the triage room with Captain Harry Beckenstein (Internist) of Brooklyn, New York; Captain Dickinson of Irvona, Pennsylvania, and Captain Grimaldo Distefano of Philadelphia, Pennsylvania, also internists. The function of the triage doctors was to evaluate all incoming casualties as to their seriousness, and to make decisions on the necessary action to be taken immediately. Among the excellent surgeons were: Captain John Vieta, general surgeon of New York City, Major Albert J. Vesper, who was executive surgical officer and my assistant chief of surgery, and Captain Phillip Morrison, general surgeon of Chicago, Illinois. All three did so much skilled and heroic surgery on our severely wounded casualties. Then there were Captain Dan Hogan, orthopedic surgeon of Kansas City, Missouri; Major Marion J. Chimera, general surgeon of Chicago, Illinois; Major Edward J. Marshall, general surgeon of Waltham, Massachusetts; Captain John W. Teahan, chief of neurosurgery of Holyoke, Massachusetts; and Captain James E. Lewis, general surgeon of Saint Louis, Missouri.

Among the internists (general medicine) who performed so admirably were Lieutenant Col. John E. Schmaltz of Media, Pennsylvania, chief of medical service; Major James J. Coll of Winstead, Connecticut, assistant chief of internal medicine; and Captain Joel T. Woodburn, post-surgical care officer of Muskogee, Oklahoma. Captain Woodburn was an unusually kind and understanding officer who took every injured man to his heart as his own son. He was very conscientious, but unfortunately he had to leave us in January of 1945 due to a hip fracture, in the line of duty.

To further complement the internal medical group were Major William P. Colpoy, Jr. of Boston, Massachusetts; Captain Brooks Brown of Silver Springs, Maryland; Captain Anthony G. Sack of Detroit, Michigan; and Captain Wallace F. Silwinski of Philadelphia, Pennsylvania.

Other officers in their specialized fields who helped in the overall effort of caring for the wounded in such skillful and admirable fashion were Captain Harold Wilt, chief of Pathology and laboratory, from Stanford, Connecticut and Captain Paul Kundahl, anesthesiologist from Seattle, Washington.

The dental officers who were very efficient and skillful and always more than willing to fulfill their duties were Major Linus M. Edwards, dental and maxillo-facial surgeon from Durham, North Carolina, who was a former infantry line officer, always militarily correct. Captain J. Van Dyke of Belvidere, Illinois, who also was indispensable in administering anesthesia and was continually cheering everyone up with his wry wit. Among the very competent medical administrative officers were Captain Russell Kurth of Bloomington, Illinois; Captain Walker C. Reeves of San Antonio, Texas; Captain Edward Conroys of Quakerton, Pennsylvania, and First Lieutenant William Pate from Louisville, Kentucky. The Ordinance officer was Lieutenant Van Gundy of Springfield, Illinois, and the Warrant Officer was James Shalda, Maple City, Michigan. Major Clifford N. Brown, efficient, correct, and a splendid M.A.C. officer who knew the army rules and regulations as his bible, was a regular who kept his own counsel. Our Chaplain, Captain Donald J. Backenstose from Bethel, Pennsylvania, administered great solace and comfort to many, and fortified our morale. He held services wherever he could—in a field, tent, or on any occasion, catch as catch could. He gave encouragement to all the wounded of every denomination. There were many more officers who also did outstanding work and gave of themselves regardless of time or fatigue. I would like to give full praise to every one of our heroic men who worked under fire at all times regardless of their personal feelings, and gave everything they could to help those heroic soldiers who were fighting for our nation. I doubt if any will ever know and realize the real fortitude a combat soldier needs and must have to endure to live and to win, unless they have been there in hand to hand combat.

—*Wallace Harry Graham*

CHRONOLOGY (POST-WAR)

1945 • September 12: Wallace H. Graham, M.D. takes the position of President Truman's Physician, after turning it down once, then accepting.
• Received Distinguished Alumnus Award from Creighton University in Omaha, Nebraska, and Central Missouri State University in Warrensburg, Missouri, among other accolades.
• Graham establishes the first medical office in the White House.
• Appointed as Chief of Surgery, Walter Reed Army Medical Center, Washington, D.C.

1946 • Attained rank of Brigadier General (1-star) U.S. Army
• Accompanied President Truman and Prime Minister Winston Churchill to Fulton, Missouri for the "Iron Curtain" Speech

1951 • Wallace and Velma's third child, Bruce Douglas is born on January 31.
• Dr. Graham is awarded Major General (2-star) U.S. Air Force and completes qualifications to become a flight surgeon.

1953 • Moved back to Kansas City, Missouri and started general surgical and family practice.

1970 • Retired from the Air Force Reserves.

1979 • Retired from medical practice.

AFTERWORD

When my dad, Wallace H. Graham, M.D. wrote this memoir, he revealed a level of modesty by leaving out some noteworthy achievements and awards his family and others esteemed. Details about duties and place are prevalent throughout his autobiographical account. But not written about during that difficult war service are some of the more emotional points and his own heroic effort. He and his unit were commended for outstanding service to the wounded. He was awarded five major campaign stars.

This writing ends before being appointed President Truman's personal White House physician and how that came about.

After the end of World War II in 1945, Dr. Graham was summoned to Potsdam, Germany, just outside Berlin, and was asked to be President Truman's personal physician. He first rejected the offer, saying he wanted to return to Kansas City and practice medicine. A day later, however, he was informed that you do not say "no" to the chief. So, following orders, he accepted his duty as a privilege and an honor.

Dr. Graham's family moved from Kansas City to join him in Washington, D.C. where they took up residence at Walter Reed Army Base and remained for eight years.

During the time Graham was in Washington, D.C., President Truman promoted him to Brigadier General in the United States Army. He was also awarded numerous foreign honors for his unfailing service to comrades and enemies alike on foreign soil. Among the honors received were the Bronze Star and Croix de Guerre.

After establishing the first medical office in the White House with the blessing of President Truman, Dr. Graham came to be not only Truman's personal physician, but also his confidant and dedicated advisor.

Having been specially trained in surgical procedure and practices, Graham was promoted to Chief of Surgery at Walter Reed Army Hospital and also had numerous White House staff as patients. He checked the medical status of President Truman on a daily basis.

Dr. Wallace Graham's duties in the White House as the President's physician took him to numerous countries to treat officials with medical needs. The president often requested Dr. Graham to provide medical services for foreign heads of state, including King Ibn Saud, of Saudi Arabia. Truman sent him as a kind of emissary which helped soothe relations and promote good will. Also among the dignitaries treated was Ambassador Manuel DeMoya of the Dominican Republic. DeMoya's family and ours became lasting friends.

On March 5, 1946, President Truman asked my father to accompany him on the train to Fulton to attend Winston Churchill's famous "Iron Curtain" speech at Westminster College. Dr. Graham was more than happy to share the window seat on the train and visit with Mr. Churchill and the President.

The doctor would prescribe good doses of rest and relaxation for the president throughout his eight years. This included trips to Key West, Florida to the "Little White House," sea cruises on the *Williamsburg,* and visits to Shangri-La, the retreat run by the United States Navy. The name was changed to Camp David during Eisenhower's term as President. When Truman was not using the mountain hideaway, he freely let others use it, including Dr. Graham and his family.

Trips to Key West with the President on the *Williamsburg* were relaxing times which were shared with the presidential family, consisting of other top aides and key people in the entourage.

For a short time, he took on the professorial role as lecturer of surgery in Washington, D.C. at George Washington School of Medicine. He also published articles on various medical procedures.

January 31, 1951, the Graham family welcomed a third child, Bruce, to the family. As Graham had already transferred to the United States Air Force Reserves, President Truman soon recommended a promotion to Major General in the Air Force. Dr. Graham subsequently completed hours at Richards Gebaur Air Force Base, where he achieved flight surgeon status.

After President Truman's tenure ended in 1953, the Graham family moved back to Kansas City. My father continued his military career as Major General in the Air Force Reserves where he built his own practice alongside his father, Dr. James Walter Graham, and continued to treat the Truman family in Independence, Missouri until their deaths.

Wallace Graham had diverse interests and engaged in many activities, including bee-keeping, and growing plants of all kinds. He took a special pride in his orchids, which he collected and nurtured. He delighted in having a large variety of pets, many of which were gifts from foreign dignitaries and indigenous to their country of origin.

From an early age, he was in Boy Scouts and rose to Eagle Scout, and tribe of Mic-O-Say. Graham attributed many of his skills to his active years in scouting, and showed his support for the organization. He also supported the KCMO Golden Gloves organization, of which he held a championship from his younger years. Following suit, his oldest son, Wally, while at Southwest High School, became Kansas City Golden Gloves Champion in 1956. To help aspiring young men, Dr. Graham established a boxing scholarship program. He was team physician for the Golden Gloves, as well as for the Southwest High School wrestling team where his youngest son, Bruce wrestled.

A good-will mission to Antiqua was made to help a poor community in need of surgeons. It was gratifying and worthwhile to him.

In retirement he stayed active with orchids in his greenhouse, and enjoyed fishing. He caught many prize fish in the lakes of Minnesota and rivers of Canada.

Dr. Graham had a very large and respected family and general surgical practice in Kansas City. He and my mother continued a loving relationship for just over sixty years.

Wallace Harry Graham passed away January 4, 1996 at age eighty-five.

—*HEATHER GRAHAM FOOTE*

PHOTO GALLERY TWO

Wallace H. Graham, M.D.
Now in official capacity as President Truman's physician,
in his White House medical office.
1946

CITE COL. WALLACE GRAHAM.

President's Physician Will Be Honored in France Today.

WASHINGTON, May 1.(AP)—Col. Wallace H. Graham of Kansas City, personal physician of President Truman, will receive the Chevalier of the Legion of Honor and the Croix de Guerre tomorrow for services in Normandy. Graham, chief of the 24th evacuation hospital's surgical service, was cited for personally caring for wounded French soldiers.

Colonel Graham, son of Dr. and Mrs. J. W. Graham, 5731 Troost avenue, is a graduate of Paseo high school, the University of Missouri, and the medical school of Creighton university. Since that time he has taken special training in surgery at Harvard university and studied in Vienna, Budapest and Edinburgh. He at one time served on the staff of the General hospital here. While he served in the army, Colonel Graham's wife and two children lived at 622 West Fifty-ninth street terrace.

Truman's Physician To Get French Award

Col. Wallace H. Graham, of Kansas City, Mo., personal physician to President Truman, will receive the Chavalier of the Legion Honor and the Croix De Guerre today for services in Normandy. Graham, chief of the twenty-fourth evacuation hospital's surgical service, was cited for personally caring for wounded French soldiers.

Colonel Wallace Graham being presented with the Cross of Chevalier of the Legion of Honor and the Croix de Guerre with Palm from the French Government, by Major General Auguste Brossin de Saint-Didier, Military Attaché of the French Embassy in Washington, D.C. May 2, 1946

Receiving medal from
Ambassador Silvercruz
Croix de Guerre of Belgium

RECIPIENT OF FOLLOWING HONORS AND DECORATIONS:

Bronze Star

Purple Heart

France--   Legion d'Honneur, Commander and Chevalier
            Croix de Guerre, witg Palm
Belgium--   Order Leopold I, Commander
            Order Leopold II, Grand Officer
            Croix de Guerre, with Palm
Great Britain-- Distinguished Service Order

Netherlands-- Order of Orange Nassau, Commander

Greece-- Order of the Phoenix, Grand Officer

Mexico-- Medical Distinction
         Medical Citation

Peru-- Medical Distinction

Dominican Republic-- Order of Juan Pablo Duarte, Grand Officer

Nicaragua-- Order Military Merit, First Class

Brazil-- Order of Military Merit, First Class

Cuba-- Order Military Merit, First Class
       Order of Carlos Finlay, Grand Officer

Italy-- Order Italian Star of Solidarity, Second Class

World War II Victory Medal

Ribbons: Europe, Africa, Middle East Theater Ribbons
          Occupation of Germany ribbon
          American Theater and American Defense ribbons (with
          battle participation award)

Elected to Hall of Fame of Creighton University 1945

261

General Graham with
President Truman in front of
Walter Reed Army Hospital
Washington, D.C.

TRUMAN VISITS WOUNDED GI'S—President
Truman is shown leaving Walter Reed hospital in Washington where
he visited wounded army men in a pre-Christmas tour of veterans'
facilities. Earlier yesterday he had visited the navy hospital at
Bethesda, Md. Accompanying the President is Col. Wallace H.
Graham, his physician—(Wirephoto).

General Graham, M.D.
with President Truman on
the *Williamsburg*

262

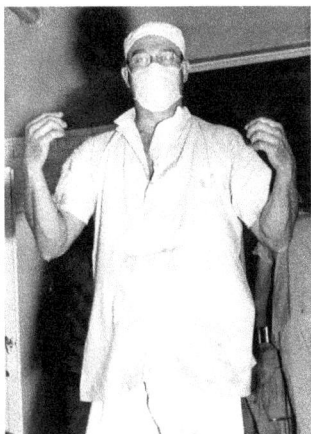

Dr. Graham, Surgeon,
Scrubbed up for surgery at
Walter Reed Army Hospital
Washington, D.C. 1946

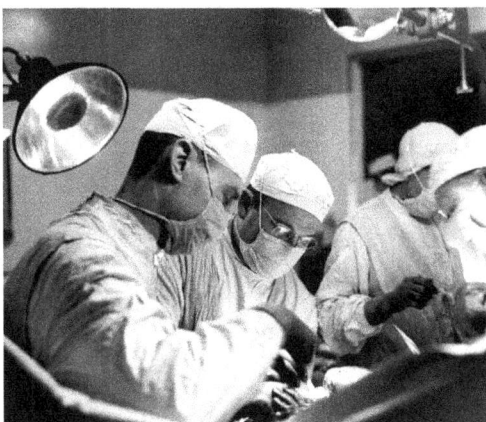

Dr. Graham (2nd from
left), performing surgery at
Walter Reed Army Hospital,
Washington, D.C. 1946

Brigadier General Graham, M.D.
U.S. Army; September 1946

General Wallace Graham, M.D.
with Velma, his wife
1946

General Wallace Graham, M.D.
riding in car with President Truman
1946

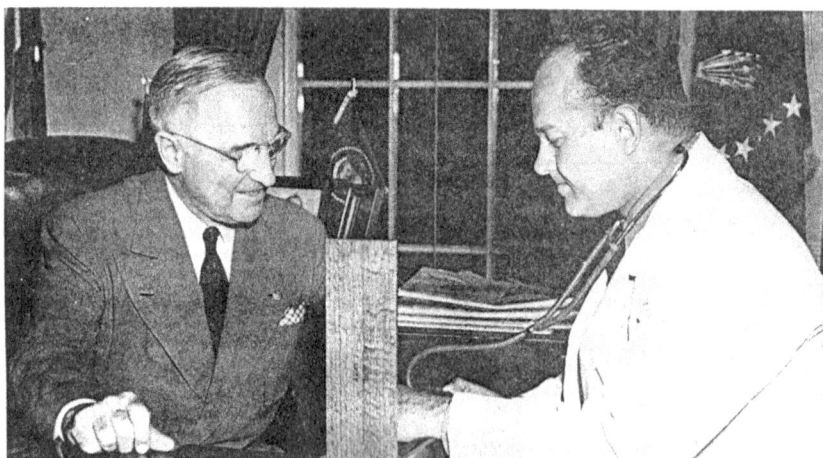

Dr. Wallace Harry Graham, Alpha '32, treats President Harry S Truman in the Oval Office during Truman's term as the nation's chief executive. Dr. Graham was awarded the Fraternity's Distinguished Achievement Award in 1991.

Distinguished Achievement Winner
Wallace Graham served Truman

Wallace Harry Graham, Alpha '32, was presented the Fraternity's Distinguished Achievement Award at the 1991 national meeting in Chicago.

Gen. Graham, a resident of Kansas City, who still holds an active commission with the U.S. Air Force Medical Corps (permanent grade, active reserve), served as personal physician to President Harry S Truman from 1945-53.

His government service was long and distinguished. After service during World War II as chief of surgery, 24th Evac. Hospital, Washington, D.C., he served as Chief of Section, Surgery, Walter Reed Army Hospital in Washington from 1945-53.

He was a professional lecturer in surgery at George Washington University School of Medicine from 1946-53 and served as a member of Presidential Special Missions to the Middle East in 1948 and 1951, Guatemala Ciy in 1950, and Nicaragua in 1951.

He was founder of the Westport Clinic and Research Foundation in Kansas City in 1955 and served on the surgical staffs of several Kaansas City area hospitals. He holds various medical association memberships and honorary memberships.

A highly-decorated military man, he holds honors from numerous foreign countries.

He holds degrees from Central Missouri State College, Creighton University, the University of Vienna, the University of Budapest, Royal College of Surgeons in Edinburgh, Scotland and the Graduate School of Aviation Medicine at Randolph Field, Texas.

Gen Graham married Velma R. Hill in 1935 and they have three children, Wallace Scott, Heaher ellen and Bruce Douglas.

He accepted the Fraternity's highest alumni honor for distinguished service in his career in full military uniform.

Dr. Graham shown taking President Truman's blood pressure in the Oval Office in 1946

264

Key West, Florida, 4 March 1948

Back row: Wallace H. Graham, Robert Dennison, Stanley Woodward, Clark Clifford, Eben Ayers, William Hassett, Robert Landry
Front Row: Harry Vaughan, William Leahy, President Harry Truman, John Steelman, Matt Connelly

Key West, Florida, 13 March 1949

Back row: Mr. William Bray, Assistant Labor; Robert Landry, Air Force Aide; Adm. Dennison, Naval Aide; Mr. Stanley Woodward, Mr. Charles Ross, Press Secty; Gen. Harry H. Vaughan, Military Aide; Gen. Wallace H. Graham, Physician to the Pres.; Mr. Eben Ayers, Press Assistant
Front row: Mr. John Steelman, Labor relations; Chief Justice Vinson, US Supreme Court; President Truman; Adm. Leahy; Mr. Wm. D. Hassett, Pres. Sec. correspondence

President Harry Truman and General MacArthur. General Wallace H. Graham in background. Wake Island October 15, 1950

General Wallace Graham, standing King Ibn Saud, sitting 1950

General Wallace Graham receiving sword from King Ibn Saud 1950

"When our friend, General Harry Vaughan found out that Daddy's medals were in a bureau drawer, he asked his daughter, Janet, an artist, if she would make a suitable display for them. She did an excellent job."

—*Heather Graham Foote, daughter*

Legend of medals and honors shown in photo on opposing page:

FOREIGN DECORATIONS

1. Belgium	Order Leopold II	Grand Officer
2. Greece	Order of the Phoenix	" "
3. France	Legion d'Honneur	Commander
4.&7.Dominican Rep.	Order Juan Pablo Duarte	Grand Officer
5. Cuba	Order of Carlos Finlay	" "
6. Brazil	Order of Military Merit	First Class
8. Cuba	Order Military Merit	" "
9. Belgium	Order Leopold I	Commander
10.France	Legion d'Honneur	Chevalier
11.Great Britain	Distinguished Service Order	
12.Netherlands	Order of Orange Nassau	Commander
13.France	Croix de Guerre	With Palm
14.Nicaragua	Order Military Merit	First Class
15.Belgium	Croix de Guerre	With Palm
16.Mexico	Medical Distinction	
17.Mexico	Medical Citation	
18.Peru	Medical Distinction	
19.		
20.		

Left- French forgier   Right- Belgian forgier

Major General Wallace Graham, M.D.
United States Air Force

Made in United States of America
Reprinted from Medical Annals of the District of Columbia
Vol. XVIII, No. 10, October, 1949

CARCINOMA IN YOUNG ADULTS*

BRIGADIER GENERAL WALLACE H.
GRAHAM, M.C., U.S.A.F.R.

*Resident Surgeon, Walter Reed General Hospital; Professorial
Lecturer in Surgery, George Washington University School of
Medicine*

*W*E SURGEONS in the military service are unique, to a certain extent, in that we have large numbers of patients within the age group which are considered to be young, active, and comparatively healthy individuals.

From the age of 16 onward nutrition is adult in type and growth is becoming more stabilized. Tumors which have been peculiar to childhood decrease, apart from sporadic cases, while the precocious adult-type neoplasms may occur from then onward. We must search adequately for those cell rests of the embryonal nidus in the age group from 18 to 30, in which the early carcinomas may occur.

I shall not consider the malignant neoplasms of early childhood which, in certain types, are rather rare in the latter years of life, such as retinoblastoma, malignant neurocytoma, and adenosarcoma of the kidney. As a matter of fact, the most common tumors in youth, say between the ages of 15 and 35, are the various types of sarcoma of bone, since the greatest change in the bones, and almost the entire process of osteogenesis, is during this early period, mainly between 16 and 25. Actually, the incidence of carcinoma reaches the peak after the age of 40. However, the site of the carcinoma and the type must be considered.

CARCINOMA OF THE GASTROINTESTINAL TRACT

In youth we do not note the marked number of disabilities to which it is liable. For instance, we do not note constipation as often as in later life, nor do we note the multitudinous cases of

* Read before the Society, April 13, 1949, as part of a Symposium on Cancer.

diverticulosis and diverticulitis. The frequency in the different parts of the colon is the same in young adults as it is in the older age groups. My study of a series of 200 cases of carcinoma of the colon in young adults shows that the tumor has been in the pelvic colon in 107, in the descending colon in 32, in the ascending colon in 20, in the transverse colon in 11, in the cecum in 11, in the splenic flexure in 10, and in the hepatic flexure in 2. The type carcinoma does not differ from one age to another. Clinically, we generally distinguish two types: one, an annular scirrhous carcinoma, typically met in the distal part of the colon and generally going on to obstruction; the other the fungating, ulcerative tumor, typically met in the proximal part of the colon, which is very likely to bleed, break down easily, cause anemia and weakness, but generally does not obstruct the bowel until very late.

From the pathologic standpoint we encounter the polypoid type of malignant papilloma, of comparatively slow growth, which in young people may spread early and far. The signet-ringed mucoid carcinoma, which of course spreads rapidly with great malignancy, infiltrating speedily and filling the lymphatics with fast-growing cells is occasionally seen. It is formidable to the eye but is quite favorable for surgery if discovered in an early stage. The tendency for cancer to spread circumferentially is not quite the same in all ages. The tumor is found around the wall of the colon, forming an annular constriction, and this disease does not tend to spread longitudinally except in cases of mucoid carcinoma, in which submucous spread along the bowel is a feature. Metastasis to the liver by the blood stream is very prone to occur when the

Examples of the many published medical works of Dr. Graham

Partial list of other publications by Dr. Graham

1942: "Appendicitis and Gastro-Enteritis" —*The Military Surgeon*

1947: "Surgical Management of Vascular Injuries in Combat"
—*Mississippi Valley Medical Journal*

1948: "Management of Injuries to Genito-Urinary System During War"
—*The Journal Of Urology*

1950: "The Importance of Complete and Scientific Medical Records from the Standpoint of Medical Science" —*Bulletin American College of Surgeons*

1951: "Carcinoma in Young Adults"
—*District of Columbia Medical Journal*

1953: "Acute Infections & Traumatic Injuries of the Hand"
(Contributing writer) —*Emergency Surgery,* by Bernard J. Ficarra;
F.A. Davis Co., Philadelphia, PA 1953.

IMPORTANT PROFESSIONAL POSITIONS FROM BEGINNING
OF CAREER TO PRESENT, AND TEACHING AND HOSPITAL
CONNECTIONS:

Fellow of American College of Surgeons

Fellow of International College of Surgeons

Chief of Surgery-- 24th Evacuation Hospital 1942-45

Chief of Section of Surgery--Walter Reed Hosp. Wash.D.C.
1945-1953

Personal Physician to President of the United States,
Harry S. Truman-- 1945-1953

Professorial Lecturer in Surg. Geo. Washington Univ.School
of Medicine--1946-1953

Member of Presidential Special Mission to:
Middle East-- 1948, 1951
Guatemala City--1950
Nicaragua--1951

Delegate to International Symposium of High Altitude Biology
Lima, Peru, 1949

U.S.Air Force Delegate to International College of Medicine--
Mexico City 1950

Special Assistant to Surgeon General--U.S.Air Force (1953 to
Special Surgical Consultant to Surgeon General--U.S.A.F.present)

Maj.General, U.S.A.F. Medical Corps (permanent grade,active
Reserve) 1953

Founder of Westport Clinic and Research Foundation 1955

Missouri State Surgeon of Medical Reserve 1959-1960
Delegate to National Securities Council-- 1960

On surgical staffs of Research Hospital, Menorah Hospital,
Baptist Memorial Hospital--of Kansas City, Missouri, and
St.Margaret's Hospital of Kansas City, Kansas

Below is the transcription of President Harry Truman's handwritten inscription to Major General Wallace Harry Graham, M.D. on the professional photograph at right:

To Major General Wallace Graham, the best doctor and the kindest man there is, who has been invaluable to me and my family with kindest regards for a happy and prosperous career.

White House,   *Harry Truman*
Jan 11, 1953

To Major General Wallace pa hrera, the best doctor and the kindest man there is who has been invaluable to me and very friendly with kindest regards + best wishes for a happy prosperous career

White House,

June 17, 1952

Harry Truman

Dr. Graham, tending his orchids,
one of his favorite hobbies.

Photos by Tom Kelley—The Washington Post

MORE THAN A HUNDRED ORCHIDS but nary a corsage! Brig. Gen. Wallace Graham, USAF, cultivates orchids when he isn't watching over the health of President Truman. The Chief Executive's personal physician has been raising orchids since he was a boy and has about 150 species to date. "But I've never cut an orchid in my life." So Mrs. Graham still buys her own corsages to wear to parties

How come orchids for a hobby? Well, 30 years ago when school boy "Wally" Graham was studying the Mendelian Theory, his dad, a Kansas City surgeon, introduced him to the hobby of cross-pollinating flowers. They started with fuchsias, then camellias before turning to orchids. And the general has been raising orchids ever since. One of his orchids will be for sale at the Air Force Fair Wednesday, 2-8 p. m., at the Fort Myer gymnasium, sponsored by the Air Force Officers' Wives' Association

Dr. Wallace H. Graham, outside his home
with pet macaw and mynah bird.
Walter Reed Army Base, Washington, D.C.

274

The Graham Family December 1952

Left to Right:
Mrs. Velma Ruth Graham, Bruce Douglas Graham, Heather Ellen Graham,
Wallace Scott Graham, General Wallace Harry Graham, M.D.

At the Graham family residence,
7108 14th Street Northwest
Washington, D.C. Walter Reed Army Base

The Graham Family 1961

Back: Heather, Mrs. Velma and Dr. Wallace Graham
Front: Wally and Bruce

At Velma's Parents, Stanley and Edna Hill's residence,
5905 Harrison Street
Kansas City, Missouri

The Graham Family 1961

Back: Dr. Wallace Graham
Front: Heather, Mrs. Velma Graham, Bruce and Wally

At the Graham Family residence,
5157 Ward Parkway
Kansas City, Missouri

20 April 1964 *Kansas City Times*

Commemoration of Prime Minister Churchill's 1946 "Iron Curtain" speech.
Westminster College Fulton, Missouri

★ ★ THE KANSAS CITY TIMES, MONDAY, APRIL

Major General Wallace H. Graham

Former President Harry S. Truman

RECALLING THE IRON CURTAIN SPEECH of 18 years ago in the Westminster college gymnasium, some of those then present were on the same platform yesterday afternoon. Seated (left to right) are Joyce Hall; Gov. John M. Dalton; Lord Harlech, British ambassador to the United States; former President Harry S. Truman, who introduced Winston Churchill the day he gave that speech; and Carl Trauernicht, president of the college board of trustees. Standing (left to right) are five men who were there when Churchill spoke: Dr. Franc McCluer, former president of Westminster; Neal S. Wood, college trustee; Maj. Gen. Wallace Graham, White House physician to Truman; Maj. Gen. Harry Vaughan, military aide to Truman; and J. Raeburn Green, trustee.

Transcript of *Kansas City Times* caption above:

RECALLING THE IRON CURTAIN SPEECH of 18 years ago in the Westminster college gymnasium, some of those then present were on the same platform yesterday afternoon. Seated (left to right) are Joyce Hall; Gov. John M. Dalton; Lord Harlech, British ambassador to the United States; former President Harry S. Truman, who introduced Winston Churchill the day he gave that speech; and Carl Trauernicht, president of the college board of trustees. Standing (left to right) are five men who were there when Churchill spoke: Dr. Franc McCluer, former president of Westminster; Neal S. Wood, college trustee; Maj. Gen. Wallace Graham, White House physician to Truman; Maj. Gen. Harry Vaughan, military aide to Truman; and J. Raeburn Green, trustee.

Major General Graham next to Major General Harry Vaughan,
standing behind President Harry Truman, seated

278

Mrs. Velma and Dr. Wallace H. Graham
50th Wedding Anniversary, 1985

Velma and Wallace Graham
holding Graham banner at Kansas City
Scottish Highland Games
Barstow School grounds
1993

President's physician
Graham cared for Truman, other world leaders

By Dwight Daniels
Missourian staff writer

Retired Air Force Maj. Gen. Wallace H. Graham says the job as President Truman's personal physician was one he never expected.

"When the call came for me to report to Potsdam (in 1945), I thought for sure they had the wrong man," the general said. "So did the presidential aides when they met me." In his combat fatigues and battered jump boots, he said he didn't look much like a physician.

"But when I met Truman, I reported in and saluted him and asked him, 'Mr. President, are you sure you know who it is you've got?' He told me, 'Certainly, I've looked at your credentials and they look all right to me.' Then I told him I might end up with his gall bladder and appendix one day. And before I finished my time with him, I had done just that. That's something he was fond of reminding me later."

Graham, 74, spoke to a gathering of 300 people Friday evening at an Air Force Reserve Officers Training Corps Dining Out, a traditional military banquet.

He described Truman as "the most easygoing patient a physician could ask for. He was considerate and kind with everyone. And fortunately for me, he was a very healthy president."

Graham's military career began with enlistment in the Army reserve in 1928. He entered the active ranks in 1941 as a first lieutenant at the outbreak of war.

But he was not the typical new lieutenant. His medical study at the University of Vienna in 1937, after he had completed his degree from Central Missouri State University the year before, left him with strong impressions of what Germany had in store for the world.

"I knew the Germans were preparing for up to eight years of war," he told the gathering of Air Force cadets, parents, university faculty and civic leaders.

"When I was in Vienna, I heard Hitler speak, and I knew the mesmerizing effect he had on the people of Germany."

In a discussion with Air Force cadets before his speech, Graham said that when Hitler's aides — Hermann Goering, leader of the Nazi air force, and Paul Joseph Goebbels, minister of propaganda — heard there was an American military man present at the Vienna speech, "They decided, for whatever reason, that I might know something. So I met both of them.

"They asked what I thought about the possibility of the U.S. going to war," the general said. "I made it clear, of course, that I was no spokesman for the U.S. government, but I did tell them that we were certainly tight with the British — that we were brothers and cousins and would stick together."

Graham told cadets his impressions of the two Nazis. Goering was "big and fat, and acted like a jolly fellow," while Goebbels was "kind of a weaselly guy who walked with a limp.

"I got the impression he didn't really like me, but that was all right with me. I didn't care about meeting him much, either. We all know what history shows about these men."

Later, as Truman's physician, Graham practiced about as much medicine on foreign heads of state as he did the president, when they requested his services from Truman.

"I was called over to Generalissimo (Joseph) Stalin's quarters at Potsdam during the Allied conference there. And he was sick — he was very white with bad stomach problems. His aides told me they thought he needed some of that new, magic 'peeniseeleen.' Well, I took a look at him, and told him through his interpreter that he didn't need any penicillin, and I gave him a double dose of paregoric and bismuth. That's all he needed. The history books say he was sick for three days."

Graham also treated Churchill — "He was polite and likeable but a bit gruff about taking his medicine. I told him he was so fat he wouldn't feel a thing" — Arabian King Ibn Saud and Crown Prince Saud el Saud, Prince Bernhardt of the Netherlands, and others.

Of his diplomatic surgery, he said, "I didn't mind the travel and, thankfully, nobody ever died under the scalpel."

Graham, who was wounded four times in the war, told the cadets that they are "the bullwark and the backbone of this great nation of ours.

"It is up to you cadets, as the representatives of our military power, to deter any Soviet aggression. You must serve as strong defenders of our freedom and human rights. Any failure to except this challenge could lead to disaster for the United States."

Wallace Graham
'They had the wrong man'

Dr. Graham continued tending his
orchids through retirement.

Among his other interests,
Dr. Graham enjoyed competition
fishing in his retirement.

Clipping from the *Sunday Star,* October 29, 1972:

Kansas City Doctor Scores High

A Kansas City physician, Dr. Wallace H. Graham, 5157 Ward
Parkway, has become the first nonresident holder of the Master
Angler gold award of Manitoba.

Dr. Graham is the second angler to earn the coveted gold
badge since Master Angler awards were instituted in 1958. To
qualify for a gold the fisherman must catch trophy size fish of 10
different species in Manitoba waters.

THE KANSAS CITY STAR.

Vol. 116, Wednesday, January 10, 1996, No. 115

A Capital Cities/ABC Inc., Newspaper

ROBERT C. WOODWORTH
President and Publisher

WESLEY R. TURNER
Executive Vice President and General Manager
R. RICHARD HOOD
Vice President and Editor, Editorial Page
DELL CAMPBELL
Vice President, Circulation/Operations
MICHAEL R. PETRAK
Vice President, Marketing/Advertising

ARTHUR S. BRISBANE
Vice President and Editor
SHARON LINDENBAUM
Vice President, Finance
RALPH W. ROWE, JR.
Vice President, Promotion
CHET WAKEFIELD
Vice President, Information Management/Production

FRAN STOWELL
Vice President, Human Resources

Dr. Wallace Graham

Harry S. Truman's personal physician, Wallace H. Graham, was a generous man with a kindly disposition.

And he was fiercely loyal to his most famous patient. In fact, he treated not just the late president but also Bess Truman throughout their long and healthy retirement years.

Graham, now gone at age 85, was a military surgeon with a deep desire to serve people (from kings to paupers). He was a man of wide interests and enthusiasms. And his ability to work hard impressed even the hard-working president for whom he cared.

Beyond his medical profession, he worked for many years with the Golden Gloves boxing program, especially its scholarship efforts, and was the physician for the Southwest High School wrestling team in the late 1960s.

Like his most famous patient, Wallace Graham was unpretentious and could tell great stories. No doubt his engaging, unfeigned personality endeared him to the Trumans — as did his professional skill. In the end he was much more than a man who happened to be picked for a famous job. He was an important contributor to his times and his profession.

Reprinted with permission

Index: Memoir and Related Material

Wallace Harry Graham

Brown shirts, 81, 112
Browning machine gun, 43, 167
Bruce, Lena, 36
Bruce, John, 123
Burgess, Martha, 36
Buzz Bombs (*see* Screaming Mimi)
C.M.T.C. Camp, 43
Café Edison, 88
Cake, Margaret, 184, 219, 248
Calloway, Cab, 42
Calvert, F.W., 54
Canadian troops, 123, 234, 245
Canaris (Admiral, Germany), 177
Carmen, G.G., 36
Carpenter, Elton, 44, 76
Cassidy (Lieutenant), 44, 148
Catania, Nancy, 66
Central Missouri State College, vii, 51
Champam (Lieutenant), 248
Charleston, the (dance), 41-42
Chimera, Marion J., 219, 228, 249
Choltitz, Dietrich von, 223-24
Chorinnini (Dozent), 85, 86
Churchill, Winston, 219, 279
Civil War, The, 22
Clark, Dick, 32
Clifford, Clark, 176, **267**
Coen, Junior, 36-37
Cogley, John Phillip, 66
Coll, James J., 198, 215, 219, 249
Colorado, Yuma, vii, 13-14, 19-21
Colpoy, William P., Jr., 249
Connecticut
    Stanford, 250
    Winstead, 249
Conroys, Edward, 250
Constant, Paul C., 36
Consumer Ice Company, 45
Coppaken, Martin "Marty", 52, 58
Country Club 63rd Street Police Station, 27
Creighton Medical School, iii, vii, 59, *133*
Creighton University, 59
Cross of Lorraine, 222
Cullen, John, 155
Czechoslovakia, 83, 98
    Prague, 83, 90
D-Day, iii, 174, 176-79, 181, 197
Daniels, K.O., 41-42
Davis Cup, 37

De Gaulle, 222
De Havilland Mosquito (plane), 212
Deutsche (Professor), 85, 87
Dickinson (Captain), 249
Distefano, Grimaldo, 215, 247, 249
Donnelly, Ed, 24, 30, 32
Donofrio, Doris, 249
Dorsey, Jimmy, 42
Dowdy, Mrs., 36
Drome (Captain, French), 223
Easy Red, viii, 174, 181-82, 189
Echles, Ora A., 36
Edwards, Linus M., 181, 215, 250
Edwards, Ward, 54
Eib, George, 32
Eib, Harry Alvin, 32
Eisenhower (General), 176, 215, 223, 254
El Torreon Ballroom, the, 42
Electric Park, 42
Ellington, Duke, 42
Enders, Warren H., 219
England, iii, 114-15, 117, 147, 171, 179-80,
    185, 187, 192, 204, 212-14, 232, 246
    Birmingham, 170
    Bristol, 170, 172, 246
    Carlisle, 170
    Cheddar, 170-74
    Cheddar Gorge, 170, 172
    London, 119, 172, 246
    Somerset, 170
Ensor-Crawford, 248
Ensworth Hospital, 1
Evans (Sergeant), 244
Fairyland Park, 43
Finster, Hans, 85
Fisher, Raymond "Ray", 36, 38
Foote, Heather Graham, (*see also* Graham,
    Heather Ellen) ii
Foote, Jerry, 41
Foster, Earl, 53
Foster, John, 152
Foster, Kathryn, 243-44
Fox, Henry, 40
Fox, Henry H., Jr., 40
Fox, Kenneth L., 40
France
    Caen, 177, 183, 209
    Calvados, 214
    Carentan, 177, 190-91, 197-98,

Index: Post-War Era Material